LOST DOWN MEMORY LANE

– CARING FOR ALZHEIMER'S –
A PERSONAL JOURNEY

DAWN FANSHAWE

WESTBOW
PRESS®
A DIVISION OF THOMAS NELSON
& ZONDERVAN

Front cover image by:
Michael Tolleson
Autistic Savant Artist
Kent, Washington, USA
www.michaeltollesonartist.com

Photography by Alexander O'Riordan and Debbie Haynes

WestBow Press books may be ordered through booksellers or by contacting:

WestBow Press
A Division of Thomas Nelson & Zondervan
1663 Liberty Drive
Bloomington, IN 47403
www.westbowpress.com
1 (866) 928-1240

ISBN: 978-1-5127-0603-1 (sc)
ISBN: 978-1-5127-0605-5 (hc)
ISBN: 978-1-5127-0604-8 (e)

Library of Congress Control Number: 2015912219

Print information available on the last page.

WestBow Press rev. date: 08/13/2015

CONTENTS

ACKNOWLEDGEMENTS

I thank my mum and my dad, for giving me life.

I thank God for protecting me and giving me new, abundant life in Him.

I thank all my family and friends, whose love and encouragement have given my life joy and purpose – particularly Simon, Joshua, Conor, Monica, Debbie, Catherine and Julia.

I thank my Church family for their love, support, wisdom and prayers.

I also acknowledge my gratitude to the NHS and Council Services (in Orkney and Nottinghamshire)

I thank the agencies and voluntary organisations and support groups that have supported my mother and supported me, as her carer, over these years of her increasing need.

Particular acknowledgments go to the residents of the island of Graemsay, who loved and supported Avril in her own home on the island she adored.

I also want to acknowledge the commitment, sacrifice and practical love shown by all you millions of carers, who make such a profound and positive difference in our society – especially to your own family.

You carers are the heroes. I dedicate this book to you.

Introduction

Carers Trust – key facts:

- There are almost seven million carers in the UK – that is one in ten people. This is rising.
- Three in five people will be carers at some point in their lives in the UK.
- Over the next 30 years, the number of carers will increase by 3.4 million (around 60%).
- *Alzheimer's disease* is the most common form of dementia affecting around 496,000 people in the UK.

(* See Note 1)

Over these past few years I have met some fantastic carers – ordinary people who have answered 'yes' to a call of duty and compassion for a loved one. Many have sacrificed careers, livelihoods and their life as they knew it, to care for a parent, child or spouse.

This book is an in-depth picture of a journey through early-onset Alzheimer's. Mum was in her early fifties when she was diagnosed.

It is about the journey, not just of the sufferer and carer, but of the dynamics and issues faced by the whole family, and friends, mourning the gradual loss of the loved one.

Unfortunately, you will become only briefly acquainted with some of these other fabulous people, who feature far more significantly in my life than in these pages.

My mother, Avril, is the main focus in these memoirs, but it is our story, our journey, discovered through my eyes.

It is not a story for gossip or blame, but an acknowledgment of the frailty and beauty of what is to be human and the choices we make in honesty and love.

After a very dysfunctional childhood, my mother disowned me and kicked me out of her home.

But by the grace of a merciful God, our story became one of forgiveness, healing and restoration, as I took her into my home and become a mother to her.

I am not telling you how to be a carer. I am not a super-hero. I make many mistakes.

I am damaged goods in recovery. A healing work in progress.

If you are a carer, as I am, I want to encourage you to find all the support that you can get, to make your life, as a carer, as comfortable as is possible.

You, your health and your well-being are of utmost importance. If you neglect your other relationships (with God, your *self* and family and friends) everyone will suffer.

You do not want to become tired, impatient, sick or resentful (as I sometimes have), so stay close to your source of all love, health, peace and joy.

I have tried to include advice and information to help make it easier to find support, but I am aware that things change so rapidly.

Whether you live in the UK, or elsewhere in the world, health and social care support will vary with the seasons. Website addresses change. Support structures, funded by local government and charities, are here today and gone tomorrow. Some benefits depend upon a post-code lottery. Different councils have different provision.

So I advise you to check the internet regularly for support available to carers. Apply for whatever support may be available.

In the UK, the first port of call should be the GP, but you will also find support from local government, churches, charities, community centres, care-homes and other institutions. (See Appendix 2)

Please, never feel guilty for admitting that you need support.

Appendix 1 and 2 contain some facts about dementia along with information and contact details to help you navigate some of the UK support services that have made this part of my journey much more bearable.

Appendix 3 contains some of the personal tributes written for her funeral.

The story is true, but most proper names have been fictionalised for their privacy.

It is not how we die, but how we live that matters.

PROLOGUE

We all forget things from time to time. We forget a birthday, lose the keys, walk into a room and forget what we came in for. It is normal. We 'rack our brains' for that word 'on-the-tip-of-our-tongue' – we know it's in there somewhere, but sometimes we have to 'dig deep'.

So we write notes, keep diaries, calendars, tallies, address books; we write memos, take photographs, buy souvenirs – a whole industry of 'aide memoirs' available to make sure we remember those things that are important to us. But that is not because we have dementia, or because we are stupid; it is because our lives and brains are so busy and so preoccupied with processing such immense amounts of information.

Dementia is very different.

So I am trying to determine now, in retrospect, when Mum's dementia first became apparent.

Mum (Avril) was by nature a bit scatty and nearly always late for something. She was "four foot eleven and three quarters" and always a slightly bonny lady, with short legs, a pretty face and long brown wavy hair. She was outwardly friendly, quite capable practically, always busying, stubborn, long-suffering and self-contained.

My father was comparably very tall at five-foot-ten-inches; also handsome, fair-haired and dangerously unpredictable. Outwardly a quiet man, a 'dark-horse', he was a depressive, emotionally damaged in childhood and, always hurting, he avoided the company of others. He was very talented as a mechanic and a maker of things, but was uneducated academically and had no self-confidence.

Mum and Dad moved from Nottingham in 1987 to a little croft on Graemsay, a small, remote island in Orkney.

Having started a family very early in life, by the age of thirty-six, their two children, Debbie and I, had both left home.

There were about twenty-three people living on Graemsay when my parents moved there. They had a two-roomed croft, land (including some of the beach), a huge barn, byers, 'bothies' and a well. There was no running water or electricity at the croft, and no shop, church or amenities (except the Post Office) on the island. There was a boat running three times a week over to neighbouring Hoy and to mainland Orkney. In the middle of the island near the school (which was open for only one child at that time and has since closed) there was a telephone kiosk. For provisions, one had to phone to order from the Mainland shops and wait for the boat to bring them over.

Mum grew vegetables and they lived a frugal 'good-life' in this remote corner of the world.

In April 1995, aged forty-nine, Dad died, just five days before Mum's forty-ninth birthday. They had been married for thirty-two years.

Dad's sister Monica went to keep Mum company in 1996 and lived there for two years. She found Mum 'very mean spirited and childish', but in retrospect she thinks that it was the first signs of the disease affecting Mum's behaviour.

But when it began I am not sure.

"Not firing on all cylinders"; "The wiring has come loose"; "Not the full ticket"; "muddled" - these were some of the expressions used to describe a noticeable change in Mum by early 1999. She began to lose everything, even herself on several occasions. She was fifty-two years old.

Her sister, Julia, first noticed that something was wrong with Mum as early as 1996, when Mum stayed with her in Nottingham. In total Mum missed five connections on that journey from Orkney to Nottingham. Several times that week Mum went visiting friends, but forgot to come back for dinner or say she was going out. Julia did not suspect Alzheimer's, but she knew that Avril was not her usual self. That was already eleven years ago.

In February 1999, Mum came down to London to help me look after my children. I was a single mum to Joshua and Conor and a full time primary school teacher. Mum stayed with me for a couple of weeks. One very rainy day in school I was distracted by a bedraggled sight out of my classroom window - Mum was standing in the playground with Conor in the pushchair – both of them soaked. Mum was crying because she had not been able to unlock my front door.

At the end of her stay with me she was to catch the late coach up to Nottingham. A friend dropped her off in Victoria, but three hours later, in the early hours of the morning, my doorbell rang and I found a very frightened, tear-stained Mammy. She had the wrong day. Instead of phoning me, she had started to walk the streets of Victoria, her luggage in hand, with no idea where she was going. After being stopped by a few strange men, she began to panic, but fortunately had had the wherewithal to hail a cab.

Back in Nottingham she was staying with Julia again. It was quite obvious to her by now that there was definitely something wrong with 'her Av'. Julia returned from work on two occasions to find her front door wide open. One evening Mum did not return from her day out, but eventually, about 22:00, a kind man unknown to them phoned Julia to say that a very lost Avril had knocked on his door. A few days later Mum did it again, this time knocking on a different stranger's door. She clearly had no sense of direction and was struggling with coordination.

She would get very frustrated with her mistakes and would chide herself constantly for being "a stupid woman".

I didn't see enough to be concerned from that distance. In Orkney she was safe.

Mum did not sound troubled in general and usually spoke on the phone with humour and sense.

I always thought that dementia happened to 'old people'. My definition of old changes year by year as *I* grow older, but I never suspected that dementia could begin in someone in their fifties.

I did not see her again until I went to Graemsay in the Summer of 2001.

Mum had had the job as Post Mistress on Graemsay for several years. By then Mum's ability to balance the books was suffering. One morning whilst I was there, the total morning's business had been the sale of *one* stamp. Instead of dealing with that logically, she tipped the whole bag of stamps onto the floor and began to count them all. She repeatedly lost count and spent several hours becoming more and more frustrated with the task and with herself. But she would not take any advice.

Over the next few months Roger, a friend on the island, began to take over the book-keeping, as Mum would have the day's accounts thousands of pounds wrong. Eventually she was asked to resign from the Post Office.

The people of Graemsay were very patient and good to Mum. I am very grateful that they enabled her to stay in her beloved home for so long.

I don't know when Mum was actually diagnosed with Alzheimer's, but she was already taking Aricept, prescribed by a consultant, in 2002 (aged fifty-five).

I visited again in 2003. Mum could still just about play the guitar and we enjoyed a memorable sing-along. I also witnessed the demise of her treacherous driving. She refused to wear her glasses, despite seeing nothing through the windscreen. I got into the car with her and as she reversed up the rough path, foot down hard, wheels screeching, when suddenly the front of the car strained and ripped off, pulling half of the lodged dry-stone wall from its ancient site. I was not sorry to see the end of the driving.

After that Mum began to exhibit more signs of confusion and disorientation with time and space. I began to get phone calls from concerned residents on Graemsay, informing me of peculiar incidents. She would wander the island and turn up at other houses in her nightwear, sometimes 'just visiting', in the middle of the night. She had lost all sense of time and would forget to eat or drink, or forget that she *had* just eaten. There were reports of stores of food gone bad. Were it not for the cats, the place would have been infested with vermin.

As Mum's condition became more desperate, I finally began to wonder what I should do. Her writing was deteriorating, cards becoming a thing of the past. She no longer called us, we phoned her.

I arranged Community Care Services for her on the island, providing her an hour's daily home help. There could only be limited resources on an island of twenty-three inhabitants. I knew they were a little 'put upon' and worried about her, but what could I do? I could hardly stick her in my flat in London could I?

What was the worst that could happen? She could leave the gas on; put something on the storage heater at night; go out in her nightie, fall in a ditch and die of hypothermia...

Lots of potential dangers, as there are for all of us.

It was easy to minimise these concerns a thousand miles away. Mammy was happy there. She always said how lucky she was to be somewhere so safe and quiet and beautiful...

I went up again in 2005 – she was unkempt and smelly and quite dependent on others to cook, clean and order her life. But I still felt unable to help. It was her life, she loved her home and I had nothing better to offer her.

In August 2006, two months after our marriage, Simon, my family and I moved from London into a large Victorian house in Nottingham. We invited Mum to stay for our first Christmas there. (My last Christmas with my mum had been in 1982). She was fully escorted, by Roger and myself, door to door.

Whilst she was here, Orkney Social services phoned me to say that Mum would now have to go into a home.

She would not be able to return to the home she loved.

I felt I had no excuse and no choice but to keep her with us.

She had to stay here until we could find somewhere local and safe.

Mum could not even pour herself a glass of water.

I felt daunted, disappointed and overwhelmed.

But this was my mum and it was my job to honour her.

Like the rest of humanity, I have no idea what the future holds, so I have to take one day at a time and do my best by the grace of God.

Avril Haynes (here aged 49) 1946 - 2011

PART 1

Day to Day: Coming to Terms with Caring.

CHAPTER 1

June 2007

Yesterday Mum did so well with the new regime. I'd left the clothes out in the right order (as discussed with the occupational therapist, OT) and down the stairs she waddled, all dressed and smiling. I felt so pleased.

"Breakfast, Mammy?"

Later we had tried another of the OT's suggestions: I gave her a long broom and asked her to sweep the kitchen. She seemed happy and, after I removed precariously balanced potential disasters, I left her to it, to do my exercises before Simon returned.

Mammy had swept the floor and there was a satisfying pile of debris to show for it. Full of praise, I issued her with a dustpan and, with lots of direction, she managed to finish the job. Success number two.

But then she forgets it all and moans, "Can I *do* anything?" (I wish she wouldn't phrase it like that.) "I'm just *hanging about* again!"

"Conor is watching TV. I suppose you could find the sitting room and join him."

She found him this time.

But this is a new day. A screen of long hair sways behind another screen of cereal boxes: the boy is shoveling his way through a bucket-full of breakfast. The boy is Josh, my oldest son. He is twelve years old and enormous. They call him 'The Tree' at school. He's a handsome, hairy, 5' 10", size 11 shoe, hormonal, a 'GREB', apparently. He doesn't have the same people-skills as others, but he is talented, clever and lovely. He has Asperger's' Syndrome, but it's not always obvious.

Conor is stirring. He is ten years old and an entertaining charmer. He'll have to go to school alone today, as my husband, Simon, is working out of the house. Simon works at the Science Park, just a stone's throw from Gibbons Street, where the mechanics' yard used to be that my Dad and Grandad owned.

On automatic pilot I open the dishwasher to begin the morning rituals

It's 'Broad Glade Day Centre' today and they collect anytime between 8:30 and 9:00. It is a recently built residential care home and day centre, just a twenty-minute walk from our house. Mum is taken there by minibus on Thursdays and Fridays, but she doesn't like to go. I cannot leave Mum in the house alone, and I need a break from her sometimes.

I'd better see how she's doing with the dressing today.

"There you are at last," she sighs with that inimitable hard-done-to tone. "I wondered where you were. It was a *long* night."

"Mammy, why didn't you get up and get dressed? We left all your clean clothes there for you to put on when you got up, like you did yesterday. You did really well yesterday."

"But you didn't come. I was waiting for you. And nobody came. So I went back to bed."

"Remember the occupational therapist? You want to be independent with getting yourself up and dressed in the morning, so you don't have to wait for anyone. Yesterday you did it really well. Here are your clothes for today.

I'm making sandwiches for the boys. You get these clothes on and come down for breakfast. Okay?"

Grump. Sulk. She's not happy, but I'm not going to let anyone get to me today.

Josh is late. Why do children hate wearing waterproofs? I suppose Josh loves the rain and can't see what's wrong with wearing it all day. And Conor just likes to be contrary.

Mum's not down yet, so I'll intervene again.

Good, the nightie is off, but the top is inside out and she looks upset.

"Shall I put that the right way round, Mammy? It's a bit tricky like that." We'll try teamwork today. I'll leave her to don her slip-on shoes independently and I'll put the landing light on.

"I'll go and make your breakfast, Mammy. Come down when the shoes are on."

Conor is very cuddly this morning. He's been good and got dressed, shoes on *and* hair brushed.

"Conor, when Nana comes down, go and greet her, 'cos she's a bit grumpy this morning."

"Morning Nana," he beams, sidling up and giving her a warm hug.

Conor is so good with her. He's a bit cheeky, but he gives her so much time – mutually beneficial of course, as *he* needs an audience and *she* needs entertaining. It couldn't have been better really.

* * *

I feel guilty.

Why? Not doing something for somebody else, I suppose. The boys are at school, Mum is at the day centre, Simon is at work and I am 'free'. Cleaning the house, cooking or shopping – these are guilt-free, but reading a book, swimming, even making coffee just for me seems – naughty? Self-indulgent? Selfish? And now I'm writing, just for me. A day of indulgences.

I feel the need to justify myself. You see, I did sort the washing and tidy the breakfast stuff. I also made up a black grout to replace some loose tiles and cleaned the hall. Is that enough?

Guilt, but not a guilty conscience, not about these issues. I have done nothing wrong.

Conscience kicks in when my brain, heart and spirit *know* I've done something not loving – which is more often than one would hope. But guilt feelings seem almost masochistic. They are not helpful, as far as I can see, so I think I should choose to ignore them.

The really big, bad thoughts are about coping, or not, with Mammy.

I can't fetch Conor from school today, because Mum gets delivered home any time after 15:00 on a Thursday and I have to be here. I can do the shopping locally when she's back, as she'll enjoy the activity, and that gives me more peace now – it's okay, Dawn. Go and make that coffee.

* * *

Simon and I met on a Christian connections website. We both knew we were looking for a serious, long-term partner and marriage. He is hoping for children and I am prepared to honour that, God willing. Simon is a gentleman with (undiagnosed) Asperger's Syndrome, which presents itself, when his guard is down, in a repertoire of peculiar physical habits and mannerisms. I trust him, respect him and love him. At the time we met, he mostly worked from home, writing computer software programmes for large scientific installations. He's an electrical engineer. He had his own home and was clearly practical as well as a computer whiz.

Josh didn't want me to marry anybody, but thought Simon was cool. Conor was looking forward to the whole thing, especially the outfits and the party.

I was living in Kilburn, London, but had been considering moving back to Nottingham, so during the wedding preparations, we also searched out a property in Nottingham.

Mums are supposed to be at weddings – especially your own. She said she wanted to come, so we put lots of thought into it and she came, with an escort, to our wedding, staying with me in my little flat, along with Uncle-Tom-Cobbly-and-all.

If Mum was at a loss as to what to do, she'd be in the loo, and as we only had one loo…

It was hard work and fun, with all the last minute vanities and butterflies.

It was a wonderful wedding - everyone said so.

We moved into a house in Nottingham on August 15th 2006. It is a lovely Victorian house with traditional features: high ceilings, cornices, fireplaces, and pretty little tiles. And here I am:

> Changed.
> Married.
> New schools, new home, new family
>   member/structure/dynamics.
> New role for me as a house wife and carer.
> No income for me.

Challenges, losses, gains, freedoms, promises, hope.

"I know the plans I have for you,..plans to give you hope and a future." (Jeremiah: 29:11) NIV

I'm holding on to that.

CHAPTER 2

Mum was born in April 1946, Dad in December 1945, both just after the war, and in the days of rationing and frugality. Mum grew up in the Meadows area of Nottingham and would have been eight years old when rationing came to an end. Both of Mum's parents were involved in the war effort. Nana was in the land army and Granddad was a panel beater for the air force.

Mum had a passion for music, loving the rock 'n' roll, especially Elvis. Like many young people at that time, Mum bought as many of the latest records as she could afford. She had to sell her records a few years after she married, because Dad did not share her passion for Elvis. Besides, they really needed the money. I think it nearly broke her heart.

At sixteen, Mum - Avril - was pregnant with Debbie. That was a terrible shock to her mum, who was known as "The Duchess", because she was 'a bit above the norm' and wore fancy clothes. (Dad didn't like her much and called her "fir coats and no knickers".) Mum had worked for six months as a typing clerk in a small office at Raleigh Industries. Being pregnant and unmarried was still considered very shameful, although Nana had Mum before she was married. Anyway, Debbie was born in May 1963, just as Mum had turned seventeen. The three of them got married that Summer. Then they moved into Dad's mum's house and his big sister, Monica, moved out.

Less than two years later, after the birth and loss of Mum's second baby, Avril, I was born.

In those days, Dad rarely worked and what he did earn he often drank away. Mum was busy with us and Dad was too proud to claim any benefits. It was not a healthy pride; it was a snobby, arrogant pride that he learned from his mother, who would rather make her daughter work two jobs than claim help for herself. I remember as a child being almost proud of the poverty they endured in their early marriage, and loved to hear of their diet of dried NHS milk (which presumably was for us babies) and the molasses, cod-liver oil, salad-cream and bread. Mum hated salad-cream.

I knew that there had been a fire. Mammy wore polo-necked jumpers for most of my childhood, due to the severe scarring all over her chest, neck and upper arms.

The story was that she *had been painting a reclaimed dolls pram in front of the open fire and had knocked over the bottle of turpentine, which had brought the fire over to her and up she'd gone in flames.* It was an horrendous story, *but Daddy was the hero that heard her screams and came to the rescue. He threw her to the ground, wrapped her in a large rug and saved the day. Apparently his hands were terribly burned and wrapped in bandages too.*

A couple of weeks ago, Conor said to me that "Granddad had burnt Nana." Somewhat surprised, I told him the story that we all knew, of Granddad, the Hero. He insisted that Nana had told him, so I asked *her* how the fire had started. She must have forgotten the original story, because she became very sorrowful and told us how Daddy had deliberately set fire to her himself. (He must have soaked her in turpentine, for the story they later used to have been believed.)

She said that he had set her alight and stood to watch her burn.

How terrified must she have felt to have the man she adored, crazed in such an atrocious act, in front of her, whilst the heat of the flames were all around her?

She was in hospital for many months.

Why she didn't leave him then – for her own safety and that of her little children, who must have been upstairs sleeping – is part of who she is and her weakness (or strength?). She says that he was hurting more than she was and that he didn't want to live. Somehow she doesn't seem to have taken it as personally as one might expect. She stuck by his story and she stuck by him. But then, if he tried to kill her once, I guess he might do it again if she upset him or got him into trouble. So at everyone else's expense, she protected him. Always.

* * *

"HELLOA!" someone calls.

Mum's back and they need to speak to me. *I'm* on the receiving end of behaviour reports now.

"She was a bit out of sorts today. She was teary this morning. Thought you might know what it was about?"

"Not really, she had a bit of trouble getting ready this morning and got a bit upset…"

"And she seemed to have trouble with her lunch, co-ordinating everything. She couldn't pick the glass up properly?"

What do I say? Co-ordination is definitely a growing problem.

"Well, thank you very much!"

And I am really grateful for those precious few hours when there is just me and no one hovering behind me, or waiting for me. I am so selfish.

She was back in time for us to go and meet Conor from school and get the bits-and-bobs from the Cooperative store as well.

I did ask first and she said "No", but I really should have insisted that she used the loo before we went out. It can be very distressing for us both when she suddenly needs the toilet in the middle of the street.

* * *

Mammy was a great help this morning. She remembered the clothes routine and was already dressed and downstairs when I trundled down.

'Tree' was there, grunting his way through his second bucket of cereal. Then Conor came down dressed, washed, and brushed too.

What a morning. And it wasn't even 8:00.

Mammy was smiling when I greeted her. She knew she'd done well. I told her so.

Conor is being very good about me not doing all the school runs this week. Soon he'll be like his brother and find it highly embarrassing to have me anywhere near the school. At the moment he still enjoys the Nottingham novelty of me being a parent in the playground to walk him home.

However, it is 'The Broad Glade Day Centre' again today and they don't fetch Mum until after 9:00 on a Friday. They have to vary the rounds and give everyone earlier and later shifts - to be fair to all.

Time to ourselves, mother and daughter, and I have a delicate announcement to make. Shocking really, but because I dread the response and disappointment from Mum, I have also neglected to prepare myself for the weekend ahead.

"I have to get things ready for a wedding this weekend, Mammy." I pause to watch the response, but all seems clear.

"It's somewhere up… Yorkshire way, I think. It's in a house called 'Sledmere'.

I showed Mammy the painting in the sitting room of a former 'Sir Richard' posing in his hunting gear in one of the rooms at 'Sledmere'; at 'the Big House'. I've never been there.

"Will there be someone here then?" she managed.

"No, I couldn't get anyone to come here this time, but you will be able to stay for the night at 'The Broad Glade Day Centre' – like you did at Easter. You will be well looked after again. Is that okay?"

I was dreading telling her.

"But that's not until tomorrow and I have to sort out what I'm going to wear for such a grand occasion. I need your help. Would you mind coming to advise me?"

The power of words to build up or to tear down sometimes astounds me. And the way we use and abuse their magic astounds me still more. I got it right this time though and she followed me up the stairs to offer me her wisdom.

I got the go ahead for the outfit and we came outside to wait for the bus.

The rain has stopped and we survey the sagging garden. The smell of green is rich.

It's already 10 O'clock.

"No, you don't need anything else. You are not staying there tonight. I'll see you at teatime, later, today. Have a lovely time."

Ah, bless her. I'm so glad I've told her now.

As I wave her off, I soak in the smells. I love my garden. The vegetables are nearly flattened under the weight of rain.

I bought a beautiful Calla lily yesterday with flowers of the deepest cherry purple and freckly leaves. It needs partial shade and prefers to be brought in for the winter (can't blame it for that, can you?). It looks like a meadow out in the front garden.

When I'm gardening I feel very much alive and at home.

It's been about five weeks since the front garden was shaved and weeded and it's now the middle of June. I wanted to weed it and tame it a little, but I'm so pathetic, I don't have the heart. I look at those little plants squeezing between the paving stones and think, "Ah, it's worked so hard and will probably have a little yellow flower on it." So I clear away that which is obviously dead and wander around my mini-meadow, wishing I could see the overshadowed plants that were intended to be pride of place. Still, they'll all have their glory.

The sky is brightening and a hazy sunshine promises another lick of warmth. The cobwebs are dazzling as they bounce with the weight of the raindrops. The buoyancy and strength of the webs are amazing, as they move to the rhythm of the ground, shaken by the trucks going along the main road.

But I'm sure my garden must reflect me, as does the house, always in a state of needing stuff doing; everything in it's place, but I'm the only one that remembers where that place is.

I was thinking about Isabelle. She has been my best friend since we were twelve.

She is the sister I chose.

When I was disowned by my own family, Isabelle and her father ('Pa') took me in, and their home became mine.

Isabelle is married to Brian and they have two children, Bruno, aged nine and Violet, aged seven.

Her garden is years more established and about 4 times bigger than mine is and it looks out across a magnificent vista for miles. *She* pulls the weeds out.

She's very 'out with the old, in with the new' and 'if it doesn't fit, give it to someone it does', sort of girl. She She is straight talking, efficient, looks great, knows me and still loves me.

We both seek integrity in ourselves and share Christian values, vision and purpose. And I love her.

I must go and do something domestic. No one noticed I'd done the tiles. I don't suppose anyone would notice if I didn't vacuum the place for another week. Isabelle would.

If anyone asks, I can now justify my day. I cleaned upstairs, and did some painting and some gardening.

The gardening? You can't really quantify it, can you? Not without sounding really nerdy (and I might just verge on that). I decided the indoor plants looked in need of a breeze and a bit of a photosynthesis boost. I needed some myself and stripped to my vest, but I seem to have embarrassed the sun into hiding again and the rain has returned, just in time for everyone's homecoming.

* * *

I have been brought up to love gardening and exploring the world of nature, especially when we lived in a tiny caravan space for nearly four years when I was an infant.

Fire damage and bad memories were probably as much why we left Nana's house as anything. We will never really know now. Mum was in denial then and has dementia now.

It was an unusual life at the caravan. The only time we were allowed to spend indoors was meals and bedtime. The caravan really was small. I'd say it was twenty foot long by seven foot wide. My parents' bed folded away into the wall and Debbie and I slept, head to toe, on a wooden seat that ran the width of the back of the caravan.

Debbie was sleeping with her ten-year old knees bent long before we left the caravan.

But we learned all about the great outdoors. We climbed trees and lived in them. We scratched buckets in the well for water. One summer, the water was so low that Mum had to dangle me by my feet and I had to scrape the water and frogs from the bottom of the well.

We made fabulous dens in the underworld of stream-side hedgerows, weaving doors, mats and shelves out of long summer grass, and had parties of home-baked scones when our friend from the club used to come and play.

Sometimes we would spend so long up the trees, that we wouldn't notice the cows returning to the field. Once we were chased home by some excited bulls (after dreaming in the branches for too long) and ran down through the field and under the barbed wire to safety.

They were long childhood summer days, when we explored as many possibilities as young girls would dare and certainly wouldn't have admitted.

Daddy had a pick-up truck, called Marigold, with stenciled flowers sprayed on, real hippie style. Mum would walk her bicycle to the village school with us in the morning and cycle home afterwards, but some days Dad would come to the square to meet us at home time and us kids would rattle home in the back of the truck with the bike, whilst Mum rode in the front. We loved that.

I am grateful for those unusual experiences we enjoyed at the caravan, and how we learned to work with nature, improvise, reuse and recycle. Nothing was ever wasted. I did learn to appreciate the value of things.

I wanted to be in the circus. I practised balancing a broom on my finger for weeks. I was good at hula hooping too.

We had a lean-to shelter at the side of the caravan, where much of our stuff was stored and where we often took refuge when the evenings were inclement and dark. There always seemed to be a mysterious glow around the caravan at night, that gave those long evenings a scary, but magical quality.

My stilts lived in the lean-to. They were great and at least twice my height. I had to climb onto the roof of the caravan to get onto them. I would totter like a peacock all over the campsite, then gracefully use the sticks to propel myself forwards until I could jump down. Anyone who saw me thought it was amazing, which encouraged me greatly.

I loved to be a tomboy, show my strength and to do clever circus tricks, or anything that might impress my dad, but I ended up quite impressed myself, so that was all right.

One day my stilt expeditions came to an abrupt end. I was daring to 'stilt-walk' over the table and chairs in the lean-to, but the stilts were not quite tall enough to go that wide and they slipped, leaving me impaled on the spire on the back of a chair. I suffered a lot of pain for about a year, but I was never taken to the doctor. I am still scarred inside to this day. I don't know whether it was that experience, or the fact that we had to go about a hundred yards to the toilet blocks, but I spent most of my childhood with headaches, nosebleeds and severe constipation. I hated going unaccompanied to the smelly toilets. I dreaded the daddy-long-legs that flopped all over you as you went through the door and I hated the pain when I tried to wee.

I still suffer from constipation if I am away from home.

Not having a bathroom, at night we shared a bowl of warm water, taking turns to wash our top half, then to stand in the bowl and wash the bottom half. This was a habit we continued right until Debbie and I left home at seventeen years of age, despite the fact that the house we then lived in had a perfectly good bathroom.

Another vivid memory of the caravan was of Debbie and I being woken one night by Mum screaming, "No, Malc, please!" When we dared to peep around the curtain, Dad had the hunting rifle up, pointing and threatening to shoot Mum. Shortly afterwards he came through to us with an offering of pickled vegetables and told us we were having nightmares. We certainly were. He was drunk.

Daddy used to get drunk at the club in Calverton and would still drive the car, even after fourteen pints. Twice he overturned the car (avoiding a dog in the road) and landed in a ditch. He smoked in those days too.

Once, Dad left my Mum, and left me with a rare and beautiful memory of Mum taking each of us girls onto her knees and holding us. We were eating ginger-nut cookies, and Mum cried and said she loved us and was sorry for everything. I was not sorry for that moment, I thought the good life had finally begun.

He came back very soon. Daddy was formidable. He could be fun, but it was all so unpredictable. Unpredictable and with the power to kill.

* * *

During my more recent adult life, I have attempted to feel appropriate anger and allow it to play its intended role in the healthy balance of life. Anger was so repressed in me and I am still on a healing journey to own and understand it. I can identify two of the first and last times that my anger was spontaneously expressed and the reason for me deciding that anger was dangerous and to be hidden at all times.

1) A weekly treat, at the caravan, was a yoghurt from the milkman. I usually had apricot, but one week I chose strawberry. As I got near the end of my yoghurt, I came across an enormous lump of pure strawberry and eased it proudly and gently from the pot with my spoon. Daddy was in a 'good mood' and began to tease me, saying he thought it was a dead spider and he should take a closer look. I knew he was teasing and I was laughing, but still, you didn't argue. He peered closer, looking more and more concerned and then, snap! He had eaten it. I was shocked, and without thinking I took some more yoghurt on the spoon and flicked it at him.

I would never do that again. I was spanked with a wooden brush, roared at and made to sit on the caravan tow bar for the whole day until bedtime.

2) I also remember one occasion when Daddy came to the square to pick us all up after school. He was teasing again, chasing me and dodging, but I caught him and kicked his shin (probably on purpose, but I don't know). Well, he kicked me so hard that I was propelled several feet and lay crying on the floor.

I remember that day as the one when I resigned all anger. I knew it was better unsaid, unfelt, buried.

* * *

Mum was always around, but as we were indoors so rarely, I recall little about her. I do remember that we had a dog called Jackie, that my mum loved. One day we came home from school to find Mum crying inconsolably, because another caravan-owner had put poison on the garden and Jackie was lying dead. Daddy was very angry.

Mum loved the animals and the garden. She had a fabulous array of aromatic wallflowers and pinks, lupines and marigolds. To this day, I adore wallflowers and the scent of them immediately transports me back to caravan days.

Mammy also taught me to sew and to knit. At the caravan, Debbie and I would sit in the lean-to and make little fur cats and cushions, to put in empty sweet tins as presents for our friends.

One of the things that did impress me about my mum, when I was little, was that she was academic. Dad could neither read nor write when he left school, but Mum had taught me reading, writing, and speaking French, before I even went to school. It was fun. I enjoyed learning and I did think I was very smart when I first went to school.

When eventually I went to University to do my teacher training degree, my first essay was entitled "My education so far." I was astounded at how little I could actually remember of those formative years at school, and at how much more I had learned at home. It had a profound affect on my approach to teaching primary school children thereafter. What was significant for me was that I loved learning and it made me feel good about myself. It was something I could do, something I could get right and be praised for and I quickly learned to appreciate that praise, and to rely on it for my growth. I am very grateful that I had that foundation of learning.

Although my memory of primary school is scant and was later overshadowed by home circumstances, school was my sanctuary, and my joyful world. I was content, because I worked hard and my best was good enough to please my teachers. They at least seemed to like me. It was this experience that moved me to want to be a teacher – to give as much love, esteem and confidence to children as I could.

I was sad when home time came. I hated weekends and dreaded holidays.

Chapter 3

Mum is just home and I get the impression that her day was a bit of "this and that, and some of the others as well".

"Can I do anything?" she pleads.

I rescued all the tiny soldiers from the dining room floor – the ones that didn't stick in my toes this morning – and gave Mammy the big broom again.

She has been sweeping for ages and looks happy with herself. Now Conor is entertaining her with more of his guessing games.

I finally cleaned the kitchen windows, but I was distracted by the birds and cut my finger on a piece of stained glass. That brought me sharply back to reality. The birds are so fascinating though. The other day I took a series of photographs of a song thrush smashing a snail against small stones and eating the insides. It wasn't in the least bothered by me. I'd hoped to hear its song, now that I could identify it in front of me, but it was too busy to sing.

I wish I could remember all the funny things that Mammy says. The twists and turns of phrase are so amusing in themselves, but somehow I lose them immediately.

The only one I can remember just now is a bath time one, but we have similar variations on that theme every bath time.

"How can water be so *wet*?"

I keep saying that I must get her a rubber duck – although I suppose they're made of plastic now. She asks for one every time she's in the bath.

"Where's my duggy thingy? You know what I mean!" she laughs.

* * *

Our weekend away was fantastic. The welcome, the host, the house, and the grounds of Sledmere were all superb. The inn was cozy and friendly, and to go to Mass in the family chapel was a very special end to the occasion. Now at last I can identify the rooms depicted in the painting we have in our 'drawing room', and Conor was delighted to go back to school with the tour-guide to the house and spout about his posh relatives-in -law.

It is taking some concentration, but I am slowly managing to piece together the whys and wherefores of the family that I have become one with.

I had over twenty-four hours without Mammy. It was good for us all, I think. She looked so pleased to see Conor and I coming to collect her again and looked very well.

Saturday morning hadn't been quite so easy. Her things were packed and she had been told several times about the overnight stay at the care-home. She was clearly anxious. I went to bath her, this time using the new seat that the occupational therapist had got for Mum's safety. We had the rubber duck banter and she got in, or rather, she squeezed herself into the space in the water, to the back of the seat. Suit yourself I mused, removing the seat.

She enjoys the hair-washing/head massage now.

"Have you done this before?" "Who does yours?" are typical comments.

Well, all was going swimmingly, as they say, until it was time to get out. We have had some problems at this point before, which is why we were experimenting with the bath seat, but this day was different.

"There's nothing to hold on to," is a frequent complaint.

After fifteen minutes, I suggested finding a handsome fireman, or two, but it didn't help. I tried very simple instructions. Then I left the room in case I was intimidating her (because she could never do things when Daddy was watching her). I had long since let the water out of the equation, but after about forty minutes, I knelt down, apologized, hugged her and prayed. Then I turned her knees to the side and this time she let me lead her up and out of the bath. Phew.

Shower or bath-seat from now on.

* * *

Another busy morning. The OT came to go through the getting dressed routine with Mammy, and to see if she could suggest any new ideas to make life easier for her. I had to remember to have her come down for breakfast in her dressing gown.

I took Conor to school and came back to find Mum dressed and ready to go to the bathroom for a wash. Then I got the call from the 'grab-rail' people to ask could they come this morning. I suggested 10:30, thinking I'd be back by then.

Mum goes to another day centre on Wednesdays, just a ten minute walk in the other direction. The OT had been very thorough and has a lovely way about her. She nods as she speaks and you find yourself nodding and agreeing with everything she says, whilst also feeling very much affirmed. We seem to be doing everything as well as we can with the morning routine, but we are going to have to devise some way for Mum to know whether it's time to get up when she wakes, because it does stress her out.

This morning we had another "long night" with "so many things happening...people and things moving about all over the place, so I just *stayed there* in bed!"

Not a good night for Mum and then the trauma of having a stranger go through the getting dressed scenario with you – albeit a lovely stranger. Poor Mum was looking rather jaded. Then, I had to rush her from the bathroom, and trot down to the day centre, before the man from the 'grab-rails' was due.

I had left a note to say I'd be "just a jiffy" and he was there waiting when I got back, puffing and panting from my little run.

Anyway, that's another few jobs done. The OT will be back next week to see if she can be more successful than I was doing some artistic endeavours with Mum.

Mum used to paint in the Orkney Isles.

I ordered a monthly watercolour magazine for her, years ago, and sent her a posh set of watercolour paints and pencils one Christmas. Later she also did an evening art course in Stromness with a good friend, called Tony. It seems she was reluctant to have an audience whilst working, and so did very little during the actual lessons.

I understand that feeling. I really dislike anybody watching me work, even in the garden or the kitchen and definitely when being artistic.

I never got used to a grown-up audience whilst teaching either.

So I don't know how successful this planned craft exercise will be. The last time I tried with Mum, I gave her a large sheet of white paper and put four bright colours on a palette and a choice of big and small brushes. We talked it through and then I left her to it. She produced two small squiggly lines and a lot of disquiet within herself, so I abandoned that plan.

But she does like the idea of trying again, so we will.

I was struck by Mum's comment today as I rushed her down to the day centre,

"Thank you, Dawn," she said, giving my hand a little squeeze. "You are very patient. I used to think I was patient, but you are much more patient."

Thinking about how badly I'd coped the last two days, I could only say, "I'm glad you think so, but I think I need to be more patient than I am. Thank you, Mammy."

It must be so difficult for her. She was so happy in her independent world on the island (Graemsay): gardening, knitting (she once had her own knitting business and label, ORKNIT), building dry-stone walls, spending time with her friends, singing and playing guitar.

Twenty-two years ago she was running a clothes shop here in Nottingham and only five years ago she was managing the Post Office on Graemsay. Of course meanwhile she also had had a family to bring up – and I suppose she did her best at that, even if the result was not too good.

And now she can do so little for herself.

She has good days and bad days. I'm just glad she has some good days.

* * *

Yesterday, we dropped off Conor at school, went to see Isabelle's mother, Pat, and then headed for the TAB (Take-a-Break) carer's group. We had to find a toilet for Mum halfway there, but made it. Mammy was especially confused this morning and my patience was flagging. The TAB are such a lovely group of odds and ends, a whole range of ages from a seventeen month-old sweetie, through the whole spectrum up to the oldest, Jack, at ninety-seven. Olive just had her ninetieth birthday and is a bundle of smiles and encouragement.

The TAB consists of carers and the cared for, with a wide range of care needs. Real people, unpretentious, kind, daft and, above all, supportive of one another. I am very much a newcomer, but they have really welcomed us both.

It was they who organised yesterday's trip to West Midlands Safari Park.

Mammy didn't seem to like the coach journey, although it was straight forward (except for the necessary right and left turns), but Mammy had me round the bend. She was huffing, muttering and shaking her head, sure that the driver had got it all wrong and was going around in circles. After about an hour and a half, she looked about to burst with frustration, wondering "why has he brought us all this way and now we're back where we started from, and haven't done anything!"

She would not be reassured that in fact we were approaching Kidderminster and not far from the Safari Park. She had that "*I know I'm right and you'll see*" expression, that I remember so well.

Then of course there was the prudent toilet-stop at the first car-park and back into the coach again. That took some explaining.

Unfortunately, it didn't then all become clear, because whilst the driver reeled off the names of the species of animals that we were about to see, and the rest of the crew cooed, poor Mammy could *see* nothing.

I was excitedly saying, "Ooh, look this way, Mammy. Here's a white tiger/ a shabbily dressed camel/ a rhinoceros/ an elephant...", whilst Mammy became more and more cross and frazzled, unable to see anything at all. The animals were staring in through the window at us, but Mammy couldn't see them. She refused to keep her glasses on and kept shaking her head and humphing. She did manage to see the zebras though, or said she did.

Eventually, at about 14:00, we were off the coach for a walkabout. We grumps had one-and-a-half hours to explore the rest of the place and Mammy finally relaxed. She enjoyed the sea lions and could appreciate the snakes, alligators and a lonesome leopard.

We ate lunch and had just two more tasks – ice cream and precautionary toilet stop before re-boarding the bus.

"Two 99s and some of that stripy fudge, please."

Mammy always used to relish a Mr Whippy ice cream, so it didn't occur to me that it might now pose a problem. Have you ever considered how unbalanced a Mr Whippy ice cream actually is? It takes some skill to hold the fragile, hollow cornet straight, whilst reaching to lick the top-heavy creamy melt from above. It proved too difficult for Mum and after a crazy few moments trying to help, I ended up carrying them both, conscious of our time running out and trying to get her to stop for licks on the way.

Toilet stop next. I hope they won't go without us.

"Mammy, you'll have to be quick, because we're already a bit late and Nottingham is a long way to walk to!"

Oh, the noises that Mammy can make. Public toilets are not the most congenial place to enjoy an ice cream, and Mum's dripped down through the cornet all over my ankles and shoes.

"Hurry up Mammy. Your ice cream has nearly melted!"

Then there was a quick hand-wash and a run for the bus. Last ones again. I gave her the remainder of the ice cream and sat down two rows behind. I'd had enough.

Someone said, "Is your mum alright with that ice cream?"

"Am I bovvered? What Mum?" are what sprang to mind.

The journey out there had been largely in silence, except for the grumbles. I had tried to make conversation, but was unsuccessful. I told her I was going to sit her next to someone else on the way back and wished I'd remembered to bring a book.

"What was your favourite animal?" I tried.

"Errr…a cat!"

I don't know whether it was an attempt to make conversation, but as we neared home she asked, "So, what are we doing tonight?"

"Same as ever," I growled selfishly, "Nothing much!"

But she does know when she is being difficult. Later she apologised again for being so mardy. I suppose anyone would be though. It must be so terribly frustrating and humiliating to be so incapacitated and still so aware of it.

Still, I need a break now and we are back just in time for me to take Conor swimming – alone. Simon is back from work and can hold the fort.

* * *

Mammy was still hard-work last night – struggling to see the film, finding dinner difficult to catch off the plate, and the shower was another one of those "I've just done that…" grumbling sessions. Take a slow, deep breath, Dawn.

I do need to talk to Simon. We have not had the opportunity to be alone recently, not awake enough to talk, anyway.

Given that yesterday was tricky, I tried to go in early enough to reassure her today, if she was up. She was up. But what a smell. I'm really not very good at dealing with the commode. Simon is excellent. His nose clearly isn't as sensitive as mine.

And what a sight. One has to laugh as well, but today it didn't seem kind to laugh. She had found her clothes and put the lovely red top on inside out. She had a shoe on one foot and a sock on the other and her trousers screwed up in a knot on her lap. I gave her a hug and sorted the trousers, then put both shoes together and gave her the other sock to put on. (We can turn the top round to show it's pretty spangly bits after breakfast, I thought to myself.)

She succeeded, but it had taken a lot out of her and she needed more hugs and encouragement.

If it were me, I constantly ask myself, how would I like to be treated?

Conor was great over breakfast, but he's very snotty and barking too. I think we're all 'barking'. He had Mammy laughing with his 'hanky' being in his pant drawer, having a bit of 'hanky panty''.

Conor is not so enthusiastic about so many journeys alone to school now. But there's not much I can do about it, unfortunately. He is old enough to go alone and I know that the angels go with him.

I might see whether Social Services can offer any more support for Mammy and myself and family? I don't like asking. They have offered us a lot of support already, but it seems to take a lot of meetings and forms to get anything underway. It is worth it though.

After all the boys had left and Mammy was rearranged, we began our regular tour of the garden, admiring all those beautiful roses, leaves and other flowers that "don't look real, do they?"

I reminded her that tomorrow we have an appointment at Neurology at the West Hospital, to see whether she has early onset epilepsy. If not, we want to know what it is that causes her occasional fainting fits. We also want to ask them what is causing her not to perceive what her eyes can, according to the optician, clearly see. Perceptively, she then commented that her eyes have difficulty when she is under stress, which is definitely something I agree with, and also when she is tired. As she stood close to tell me this, her eyes were wobbling and blinking furiously and I asked if she was stressed talking to me. She said she didn't think so, but thought that maybe she was going mad.

I think it's a fine line for all of us, between sanity and insanity, and I'm sure that we all regularly cross those lines. I appreciate it though, when she can converse with me.

She has a fabulous smile when she wants to. Two men on the bus were good enough reasons for her to want to smile today. She looked a picture in her tinted glasses with dangling gold chain, her red sparkly top and her newly washed hair. She can be such a playful flirt, and will often come back from a day centre announcing that she has "another admirer", and then be coy, shrugging dismissively when you pry further. She complains that they are "much too old" for her – being only sixty-one years young herself.

We did have a laugh last week with that. Conor, Mammy and I were in the chip-shop, waiting for our order, and a smallish, jolly-faced man walked in the door just as Conor and Mum were playing a cat and mouse game, around the pillars in the shop. Mammy emerged from behind a pillar wearing Conor's coat on top of her own, and sporting an "I'm going to gobble you up" sort of manic grin. She went straight for the man. He was fairly nimble and dodged, but Mammy went trotting after him. Conor was in screams of embarrassment and laughter, calling "NANA, I'm here!" I think she realised her blunder, but wasn't going to show that it hadn't been intentional. What a giggle.

She's followed the wrong person a few times now. She panics crossing roads and if I am not holding her hand she can easily march away with the fastest walker. Recently, I was holding her hand and a jogger-lady, with dyed orange hair, trotted past on Mum's side, looking for a space to cross the road. As she darted across the road, Mammy pulled at me to run after her. She looked at me restraining her, momentarily very confused and we both laughed.

* * *

"Every morning you renew your mercies" is a line from an ear-worm this morning. After a late, great girls' night out and a few glasses of wine, I had all the ingredients for a dodgy day today, what with the rain and a trip to the West Hospital to look forward to. But I have felt very alive and full of joy and gratitude today.

Us women sure do roller coaster with hormonal moods. I do anyway. I wrote a poem about this from my perspective:

Roller Coaster

Climbing, soaring, awesome
falling...
The excitement is breathtaking
    as the ride just begins;
the path I steadily climb,
higher and higher, the air getting thin,
exhilarating rushes of wind.
Reaching a peak it rests for a while...
the views from up here, I inhale -
the beauty, creation, the planets and stars
from this awesome height I rejoice.

With joy and with awe I would stay here forever
a sigh as my head tumbles back...
but this is the ride where high turns to low,
and this will not last,
back down I will go,
with a scream and a tear
and a moment of fear,
I will land with a thump back below!

The body has landed but the rest is still up there,
sick with no stomach and empty inside,
and now it all seems, back down on the ground,
that this is reality and that was a dream...

Climbing, soaring, awesome
falling...

Why don't I get on the nice Carousel,
that gently rotates all the time?
No ups and no downs, no loops upside down
no sickness or wobbly limbs.
I could pick a gold lion, a lamb or a horse
and wait while each animal follows its course -
round and round
round and round
round and round...

But I'm not alone on the ride of my choosing,
Jesus knows what it's like.
His highs and His lows were deeper with love
than mine ever were or will be;
and God raised Him higher and higher
and higher
and he's here even now with me.
Giving me hope
that I'm never alone,
in the climbing, the soaring
the awe and the falling
and I trust He is leading me home! Dawn.

We arrived in good time to ride the car park helter-skelter to
the seventh floor, and then had to descend the stairs on foot. This
is challenging for Mum, but she managed exceptionally well today.

We got a good rhythm going. "1,2,3…9,10 and round the bar on the flat… and 1,2…" all the way down. It generated a few smiles from the other visitors.

The West Hospital is well sign posted inside, but it still takes some concentration to get to the right block, the right floor and the right department. I got it wrong, but it didn't seem to matter and we weren't late.

The Neurologist wasn't a native English speaker and Mum found her difficult to understand, but she was very sweet to Mum, explained things well and listened well to me. She concluded that Mum has a "form of epilepsy " (not the more well known one) that is affected by frontal lobe seizures and is linked to the progression of the Alzheimer's. She will have to undergo some kind of brain wave monitor, to be sure of this diagnosis, but that won't be today. With epilepsy she will have to be on more medication, which may have side effects. She will see us again in November. Meanwhile, she said, "if she goes all stiff and purple and foams at the mouth for 5 minutes", then I am to call an ambulance. Apparently the 'wobbly eyes' is also a symptom of the Alzheimer's and nothing can be done about that.

Back up seven flights of stairs and then spinning the wheel back down again. Only £2.50 for the parking this time.

Looking through my calendar I see that today was our twenty-fifth appointment at a clinic, hospital, dentist or optician since January. That doesn't include all the regular trips to the GP. That's well over £50 in parking fees as well. I now tell Mum she's going to have to dream up a complaint with her ears, nose or kneecaps, as these are the only bits that haven't been thoroughly examined yet.

It was still early so I delivered her to the 'Broad Glade Day Centre' and went off looking for cards and presents. I went into a local gift shop and came out feeling very fortunate. No matter what your circumstances, you always manage to meet someone who has been through something worse than yourself. I mentioned my situation with Mum and realised again how very blessed I am to have such a supportive husband. Simon positively encouraged me to keep her here with us, at least until we could decide what to do. This lady's husband was refusing to let her care for her mum at home and she was heart-broken.

* * *

Mum loved her home, 'Clett', on Graemsay, where she could roam all day, and always someone would find her and bring her home again. She used to tell me she was "in the safest place in the entire world". Maybe she was, but if the local council would oust her and put her in a home, miles away from her family and friends, she would possibly wither and die, confused, angry and terribly sad. I can't think how awful it would have been.

When Simon married me last June, he suddenly had a family of four. He knew he would be taking on the boys, but neither of us expected a mother (in-law). It was a strange four months before Mum came and it seemed somehow unreal. The boys were settling in really well, which was a great relief, and Simon was hardly affected by the change of location as his work and pastimes (the computer) had come with him.

But I was very unsettled and anxious. I had busied myself with domestic and gardening projects. The big job was to rid the garden of the ground elder, which was like a huge, underground, spaghetti root-ball extending the length of the back garden. There were rosy apples relentlessly showering the garden for much of that time and I was busy finding good apple recipes. I visited friends, attended school events and became a parent governor at Joshua's secondary school, which seemed healthy for my professional development and interest.

There was also the possible luxury of Simon and I slipping away together after lunch.

I became pregnant and tried to get plenty of rest, reading and living very much in that hormonal chaos of early pregnancy. The overstated, "blooming time" of sore breasts, greasy hair, nausea and ravenous hunger.

Then, on 6th December we went for our first scan. We were so excited.

Our baby was dead.

The shock numbs all sense. There was no time to grieve.

Medical intervention was deemed necessary as I had a long journey to make to Aberdeen, to meet Mum for that first Christmas together.

So I had the surgical evacuation at the hospital and the following week fetched Mammy from Aberdeen, for our first Christmas together since I was seventeen. Roger, our friend from Graemsay, had taken Mum down to Aberdeen and booked us all in for the night. The plan was for Mum to return to Orkney with Roger on 8th January 2007. I was then going to look for supply work at local primary schools and other early years settings, but seemingly that wasn't part of the bigger picture.

"In his heart a man plans his course, but the LORD determines his steps." (Proverbs 16:9) NIV

* * *

Tonight Mammy had what I think is another fit. It didn't look all stiff and straight like the Neurologist demonstrated earlier, but she was shaky and jerky for about one minute. We were watching a film and she had begun to doze. Again she sat up suddenly, wondering momentarily where she was. I wonder how many of these episodes she actually has?

I first noticed these 'fits' on March 12th. Mum had had a shower and I was helping her dress, when suddenly she was less responsive to instructions and then began to topple backwards. I remember it all being in slow motion, as I caught her and tried to hold her upright to steady her and get a response. She became very heavy and as I tried to sit her onto the chair she began throwing her arms and head about and shaking in a jerky sort of way. My heart was pounding, but Mammy looked up at me and said "Am I ready yet?" with a big smile.

She had no idea that anything had occurred, so we came down and had breakfast. She was absolutely fine. I thought maybe she had low blood sugar. As I was putting her plate back in the kitchen, there was a slump and thud and she was out cold on the floor. Her head just missed the brick hearth by an inch. Again, swooping to her side to reassure, her arms, legs and head threw themselves about shaking jerkily and then she came back round. This time she looked very drained and was confused to find herself on the floor. I sat her down and pulled up close beside her to hold her and try to explain what had happened, and she went again, within minutes. Simon called NHS Direct and an ambulance. The paramedics took Mum to the hospital to be monitored. It was a very unnerving experience, just not knowing what might happen next and having no control. Fifteen weeks later we still don't really know what it is, or when or why it may happen again, although we do suspect epilepsy and are hopefully en route, via the neurologist, to a conclusion.

She had another episode in the bath on May 15th and that one tonight, but I'm sure she has had many more. On that first Saturday, when she went into hospital overnight, (ostensibly to be monitored, but wasn't) I phoned a couple of people from Orkney to find out whether this had been a common occurrence in the past. I discovered that several Graemsay residents had witnessed Mum's 'funny turns' and that once, after one such episode, she had even been helicoptered over to hospital in Orkney. I also learned that the doctor there had reduced Mum's dosage of Aricept because of this. Some communication between health professionals could have been useful here. When I went to collect Mum from hospital, after 'being monitored overnight', I gave the consultant this information from the islanders, and he said to discontinue the Aricept altogether, admitting that he was aware of such possible side-effects. I was particularly cross that when she came home it was obvious that she had not even been undressed for bed, and came home with the tube for the needles still in her arm.

* * *

33

Another morning and I nearly slept through it. Simon kindly let me have a Saturday lie-in, whilst he got up to see the boys off to Music School. Mammy got up very early too, but was happily being entertained by some Saturday morning programmes on the wireless. I say happy, but apparently she needed a tissue as a lady on the wireless was recounting her ordeal of when she lost a small child... I would no doubt have been blubbering too, had I been awake and listening. I emerged after 10:00 and later I asked Mammy about the child *she* lost.

There are twenty-two months between my sister and I, but between us, on 15th February, 1964, another baby girl was born and was named Avril, after her Mammy. The baby died. Mammy can't remember whether she was weeks, days or only hours old, or even whether she was born dead. She remembers that no one else was in the house, that the baby was tiny and she remembers Daddy being angry and blaming her. Apparently, the baby died minutes after being born and her sister believes it was because Mum had starved herself, in order to feed Dad and baby Debbie.

Dad can't have been angry for long, because I was conceived within the next few months.

I have very few (conscious) memories of our first house on Herbert Street. (I have had other, hypnotherapy-induced memories of that house dug out of my sub-conscious mind over the years, but they were very sad and scary.)

I remember being served privet leaves for supper once, after being warned not to eat them off the bush. I remember that the house was one of a terrace and that one winter it snowed so much that the back gate was nearly buried and Dad leapt over it with such style.

Sometimes I was so proud of my father and thought him very cool and handsome. Most clearly I remember our bedroom at Herbert Street. One morning, just after my fourth birthday, Dad sat on the edge of my little canvas camp bed and told Debbie and I that we were leaving the house and going to live in a caravan. I took a mental photograph of that room, which has never left me.

CHAPTER 4

Mammy came down in her vest and trousers, so I fetched her a top and she wanted to find her shoes, so we went hunting. She has a funny way of saying things to sound as if she has understood everything.

"It's *that* way," she grinned, with both arms out, pointing in opposite directions.

Gradually she inched her way hesitantly down the hallway and then turned, as if to come back, but I was in the way, so she continued. Recognising the stairs, she went up and straight along to the bathroom.

"I'm here", she announced. She *had* forgotten what she was looking for, so I reminded her of the mission. She remained standing.

"Is this your bedroom?" I asked, sounding surprised.

"I think so", she said, looking at the bath and peering gingerly at the label on the door. Realising it said "bathroom", she laughed.

Eventually she did find her room and had no trouble exchanging slippers for a matching pair of shoes. Well done, Mammy.

Back in the kitchen, she was hovering behind me as I prepared food for the freezer.

"Who said you could watch me?" I laughed cheekily.

"But you're my *Mummy*!" she whined in a pretend little-girl voice.

It's funny, but more than one person has introduced me as "Avril's Mum" already. I guess the roles get fixed in the brain more than the ages.

We are going out to a restaurant this evening, so I suggested a rest first, since she was up so early today.

"Do you know where to find the sitting room?" I checked.

"Of course I do…it's here, where we live!" she laughed.

I must take her for a bath soon. I wonder what adventures we'll have today?

* * *

We had a lovely evening at the restaurant, but I was a bit worried at first, because when she sat down, Mammy looked as if she was having a panic attack. A cacophony of voices and other restaurant noises enveloped us and it was all too much for her. I was trying to help her choose a main course and I thought she was going to freak out on me again.

The last time I took Mum to church in town she did freak and cry, and I had to take her out. She complained that the noise was "just so intense". It is very loud. We discussed how it felt for her and whether earplugs might be a good idea. I think it might be like it is for babies, in that they cry when there's a lot of noise that they cannot understand, but as we get older we understand the noise and can tune some of it out. Some autistic people cannot tune it out either and maybe Mum can't now? I don't suppose it's worth having the ears examined; I'm sure they'll just say that it's another symptom of the disease.

Before we went out Mum gave me a big hug and thanked me for everything and for looking after her so well.

"I hope I don't annoy you *too* much?" she said. Of course she does sometimes, but that's *my* problem.

* * *

What to do with Mum is always such a challenge, particularly if I don't know what I want to do myself.

We went out for a walk with the pretext of buying milk. Mammy was looking upset again.

"I'm so scared," she said "I can't DO anything and I don't know what's going to happen."

"It is scary. But you can walk and talk, sing and dance, eat and pray and you *can love*. That's quite a lot of stuff that you CAN do well and I think it's very important stuff. The other things we can help you with."

Mammy certainly can dance. She dances in a a very seductive, fun way and can still jive. Once, they had an outing at the 'Broad Glade Day Centre', and Mum returned with a certificate for being "a beautiful dancer and a lovely presence on the stage". She is happy when dancing, especially to rock 'n' roll. She loves blue grass too. It always surprises me how deep into the soul music must go, as many people can forget even their own name but still manage to sing-along to an old tune.

* * *

Monday again. We've done the school run, had tea and a chat with Pat (we visit her on the way home several times a week), been up to Take-a-Break, done some shopping and assessed the growth (and the storm-damage) in the garden. The air smells fabulous today, like the air you smell when hill-walking: fresh green, muddy fragrances, full of warmth, heady-sweet privet, elder flower and promise somehow?

The OT is here now, doing an activity with my crafty mum. I'm trying not to listen, but it sounds like she's taking some encouraging.

Yesterday I picked up a book and read the first chapter, called "What is Alzheimer's Disease?"

I must admit that I found this a little alarming:

"The form of Alzheimer's disease that is definitely known to be passed on...in the genes, is extremely rare. It is very unlikely... unless close relatives have developed the disease below the age of 60... If your family does... you are only at risk if your mother or father developed it. If [so]...you have a one in two chance of developing the disease...a genetic test ... could be requested to confirm whether or not you do in fact have the gene..." (page 5) [Notes 2]

Now that's not very encouraging. I will banish such thoughts and rebuke all fear. I have no intention of carrying or developing such a horrible disease. Nor Debbie.

It also says that up to the age of sixty-five, Alzheimer's disease develops in only about one person in a thousand.

One other fact that I found interesting, considering they seem to know so little about what actually causes the disease, was the description of what would be found in the brain of an Alzheimer's sufferer at their post-mortem:

"Diagnosis... usually depends on finding characteristic changes in the brain tissue...Spread throughout the brain... are deposits, or plaques, made up of an abnormal protein called beta amyloid. A further abnormality is the occurrence of tangles of twisted protein molecules within the nerve cells of the brain. Other features, also found in other dementias, are shrinkage of the brain and widespread death of cells." (Page 3)

Another thing they find in post-mortems is a lack of acetylcholine (a neurotransmitter) in the brains of people who have had Alzheimer's. That's why they prescribe Aricept, I believe.

But we don't seem to know what causes all these proteins and plaques to develop.

The book also offers a rough guide to the likely progression of the disease, in terms of symptoms. They list early, middle and late symptoms. Reading through them for a "best fit" assessment of Mum, I can tick off everything in the early and the middle lists and even put hesitant ticks on half of the symptoms listed in late symptoms. (page 10) [Notes 2]

I have listed these stages in the Appendix [App.1]

So we've got more to look forward to yet. It is all quite vague though. The last time we were at the St Peter's Wing, the doctor did a memory assessment of Mammy. She scored "nine" out of something, but apparently "less than twelve" (out of that same something) indicates a severe memory impairment. They asked lots of questions about what day, month, year, and season we are in and, mostly, she doesn't have a clue. Personally, when my own routine is disturbed, during holidays for example, I don't know what day or date it is either.

And what does it really matter?

Some new events do register and stay in her mind and recall though.

Last year when I told Mum that I was getting married, she consistently said she wanted to come. When it was arranged, apparently she told lots of people in Orkney that she was coming to my wedding.

More recently, the tragic, accidental death of our dear friend, Roger, was an event she recalled frequently over the weeks until the funeral, which we were fortunate to be able to attend. I suppose the fact that these events were so significant was the main point.

Anyway, the doctor here said that the Aricept doesn't help with severe memory loss anyway.

I looked to see what the book says about the genetic test for family members. Apparently it is a simple blood test to see whether or not I could be carrying the gene that has caused Alzheimer's disease in my mother. I probably won't do it though. I want to live in faith in God, not under a medical prognosis.

However, I might try some vitamin B12 and B1 supplements, which are supposed to help keep the brain healthy anyway.

This is all technical stuff, but I find it interesting and worth knowing. I know what to pray against for myself and my boys too. (And for my sister and her children.)

The Alzheimer's website has another simple checklist:

The seven warning signs of Alzheimer's disease are:

1. Asking the same question over and over again.
1. Asking the same question over and over again.
1. Asking the same question over and over again.
2. Repeating the same story, word for word, again and again.
3. Forgetting how to cook, or how to make repairs, or how to play cards — activities that were previously done with ease and regularity.
4. Losing one's ability to pay bills or balance one's chequebook.
5. Getting lost in familiar surroundings, or misplacing household objects.
6. Neglecting to bathe, or wearing the same clothes over again, while insisting that they have taken a bath or that their clothes are still clean.

7. Relying on someone else, such as a spouse, to make decisions or answer questions they previously would have handled themselves.

[See Appendix 2: useful websites.]

* * *

My sister, Debbie, will be coming to Nottingham next Tuesday. Debbie and I are not alike. We see the world from very different perspectives. I haven't seen her since Christmas, just before Simon and I decided that Mum would not be returning to Orkney. She has lived in Spain for about thirteen years with her three children.

She has "Enduring Power of Attorney" over Mum, so I have had to update her regularly on what's been happening medically and decisions that need to be, or have been, taken. It has been particularly difficult for the various agencies involved, because technically Debbie is supposed to give her permission, and sign the forms, for just about everything. Fortunately, however, the system is mostly humane enough to allow me, as "main carer" and "other daughter", to get on with the nitty-gritty, day-to-day stuff, without too much ceremony.

I have found the situation frustrating. Not that I want the legal as well as the practical responsibility, but when the Enduring POA was set up by Debbie and Mum, (in Orkney, under Scottish Law) I was given the impression that we had *joint*-POA. Apparently though, I only have real authority to act on Mum's behalf if either Debbie dies, or rescinds her power. She doesn't intend to do either.

Life is like that sometimes.

* * *

I would strongly advise anyone caring for a relative with dementia to make sure that POA issues are settled early on, as the dementia sufferer has to be "of sound mind" to sanction it.

* * *

One theory I have always had about Mum (but may not be true at all), is that the reason she has lost her memory is because she has lived in denial of the truth for most of her life. For much of her life, I do not know the real truth, I just know that she has hidden it. Growing up, there was so much horrible stuff happening, that both parents, but particularly Mum, would deny. They lived in a world of preferred make-belief.

My own memory of my early years is very patchy and I have used therapy to make sense of some of what I consciously remember. Experiences from my sub-conscious memory have managed to surface from their hidden depths and revealed themselves during my therapy. But I want to know what has affected me.

I wonder how much more Mum has hidden?

I do remember that Dad would beat her up quite badly at the caravan, when I was a little girl. And now we know the real story behind Mum's burns.

Later, it was me who became Dad's victim. I'm not looking forward to telling you about this next part, but it is an important part of my story. Please remember not to judge, as it is all forgiven and healed by God's grace.

I don't know when it all began, I only know when I became aware of things being uncomfortable. In good moods, Dad was very physically playful and we would tickle-fight, carry and tackle each other. Eventually, I became aware of not wanting him to tickle me in certain places, and of being embarrassed when he playfully checked that I wasn't developing "a hairy chest".

I began to dread the playful moods nearly as much as the bad moods.

One day, Dad and I went on a long bike-ride, to visit our old caravan. It felt very strange going back through the site and seeing the trickle of a stream that had once been my world of play. Somehow we got into the caravan through a window. We sat on the seat that was once Debbie's bed and mine. He began to kiss me inappropriately and to take off my clothes. I started to cry, but he continued. I was so scared, but he seemed surprised and disappointed and tried to talk me into it as he touched me and explained how he loved me and wanted to show his love; how love begins at home and this was how he needed me to help him. He said he loved me and I could help him feel better and no one needed to know; I would enjoy it if I would let him; it wasn't hurting anybody; it was good. I sobbed more and more, pulling away and going rigid and shaking. Eventually he got angry and stopped. He had not had what he had hoped for, and he was clearly disappointed and "hurt" by my "lack of love and understanding".

He let me get ready and we cycled straight home, my legs like jellied lead.

From then on I was even more terrified of him, especially being alone. Every time we were alone he would ask me again to "cuddle" him. He would plead with me and tell me why I was selfish, just like my mum, causing his depression and making him ill.

I knew I could not say yes. If ever I could speak, I would say, "What about Mum?" or "But you're my Dad!'" I didn't dare tell him that I just didn't want to.

He thought that me being his daughter made it more morally right than if he went to a stranger.

This went on for the next six years until I left home. Some days he would go on until I cried, then he would hit me and go away. Some days he just went on trying until someone else came home.

Twice he held a gun to my head, after me watching him put the bullets in, then he pulled the trigger.

Once, having packed to go on a school trip to France, Daddy played Russian Roulette as I waited, desperately praying that I would live to leave the house.

Some days I hoped that something awful might happen to me whilst I was out, like having an accident or being kidnapped, so that I would have a good excuse not to go home. And if I was dead, it would "serve them right".

Then it would no longer be my fault. It might make him happy. It might make him stop. I know it was to his credit that he didn't ever force me sexually, but I still wondered if it would have put me out of my misery if he had.

I also feared that he might stab or strangle me instead, so I used to sleep with my back to the wall, one arm covering my heart and the other shielding my neck. I still sleep more peacefully like that.

At the time, no one admitted to knowing anything. I certainly didn't dare tell a soul. As for many poor children in this world, it was the dreadful secret.

I still remember the beating I received when a policeman insisted on escorting me home (despite my protestations) after an accident I had at school. Dad had been terrified when he saw him at the door.

I often wondered whether my mum knew what he was doing. Eventually I confided in my Isabelle, but I believed that if any word of complaint got back to Dad, my life would literally end.

About five years before he died, at our last meeting in Orkney, I told Dad how devastating this had been for me, but his response was, "I'm sorry I hurt you. You were still too young."

At about the age of thirteen, I had become a Christian. I still know, as I did then, how much God had protected me throughout this time. I was also grateful that He had sent other wonderful people into my life to affirm me. I know He preserved my life.

At the age of seventeen, on a beautiful August day my lovely Nana finally gave in to the cancer that had riddled her body. I was devastated. Dad took Mum to Nana's house and then went to his yard, a motor- mechanics' business, which he had inherited from his dad a couple of years earlier. They had left me at home to mourn in peace.

I took my one cassette tape (Fleetwood Mac) out into the garden and lay in the sun, crying and thinking about Mum and Nana. After what seemed like several hours, I heard the dreadful sound of Dad's car returning. My stomach in knots again I waited, hoping he'd go to bed and leave me in the garden. He banged on the kitchen window and beckoned me in. What followed is messy, like a storm. He was ranting about me being a harlot to the neighbours, disrespectful to my Nana and a nasty thing. He whacked me repeatedly around the head and kicked me to the floor, knocking the ironing board and other furniture flying. He was mad. Arms and legs pumping, he screamed at me to get out before he killed me.

I knew he meant it and how I got to the front door and out, I don't know. I ran as fast as I could, shaking and crying until I found myself near Isabelle's house. She was away on holiday with her mother, but her Dad was at home. I stood sobbing on his doorstep, before plucking up the courage to knock.

He was very good to me and offered me sanctuary. Later that day, Mum found me and forced me to go back home, saying that she was not going to lose her mother and her daughter on the same day. I made her promise that Daddy would not touch me again. I don't think he did. He had very little to do with me for the four months after that.

When Isabelle returned, she was furious and begged me to come to live with her. Her Dad was happy with the idea and we devised a marvelous plan. One day a friend with a car came to my house when the coast was clear. We quickly loaded all my belongings and took them to Isabelle's house. Then I walked to Mum's shop to give her the house key and to tell her what I thought she should know.

It didn't go as planned. I'm not sure how I expressed what had been happening all those years, but now it was Mum's turn to be angry and thump me. She called me a deceitful liar, amongst other things, saying she had never liked me and threatened that if I didn't have everything back at home by the time Dad got home, then Dad would come and kill us all. I phoned Isabelle and told her that I had to go back, having no idea when Dad would return. We no longer had the friend and his Mini, so Isabelle and I legged it back and forth with box after box, until it was all back in order.

For the next few months at home, Mum was in charge and I had certain freedoms. At weekends I was allowed to stay at Isabelle's house. I did as many of those rebellious things that young girls are not supposed to do. We rarely stayed in at Isabelle's house, but her Dad was fabulous. She could phone him on a Sunday morning and he would always come and fetch us, from wherever we had stayed the night.

One such Sunday morning, between Christmas Day and New Year's Day, Mum saw him drive up the road with an empty van and return with us party girls about twenty minutes later. She put two and two together and made ten, deciding that we were prostitutes, drug dealers and whatever else, and that she didn't want me in her house anymore.

She had formally disowned me. I was no longer her daughter, she no longer my mother.

She typed out a contract for Isabelle's dad to sign (as I was not yet eighteen), giving him full parental rights over me. He was happy to sign it.

That was a New Year to rejoice! How happy I was to leave.

It hurt to have her disown me though.

She didn't want to face reality. Even when Dad died, the first thing she said to me, when I rushed all the way to Orkney, from London, was,

"I don't want to hear anything bad about your Dad, now or ever. Okay? I want to remember the man I loved."

Doesn't that say it all?

When he was gone, she slowly lost a grip on how to "seem to be normal" and then lost all the secrets and most of the memories. I can't blame her for wanting to forget though.

* * *

Chapter 5

I have been extra busy and a little "down-in-the-dumps", with minor irritations making me more tired than usual. My eyes and ears are sore, the head aches a lot again, the back is giving me pain and, due to decorating, the skin on my hands is cracked and stings.

On Tuesday I had to take Conor to Orthodontics at the West Hospital.

Simon had to take the day off work, so that Mum could have her "befriender" and the "sitting service", which are both on Tuesdays. The "befriending scheme" is a service provided by volunteers and organised by the Alzheimer's Society. Simply put, a volunteer will agree to visit the "service user" at a mutually convenient time each week and befriend them. The "sitting service" is a more specialist organisation, run in Nottinghamshire. These workers have some training and are paid by the local council, but they perform a similar task to the befriender.

(See Appendix 2: "Helpful Organisations")

It was a bit squirmy in orthodontics, when they put the green putty in Conor's mouth to make the shape; and fitting the tight metal rings was painful, but the rest of the day was great. They are making Conor a 'palatal arch' for when they extract his molars. He has to have eight teeth pulled out in July and he is going to need a general anaesthetic. He's still my baby and I don't like the idea at all. I hope he gets to like soup.

We didn't get back until 15:00. Mum had had a good day so far and remembered having "something yummy" to drink in a café with her befriender.

The sitting service lady came next, and Conor and I went for his last swimming lesson.

Interesting things happen when I become hormonal. Apart from the physical bits being more sensitive, the nerves cut like knives. As for making decisions, I become almost paralysed, as if facing a life-changing choice like: shall I make a pot of tea now, or when I've finished hanging the washing?

And I keep banging into things.

Yesterday and today, amidst the ongoing decorating and gardening, I've been sewing up ties, cutting Mum's hair, form-filling, ordering a disability badge for the car, and managed some prayer time. I am feeling satisfied, but there's such a lot planned that I think I'm feeling some anxiety too.

Simon's friend is staying with us tomorrow before his wedding on Saturday. Mum is coming with us to this wedding, so we all need dressing up and I have to drive. It is not easy to get "babysitters" for people like Mum, and as we are not sleeping away, Mum should be able to handle it.

Bruno and Violet's First Holy Communion is on Sunday, with a party to follow.

Debbie is coming on Tuesday, until…?

On Wednesday, the "Pension Credit people" are coming AGAIN, to ask more questions and hopefully get these forms finished.

Ana is coming on Thursday night, and on Friday, Simon and I fly out to Jersey, leaving Ana to look after the boys and Isabelle to deliver Mum to Broad Glade. Ana was one of the fantastic Au-pairs we had whilst I was working in London. She was our Au-pair for two years and then later lodged with us for another year before we left London. She still works in London and visits us regularly for holidays.

I am really looking forward to a break with Simon. It will be our first time away, just the two of us, since our honeymoon.

Yesterday we went to see Mum's dementia consultant, who I understand to be the "top dog" at the St Peter's Unit. She didn't keep us long, but what she said has knocked-me-for-six. Apparently, the OT had given her notes to the consultant, who, on reading them, doesn't feel that Mum is presenting Alzheimer's at all.

She might not have Alzheimer's?

She said that the report suggests frontal lobe deterioration, which is apparently not consistent with Alzheimer's. Frontal lobe, is also what the epilepsy specialist was talking about. So if Mum is having frontal lobe seizures, would that not cause frontal lobe deterioration?

I didn't ask these questions.

The consultant wants to refer Mum to another neurology specialist for a second opinion.

How will I feel, if I discover that Mum has had epilepsy all this time, which, had it been diagnosed and treated correctly, might not have resulted in this incapacitating dementia? Could treatment *now* halt or reverse the deterioration? Does that mean Debbie and I probably haven't inherited Alzheimer's?

I guess some of these questions will be answered in time. Meanwhile we await the "brain-wave test" (EEG) and the neurologist's "second opinion".

It does offer some additional hope though, as well as questions.

Mum had another "little episode" on Monday. She didn't faint this time, but she "blanked" and her eyes rolled whilst she shook.

Her hands and skin look white and puffy and she is coughing again quite a lot. The GP must be sick of us all by now, but we visited her again to formally get the results of the recent tests. All of it is clear.

The cough is still a big problem to Mum. We now have two more avenues to explore: asthma or something to do with "reflux" from the oesophagus into the lungs.

The dementia consultant has just phoned me. Her ears must have been burning. Like many of the professionals involved with Mum, she has shown genuine concern for *my* well-being as a carer. According to the consultant, the question of dementia-type, is "all very academic", compared to the day-to-day job of caring.

The epilepsy specialist arranging the EEG has told her of her own doubts about the Alzheimer's. Apparently in the 10% of dementia sufferers who have neither Alzheimer's nor Vascular dementia, there is a relatively rare "frontal and temporal area" dementia, which may present like Mum's does. Anyway, the EEG should uncover more of this.

I will see the epilepsy specialist to discuss findings in November. It seems a long way off.

The consultant said it sounds like Mum is having chronic seizures, which prevent oxygen reaching the brain. So, if it gets worse, medication for epilepsy would be better than whatever side-effects may result from the medication.

It is very frustrating, watching everyone doing tests all the time, but nothing conclusive happening. I think we would all feel somehow rewarded if even *one* test result would point to a definitive cause and a possible solution.

I know they are all doing their best. We all are.

I still wonder whether therapy for Mammy could be helpful. I did mention it to the consultant and she said something vague in response, so I dropped it.

* * *

The school fair on Friday was not good for Mum. She couldn't see anything on the stalls, the children were moving around too fast, the sun was too hot and she couldn't hold the hot-dog properly, and inevitably lost the sausage on the floor. I was partly to blame, as I was still agitated.

Mum had a great day out with Debbie yesterday, and even though she has no idea where she went or who with, she enjoyed doing something different. So did I. It was good knowing that someone else was caring for Mum and happy to do so. It felt strange being in the house at the boys' dinnertime though, and Mum not being there.

On the morning of our friend's wedding, I found Mum in the downstairs loo. She sometimes goes in there just to "hang about".

It was such a funny sight. She knew something wasn't quite right, which must have been why she was hiding and looking at me with a "naughty girl" kind of apology. She had put on her stripy blouse, but only fastened the top button; she had a black sock on one foot and a black shoe on the other, and nothing else, no pants or anything.

Fortunately, she was able to laugh with me as I inquired as to whether this was her "sexy get-up" for the wedding.

Suddenly she became very upset and scared again. Her inability to perform what her mind envisions sometimes bothers her so much. The frustration then cripples her and it's a downward spiral. I can only hug and reassure and blame the "whatever it is" dementia, and tell her it's not her fault.

She cries at weddings too and, although she didn't know who was getting married, this was no exception. I dressed Mum in the top and suit jacket that I got her for my wedding. She was beaming.

Taking Mum to get our food at the reception was another mistake I'll not make twice. There was so much choice and people busy foraging, that it was enough for Mammy to just to hang on to me and follow me around the table, whilst I filled our plates. Then the disco set themselves up and Mum panicked. It was too loud again, so we searched for a quieter place for her to sit. She ended up in the cloakroom, which was a shame, because she loves dancing so much. We were very late home.

Fortunately the First Holy Communions were not until 12:00 the following day. It was very special for me to witness my Goddaughter, Violet, and Bruno, receive the Eucharist for the very first time.

There were some Italian guests at the house party afterwards, and for Mum the treat seemed to be one of the Italians himself. She became so amazingly animated and sociable, and completely unlike the Mum who had arrived an hour earlier.

Later that evening, at home with two exhausted boys, Mammy asked me, "Did you have a good day? Did you do something nice?" as if we had been in different parts of the world.

I told her that we had just spent the entire weekend together, at a Wedding and at a First Holy Communion celebration.

She looked at me sceptically and then conceded, "I must have got it wrong again then?"

I did press, but she couldn't tell me what she thought she had done instead.

* * *

I'm feeling very anxious about going to Jersey, about Mammy being in Broad Glade and about Ana and the boys, and all the arrangements necessary.

And I suspect I am pregnant.

Saturday is the 07/07/07, and that was our lost baby's due date. Can I do it this time? Will I manage to care for Mum and have a baby?

How good it is to know I can cast my cares on my heavenly Father.

* * *

I'm back after a great weekend in Jersey. We managed to walk our socks off, see so many wonderful sights, and eat the most delicious seafood. I've taken so many photographs of unusual petals, shrubs and other anomalies. One of my favourite plants there is called 'Agapanthus'. I bought one from the airport and hope it will thrive in Nottingham.

The pregnancy test confirmed my suspicions. Simon knew by then and is equally excited and nervous again. I spoke to the midwife yesterday and they've booked me for an eight-week scan on 6th August.

Mammy was pleased to see us. Conor and I could see her sitting in a lounge in the respite home with two other ladies, all equally motionless and grey. Conor stuck his head in front of her, with an "Hello Nana" and she transformed magically into a bouncy, smiley and colourful young Nana.

"*Oh*, I didn't know you were coming. It's *so lovely* to see you."

Up she jumped then to give him a hug and to find me.

The man on reception took us to get her things and as we searched the whole ward for her medication, there was not another member of staff to be seen. It makes me very sad, but grateful that I have not yet been forced by circumstances, as many are, to put Mum into a home permanently.

Debbie sent me a text, after dropping Mum off at the respite home on Friday, saying that she really appreciates all we are doing for Mum and apologised for "the hard time" she gave us initially. She commented on how much Mum has improved since she last saw her at Christmas. I really did appreciate that.

* * *

Mum dressed herself this morning. Only the trousers were wrong today, and they look so funny, like a little elephant dangling it's floppy ears (pockets inside out). She wished her breakfast a "good morning" and when I mentioned "having a bath", she asked me, "Which one are we going to today?"

She loves having her head and back scrubbed now; then I sorted her crabby foot and nails and she looked fresh and comfortably pampered.

I really do enjoy her more when she is responsive and content, and when I know I'm going to have a couple of hours to myself.

* * *

Walking to pick Conor up from school, I felt completely "spaced out". It is like continuing the experience of years of feeling alone; day dreaming, anxious, hiding, hoping I won't be noticed – a numbness, only half alive, yet simultaneously tingling with sensation and nerves everywhere, too painfully alive. I think it was a coping strategy, when extremely scared or alone as a child. I lived in my own intense little world a lot, usually in dread of what might be next.

* * *

Last night, as Mum joined in with prayers, she implied that she had been thinking a lot about things and trying to get everything in good order, and although she had done well, she wanted help to do even better. I didn't ask her what she had been thinking so much about, because her prayer is not to me, but it might explain why she was so much easier for me yesterday.

I had a little reminisce this morning with Mum and Conor, because next Tuesday is his school's performance of "Joseph and his Technicolor Dream-Coat". I described to them how at my junior school, I practised for weeks for that same concert, but in the end I was not allowed to be in the performance, because "They…" I said to Conor, whilst waving an accusing finger at Mum… "wouldn't let me do *anything* after school."

* * *

I always had to be home ten minutes after the school bell had gone. We had chores to do at home: cleaning, shopping, laundry and, often, cooking the tea.

We had left the caravan when I was eight years old and moved into a large, three-bedroom Victorian house in Mapperley. There was a cellar and a secret corridor between the hallway and the dining room, which fired our imagination and was an inexhaustible catalyst for games. There were also two sitting rooms and a crooked kitchen, with a twin-tub and a mangle. Daddy decorated the rooms with multicoloured spray-paints and lots of different wallpapers, and Mum painted the moulded patterns on the doors and filled the house with sparkly brasses and knick-knacks.

I would often sit in my room doing my homework in Winter, wearing hat, scarf, coat and gloves. The windows would have frosted leaf patterns all over the insides, and I could see each nervous morning breath shiver around my bed.

We never had hot running water, except ready for the bath every fortnight, which we shared one after another. Other jobs were done by boiling kettles on the stove. Water was never wasted.

Mum looked after our basic needs for food, clothes and a roof over head and she tried to make sure that we were washed and schooled, but she couldn't provide much emotional support and was always more distant than I would have liked. I would sometimes try to trick her into kissing me goodnight by pretending to whisper something and then grabbing her round the neck. Unfortunately, she would pull away from me irritated and leave me feeling even worse.

I was envious of Debbie, being the elder of us. She seemed to have space and privileges, and apparently never got the same abuse that I suffered. She also got beatings for being naughty though. Dad always said that she was like him and that I was too much like Mammy and I drove him mad.

In 1972, Mum bought a shop. It was a drapers, called "Nine till Five". She also did dressmaking and repairs and I used to help make soft toys to sell at Easter and Christmas. I knew that it was good for us to have the shop, because otherwise we had no income at all, but I hated her being away all day and, most of all, I hated being alone in the house with my Dad.

One day, when I got home from primary school, Dad was waiting with an important question, that Debbie and I would have to answer before Mum got home from the shop. He and Mammy were going to separate, he said, and he needed to know which of us was going to stay with him and which of us with Mum. She had apparently done something "unforgivable", but he wouldn't divulge. He left Debbie and I to solve this "Catch 22", and we decided that we girls would not be separated. We were scared to tell him the truth, which was that neither of us wanted to go with him. Eventually, at the tortuous eleventh hour, we said that we would go with Mum or run away together, but we never heard anything more about the separation again.

Dad never forgot our response though.

Safety and protection were not rights that I was to know as a child at home.

Mum never had them during her married life either and I believe that must account for some of the fear and anxiety that she still experiences now.

School was my refuge and a place where I did feel safe and valued. It was the place where Dawn was accepted and encouraged and nurtured.

I dreaded going home. I hated his torturous speeches. I hated the unpredictability of what he put me through.

I was also very aware of our financial poverty. I wore clothes that were not only hand-me-downs, but had been bought in jumble sales, altered for my sister and then passed on to me. I was embarrassed by my outgrown rags and admired the pretty girls with their fancy clothes.

I saved birthday money and wages from my paper-round and eventually bought myself a £14 second-hand bike. I loved it and would play out on it after tea and ride out to the countryside in the holidays.

* * *

When I was telling these stories at breakfast, Mammy was smiling and laughing as if I was talking about someone else. I suppose I was. She was no more to blame then for making my life difficult, as she is now for what she can or can't do today.

CHAPTER 6

The current night-time routine goes something like this: Mum comes to say prayers and join our "goodnight boys time", usually in Conor's room, as Josh's room is up the second flight of stairs. Simon and I take turns to be with each child. Then I take Mum to the bathroom and for night-dress, medication and bed. Medication is only a mini aspirin (against strokes), a Simvastatin (against cholesterol build up) and two puffs of the Salbutamol (to stop the wheezing). She is usually so tired by this time that her eyes are flickering and she cannot think for herself, so getting undressed is very much a guided affair.

I put a tablet into her hand, she pops it in her mouth and then looks into her hand and at me, back and forth.

"Do you need your water?" I'll ask.

Then we get "the shakes", a few attempts to swallow and then the next tablet. Lastly, the Salbutamol. She looks surprised to see it, screws up her little nose and squishes it against the mouthpiece – she looks like a little pig, and we both laugh; it's all part of the routine.

"Suck," I instruct, "now breathe out through the nose… Suck… out through the nose…Well done!"

Nine times out of ten, she will giggle and say something along the lines of,

"What is it supposed to do?"

And I take a deep breath, smile, and explain all over again.

* * *

I awoke to the sound of Joshua's alarm this morning, at 6:30am. Mum came down then with her trousers on back to front, but that's okay, as her tummy is bigger than her bottom, so they actually fit better that way. She had her shoes and socks on and an open cardigan on top of her bra. Something else wasn't quite right though and she was particularly unresponsive.

When finally all the boys had gone and we sat down with a second cup of coffee, Mum said, "Oh yes, there's something I need to tell you."

In essence, she said that she had got up in the night, wondered where everybody was, come downstairs, looked this way and that, and had gone out onto the road to find us. Then she had come back in again, but couldn't find anyone.

"It has been such a long night." she moaned.

She clearly hadn't been out onto the road, or out of the house, because she cannot get out. She has never yet managed to open or close the front door. The door is so stiff that you need two hands, elbow grease and a knack. And it is extremely noisy to open and even more so to slam shut.

I don't think I handled it correctly. She had her story firmly in her mind. Somehow this stuck in her memory as real. Was she hallucinating? Had she dreamt it? Had she heard the road and looked out of the window? Was she remembering a childhood reality or fear? I don't know.

I tried to explain all of this, but she refused to accept it, "because I was there!" she insisted.

So I asked her to show me what she had done. This was perhaps cruel, but I didn't want her believing what was untrue. Needless to say, she couldn't even find the door, so I led her to it and asked her again to show me where she had gone. She could not open the door.

Of course, then she was frustrated that I didn't accept her story and was "scared" by her confusion. More hugs and a chance for her to release some more tears.

Maybe I should have pretended that she was right. Maybe I wanted to prove her wrong.

The bus came ten minutes later and Mammy still seemed flat, despite me trying to cheer her up. I hope she doesn't carry it with her all day.

* * *

Mum has been discontent and "bored" all day. I've had some other chores to do, but we went shopping together and visited Pat, she spoke to her sister on the phone, did a tour of the garden, had tea and cakes, and listened to 'Far from the Madding Crowd" on cassette.

By 19:00, she looked so angry and huffy, I thought she was going to burst .

"All I do is wander about, with nothing to do. Just walk about."

She cannot remember going out today, or anything else she's done, so she does believe that all she does is wander about. Sometimes I have nothing useful left to say, other than to remind her of the activities of the day.

Today she did apologise, after my explanation. She does seem to realise when she has been "mardy".

I'm also a bit anxious about Wednesday, when Conor goes for his general anaesthetic and teeth pulling.

The boys don't know I'm pregnant yet. That's the other thing on my mind; this is the start of my seventh week, and the last baby died during the seventh week, they said.

* * *

Today we've been busy all day and it has felt good. After the usual Monday routine, we walked up to the church where Mum's mum and dad both have their ashes buried. Mum and I sat contemplating in the beautifully peaceful memorial garden. Then, having discovered that the vicar lived next door, I rang the bell. He was very accommodating and took us to see the plan of the garden and the book of records - their names were there: Elsie Marjorie Cowen, died 1982 (plot A8) and James Alvin Cowen, died 1992 (B39). It felt quite strange and satisfying, that after all these years, Mum and I should end up living just a walk away from her parents' place of rest.

We have decided to get a marble, memorial flower-pot engraved with their details. Mum is very pleased with the idea and wants to pay for the work, which is fitting. Anyway, with the back pay coming from her pension, she can afford it now.

I want to be buried when the time comes.

I asked Mum, but she doesn't seem to know. It became a family discussion and Josh said he wants to be "left to nature, or fed to the lions" and Conor wants to be cremated and his ashes thrown to the wind from the top of a high mountain.

* * *

I loved my Nana and Granddad Cowen. They were the only family to ever take us on holiday and they told funny stories, sang songs, and were a bit cheeky and daring. Nana wore makeup, fur coats, perfume and lots of smiles, and she chain-smoked. She was riddled with cancer when she died, only sixty-five. Granddad was five years younger than her, wore an old-man cap, braces and smoked a pipe. He was not much liked by his own kids, but dearly loved by his grandchildren. He was seventy when he died.

Nana was a practicing Anglican and brought her children up through the church to confirmation.

I remember Mum telling me, many years ago, that she had decided at the wise old age of thirteen, that the Bible was a "bunch of contradictions and lies" and that she was a non-believer.

Years later, when Daddy died, Mum used to experience him coming to visit her and this caused her to "know that there is life after death" and accept Christianity for herself.

As she put it in a letter to her Aunt Grace, in December 1995,

"It's my first ever experience of anything 'unusual' and now I'm a firm believer!"

* * *

Last night was the "Joseph and his Technicolour Dream Coat" presentation at Conor's school. It was all a wonderful and very welcome distraction, because I was getting nervous about today.

We were up at 06:15 for Conor's general anaesthetic and operation. All were good-humoured at home and no one dawdled getting up. Then Mum collapsed again at the breakfast table and fell off her chair. We kept it low-key, as again she didn't know it had happened. Simon had taken the morning off work to help.

In the car to the hospital, Mum had another turn. Simon had to inform the day centre when he dropped her off later.

I keep a record of all her fainting fits.

Conor and I arrived at the hospital in good time. We had fun playing a game with two soft toy characters that he'd brought with him, then we had some great chairs to play in. Two and a half-hours later we were called to the operating theatre.

The anaesthetist was excellent. He kept Conor distracted beautifully whilst he put the needle in. I watched it go in, then looked at Conor and got such a shock. He was out cold. They told me to kiss him and go. His eyes were open like a corpse, and it was all I could do not to close his eyelids, or to cry as I kissed him.

"Look after him please." I whispered.

I went and prayed, marched around and drank some coffee.

He was "down" for seventy minutes, due to his little body, they said. Then he was very woozy, but he wouldn't sleep. He kept trying to stand up, only to find his legs too weak and would fall. He felt sick, and of course his mouth was still all very numb from the anaesthetic, which made drinking water and eating ice cream satisfyingly messy.

Then we had a heart tugging film to cuddle up to at home, just Conor and I.

I feel like I've been awake all night and day; that spaced out feeling again.

Mum is home from the day centre now.

Conor has a big fat lip and is complaining of a bad back.

After tending to him, suddenly I felt compelled to look out of the window, just in time to see Mum disappearing out of the back gates. I ran out and caught her at the corner, heading for the road. I should have followed her to see what she would have done, but I couldn't leave Conor, so I brought her straight back. She insisted that she knew where she was and how to get back, but I didn't have the energy to risk losing her.

CHAPTER 7

Today Mum had the "Spirometry", a breathing test to measure the force and amount of available breath. Mum does fine breathing, but it is so difficult for her to follow instructions other than the most basic.

Like last night when she had pulled off a sock with the trousers and I gave it to her and asked her to put it back on. I came back with some fresh drinking water to find her with the sock on her knee and her foot in the sleeve of the nightie. She couldn't see what was wrong, but when I explained that she had her foot in the sleeve of her nightie, she thought it was hilarious.

As far as the breathing goes, we are going to try a steroid inhaler for six weeks, to see if the cough disappears. Unfortunately, the inhaler they've given doesn't fit into the spacer device that she is used to, so we are having to learn a whole new trick.

* * *

The school holidays have begun. Today I managed to get Josh out on an important mission, so that Conor and I could pick up his birthday cake, whilst Mum was out with her befriender. The cake, designed by Conor and made by the wonderful people in the cake shop, looks fabulous. It is a "stage" with a singer, guitarist and drummer, with the name of Josh's band written across it, along with his name and age – thirteen. Then I left the boys in charge of assisting with Mum's artwork, took the car and managed to get to the drum shop in town without arousing any suspicion. There is now one birthday "Repenique" (a Samba drum) in the boot of the car, complete with strap, case and beaters. I'm very excited.

The boys have been talking lots about "Faith Camp" recently and I know Mum must have been wondering what was going to happen for her.

When the sitting service arrived, she finally pleaded, "Am I coming?"

"What, are you coming camping?" I asked.

"Yes."

"To sleep on the floor in a tent?"

"Yes."

"No, mammy, you won't be able to come with us." I said.

I imagined with a shudder how absolutely unsuitable it would be. She would hate the noise in the main meeting tent and would regularly need escorting to the toilets across the campsite. I would have to watch her twenty-four hours a day.

She knows she's not coming and she is letting me know that she resents this.

I got a phone call earlier today from the "Evening Post" to talk about the needs of carers in the light of some new money being "poured in" to help support carers. I reported that everyone in the support services had been great, but that the process was too long and disjointed. The people have been helpful, but the services are spread thinly, are rather inflexible and do not interrelate enough. They want to take a photo of me later, to put with the article in tomorrow's paper. I hope they do put in some extra support.

It's hard to believe that there are "more than 80,000 carers in Nottinghamshire - about 10% of the population."

* * *

I had a good heart-to-heart with Mum this morning.

She had had a grumpy, silent breakfast as I sat with her. Then she went into the kitchen and started chatting away. She does this a lot: talks lucidly away to herself and says nothing in company. Admittedly, a lot of it is grumbling about things that she dare not say outright, but sometimes I'd rather hear it than just feel it.

"Are you talking to me, Mammy?" I called in.

"No."

"Is it easier talking to yourself? I wish you would talk to me."

"Don't I talk to you?" she sounded concerned.

"Not nearly as much as you talk to yourself."

"I'm sorry. I don't help you very much, do I?"

"Mammy, you do. You know that the only thing that bothers me is when you are mardy and grumpy. Doing stuff for you and with you is good, but I can't handle the bad moods. We've found two day centres, so that I can do what I need to do and you can meet people and have some fun. After all, it's much better than following me around the house, looking for something to do."

"I know. I'm sorry. Sometimes I look at you and I know I've hurt you."

We had a good hug and she went off arm-in-arm with the mini-bus driver.

I hope she takes some of that sunshine to the other folk at The Broad Glade Day Centre this morning.

* * *

I knew she would remember that I was going away. She didn't even break a smile when I put a Willie Nelson tape on. I know she was feeling rotten, but I'm already feeling anxious enough about packing, camping and the baby inside.

Mammy seems to be crying for all my attention. I could hardly stay awake any longer and had to lie down.

Simon and I will at least get some time together at camp this week. I bought a double sleeping bag today.

To wash Mum's hair now, I climb onto a chair at the open shower door, otherwise the shampoo runs down to my armpits and soaks me. Sometimes I just strip off and wrap a towel around me, but this works too. Today I leaned in a bit too far and the chair tipped. Mum couldn't have stopped my fall, so I grabbed the tiles and all was well, but it shook me.

She said she was jealous of anybody who can do things for themselves. I think she is also jealous of me going away without her.

Once dry, her tears began to fall silently.

I kept telling her it was only for a week, Monica was going to visit, camping is completely unsuitable, and so on, but she kept crying all the way to the care-home.

Conor told her she was snotty and should blow her nose, but she was inconsolable today. I don't know what the care-workers thought (there were lots of them around this morning), but I'm sure they'll cheer her up and she'll have forgotten it all when we come to pick her up again.

I can turn my mind to camp now.

When I come back, it will be August and I'll have my nine-week scan on the Monday.

* * *

Camp was fabulous. This year is our seventh camp together.

The boys are so much more independent now, that I actually had a good rest as well the opportunity to pray and worship. According to Josh it was "the best camp ever". In many ways it was my best too. To have a whole week in the presence of God and His children is such a blessing. I love being able to introduce my husband to people too. We had lots of time to chat and relax in the sunshine together.

Unfortunately I had a bad sleep on the last night and in the morning I had such pain in my abdomen and back. It took hours before I realised that I was having contractions. We managed to pack up quite efficiently as the pain intensified, but it was very distressing. The journey home was a painful endurance and when I got home I was bleeding heavily and got an ambulance to the West Hospital.

Eventually the morphine calmed me down, but it still hurt; I just couldn't keep my eyelids open. I had miscarried before arriving at hospital, but they kept me in there until Monday evening.

Two beautiful babies lost to me.

They are in God's hands.

Meanwhile, Mum was supposed to come home on the Sunday, but Simon explained my predicament and they agreed to keep her for an extra day.

I wished I could have had a day or two at home alone to rest and grieve.

I think Mum had a good time. Pat, Monica and Alf had all been to see her and said she seemed to be well looked after.

I'm beginning to wonder whether she is perhaps better-off with the routines and life in the home than she is here. She rarely seems to be happy here, no matter how much we provide for her. She seems happy during the activities, but immediately becomes restless and starts to flap with that "I'm hanging about" expression.

Last Tuesday was a good example: Pat came to visit and chat, then her befriender came and they went out for a long walk, "put-the-world-to-rights" and had coffee and cakes. Mum and I toured the garden and sat out for a chat. At 14:00 the art lady came and Mum painted her papier-mâché plate; after refreshments and more friends visiting, the sitting service arrived and they had a laugh together, listened to music, had another long walk, and a drink in the pub.

At 19:30, Mum's sister phoned and I heard Mum complaining:

"Nothing much at all! I don't do anything. I've just been hanging about!"

I spoke to Julia myself and used that day as an example of what "just hanging about" often is in reality.

She's out walking with her befriender again now. I often wonder what Mum talks about to other people. I'd love to be a fly on the wall.

I want to read some alphabet and words with Mum later, because when we've done it in the past, she has enjoyed the sense of accomplishment and we've vowed to do it regularly, like so many good intentions.

* * *

It was not a good idea today. She can still read the letters of the alphabet and individual names, but cannot write anything today. She was shrinking her neck backward into her shell and when I encouraged her she would say,

"I don't know what I'm supposed to be doing!"

"It doesn't matter if you don't want to write anything today. Your reading is still good." I tried to reassure.

Then I presented some old photographs, because she usually enjoys looking at them and comments, "I haven't seen that one before" and smiles longingly as she recognises past times.

But not today. The only pictures she recognised was one of me at about six years old, and one of her mum, but she didn't recognise herself or her sister smiling proudly on either side. Now she feels inadequate again and I am exhausted.

* * *

Mum seems to be deteriorating these past few weeks.

This morning I woke her, gave her her clothes and came down to make breakfast. After twenty-five minutes she was still rolling the trousers round and round her hands. Then she screwed up her face, saying there was "such a nasty smell in here".

I said it was the commode, as she had used it in the night.

"No I didn't!" she growled at me.

"Yes you did." I retorted. "Do you want to see it?"

"I didn't use it at all… It wasn't me… I haven't been today."

"You used it in the night. No one else comes in to use it, Mammy."

"They did. I didn't."

"Whatever! Please don't argue with me, Mammy. You don't remember what you've done ten minutes ago, so you probably don't remember what you did during the night!"

"I do know…"

Nauseous, rattled and wanting to stick the commode in front of her nose, I dressed her and led the way downstairs.

Conor tried to play with her, but to no avail. I'd successfully spoiled her mood for the morning. Despite a few meagre attempts to converse, we did the school walk in near silence, holding each other's sweaty mitts.

"I'm sorry Mammy."

One aspect that has noticeably deteriorated is her proprioception. When she wants to touch a part of her body, for example, she reaches her hand outwards to external things. In the shower if I give her the soap and ask her to wash "down below", she reaches out, touching all the sides of the shower-cubicle trying to find the bits to wash.

I now have to wash her bottom for her; she doesn't even wipe it now. She screws up the clean toilet-paper and shoves it into her pockets. At the undressing end of every day, when she gives me her rolled up trousers, I tip hands-full of clean tissue into the bin. There is no point arguing, because she believes she is doing it properly and gets upset if I challenge her. Sometimes I feel the need to challenge her, but I regret it later.

I have to remind myself frequently that it isn't her fault.

Two weeks ago, Conor was with Nana in the dining room when she suddenly slumped off the chair and hit her face on the floorboards. Conor was freaked, but Nana did her usual jerks and had a nosebleed. She was a bit fazed by the blood and by finding herself on the floor, but we got her into a comfy chair in the sitting room and attended to her nose. She was complaining about her teeth, which she kept dabbing with her fingers. Suddenly she pointed in front of her to the left and exclaimed, "What's that?" I looked over towards the TV, which was switched off, and asked what she meant, but she kept pointing and saying "It hurts!"

"Touch where it hurts, Mammy"

Gradually her hand closed in towards her face and I realised that underneath her fringe a huge swelling had grown over her right eye. We applied an ice pack and phoned NHS Direct, who sent a couple of paramedics. They did a thorough check and felt around to check that nothing was broken, cracked, or out-of-place in any way. They recommended Paracetamol and sleep. Poor Mum.

The next morning she slept in, but had such a whopper of a black eye.

The following day was our planned boat trip, with the Take-a-Break group. Mammy awoke with two purple eyes, but was feeling much better in herself, so we went to the river.

She became tired very quickly and I had to answer lots of questions about Mum's panda-face. I almost began to feel guilty, as if I had given her the black eyes.

* * *

Chapter 8

We now have Mum's EEG appointment, for the twentieth of this month (EEG is Electroencephalograph, which is a test to record the electrical impulses that the brain produces whilst sending and receiving messages from the body.)

They want to do a sleep deprived EEG, which will entail keeping Mammy up all night before the test. In recent weeks, Mum becomes overwhelmed with tiredness and goes almost immediately to bed after dinner in the evenings. Some days she also wants a nap in the daytime, and becomes panicky and tearful if I don't suggest it.

I do want to know what is causing the seizures. The Consultant Neurologist called them "frontal lobe seizures with a quick recovery".

* * *

I let Mum have a relaxing day and tried to keep her gently entertained (good old Conor) and after dinner, I went to get some sleep. Simon stayed up with Mum until 03:00.

I made coffee, showered us both, had an early breakfast and listened to some lively dance music. The taxi came at 07:45 and we arrived at hospital feeling very pleased with our success.

The nurses in Neurophysiology measured Mum's head, making little crayon marks on her scalp. They asked many questions and handled Mum well, so after watching them stick the little electrodes to her head I left her, looking like an experimental hedgehog, in their capable hands.

When I returned, she was already back in the waiting room, looking rather disoriented, but free to go.

Our doctor should receive their findings in about three weeks.

* * *

It's the third of October and Mum and I are both miserable and tearful.

Since the Summer, I have not felt my usual bounce and optimism. I think I need some more help.

Mum is finding ordinary things even harder now. The OT says I should encourage Mum's independence, but more often than not the getting-dressed routine has failed. She won't ask for help or admit that she needs it when I offer, so I have to take over.

She stares at the walls and follows me around, so I have to constantly say, "Excuse me, Mammy", or physically move her to one side.

Her noise sensitivity is becoming more acute. Yesterday I played some music whilst preparing dinner in the kitchen. Mum hid in the toilet rather than say "the music is too loud." She won't say if she's cold or hungry either, but just looks at me with a hurt expression whilst I guess what's wrong.

Increasingly the answer to any question is,

"I don't know!"

Do you want tea or coffee?

"I don't know"

Why are you crying, mammy?

"I don't know"

Shall we go for a walk?

"I don't know"

Yesterday Mum had another activity-packed day and again she told her sister that she doesn't do anything. Then at prayer time, when invited to say her prayer, she complained, "Not really, I've done nothing."

"Pardon?"

"Well, I don't do anything all day!"

I wasn't very kind and said how I spend my days trying to keep her entertained and happy – for what? I might as well not bother.

Conor was angry with me,

"It's not her fault she forgets. She enjoys herself at the time. And she should be here. She entertains me."

Stress, depression, frustration, ulcers and now guilt too. I knew I was being cruel. I want her to wake up. Conor is right. My selfishness is my fault.

A couple of days ago she was crying that she just wants to be normal. It hurts her that she can't do ordinary things, like picking up a cup, or using a knife and fork.

She does persevere when eating, but not for clothes or anything else.

I get frustrated because I can't make it better, and, worst of all, I can't even make her feel better.

* * *

I went to my first of a series of eight carers' group meetings. We were asked to introduce ourselves, saying who we were caring for, something about the circumstances and what we found most difficult.

I kept mine brief and vaguely humorous, but afterwards a lady told me that, of all the stories, she found mine the most touching. She felt that having a young family at home as well was too hard, and that she was thankful that her children had not had to witness the misery of dementia.

The stories represented a whole range of caring experiences. Some for spouse or parent, some at home, some hospitalised, but all with a fairly recent diagnosis of dementia. The ways in which the dementia presented itself were unique to each family, but very recognisable. There was a hum of empathy and agreement as the listeners recognised behaviours, symptoms and traits that they too had had to deal with in some form.

* * *

Last night was my second carer's group meeting. The speaker was good at his job, but I found the content unhelpful to me, as I had already spent the last ten months battling to come to grips with much of the system. However, I was reassured that I had left no stone unturned.

I have made extra effort this week to be patient and encourage conversation. The trouble is that Mum doesn't seem to enjoy her own company, whilst I love quiet time alone. She doesn't actually know what she wants to do. I know she likes walking, visiting, eating and drinking, music and occasionally some TV. If I suggest any one of these activities, she will invariably say "Yes" and, as Conor says, she will enjoy it at the time.

Mums evening prayers have been an interesting reflection of her emotional state over these months. When she first arrived with us, she would say she couldn't find words to pray and would fluster and stammer. After a couple of months her prayers began to express how lucky she felt to be living with us and how she loves us very much. By August the prayers reflected how she felt she hadn't done well, had been selfish or mardy and how she would try harder tomorrow. I always felt the need to address these negative comments afterwards and remind her of all the good things she had done. These last three weeks her prayers have been an expression of her boredom and frustration at how useless and under-stimulated she feels.

Today I have inhaled the scent of roses and feel grateful for the chilly warmth of Autumn earth and the dancing red leaves.

I am looking at my life to see what would enrich me, make me more alive and fruitful and a better person for us all to live with.

I was breaking off the dead geranium flowers, reflecting on how they have flowered continually since I planted them out in the spring. I wondered at how difficult it is for me to prune the unfruitful parts of my life and how I try to keep all the dross and still expect to flower.

I need to nourish my own soil and do some overdue pruning.

* * *

I took the boys to Nottingham's famous "Goose Fair", whilst Simon stayed at home with Mum. The fair was great fun and when the boys felt sufficiently dizzy and sick, we began the long walk home.

I took them on a trip down my "Memory Lane". I showed them my old college, my childhood park, the shop where I did my paper-rounds and Saturday job, my old house on Porchester Road, and smiled fondly at Pa's house, where the boys used to stay when they were little. It took us two and a half-hours to explore and I came home feeling quite disorientated. Such a lot of memories.

Part of me is seeking memories to make sense of, and celebrate, the whole jigsaw of my life.

* * *

On Sunday I told Debbie how things are for Mum now and she was very supportive. She wants to help, but can't. She said she will back me if I choose to put Mum into a home.

I hate the thought of doing it, even if I believe that it will be better for Mum.

I spoke to the boys about it too, explaining that the carers in these homes have more energy, because they work eight hours a day for six days, not 24/7. Also she would have more company and we could still bring her here to play, but she wouldn't be dependent on us and she might get less bored.

Conor is fabulous with her and I acknowledged that. I thought Conor would be angry with me, but he seemed very understanding. He would miss her. He's finally got one Nana at last and she might have to go away again. But at least she wouldn't be a thousand miles away in Orkney.

I'm afraid that Mammy will be angry with me if I make her go.

I'm sure I won't be the first person to feel they have failed a loved one, when they finally admit to not being able to cope alone any more.

I don't know when I'll do it. I'm not desperate yet.

* * *

Today I told my therapist about the fire that scarred my mother. I know how terrifying it was to live with my father and how much Mammy must be still emotionally, as well as physically, scarred from those thirty-two years of marriage.

Her fear and love of him made her incapable of responding rationally and leaving. She protected him by her lies and secrecy and therefore made external help impossible. She was trapped. I feel she is still trapped.

* * *

It is a beautiful "All Saint's Day", with cool sunshine and fiery leaves whirling in the breeze. The last of our apples are lying in the fading grass and the still unripe corncobs are rustling in the wind.

Yesterday I had four hours to myself. Nobody in the house but me. I prayed, cried, read, did some correspondence and sanded and waxed another shelf. It was great.

Last week Mum was in the respite home, whilst we all went away. Simon took Mum to the home this time, because Mum doesn't seem to get as upset with other people as she does with me.

I was glad to come home. Simon and I haven't been so close since the summer; since the last miscarriage. Whether it is due to his depression, mine or Mum's, I don't know. Perhaps it's a lack of time alone together.

Simon is going walking with friends for the next three days. I hope it refreshes him.

Mum was very well after her respite. Her prayers on Saturday had returned to how wonderful we all were and how much she loved us. By Monday night, however, they were about how she "hadn't tried hard enough" and was "sorry for being mardy". Last night she had reverted to how she hadn't "done anything at all. Not a thing all day".

I have spoken to Social Services. They have put Mum's name on the long waiting-list in Broad Glade, where she has been staying for respite. It is also where the day centre is, so she is already well known there.

There is another home, even closer, that I should explore, but I haven't yet.

Mammy has every right to have her needs and wishes met, but what should happen when those needs and wishes conflict with the needs and wishes of those around her, or what if they are not good for her?

I'm not sure how responsible I should be for her every happiness, if it conflicts with our well being as a family. I know that most of my life nowadays is about keeping Mammy happy, but it isn't her fault.

It might be easier if I looked at it all differently, but I can only see things Dawn's way.

Earlier I was sharing with Mum some of the more general memories from Herbert Street, the Caravan and Porchester Road (our three homes as a family together), but she remembers nothing. I asked if that was frightening, not knowing what your past is, what you did yesterday or what you will do tomorrow. She acknowledged that it's scary, but wanted to express the frustration she feels about knowing what she wants to do or say and realising that she has got it wrong, without knowing why. It must be so frustrating, confusing and very lonely in a space with no memories to keep you company.

* * *

Mammy is very tearful again today.

She couldn't get dressed and after breakfast she said she would like to read, because she "should be able to". It was distressing for her to see that she can't do it anymore. We looked at one of Conor's birthday cards to illustrate that even if she reads one word, she has forgotten it after reading the next one. Nor does she read across the page, she reads random words vertically down a text, so comprehension is impossible. But she was positive and said,

"I'm gonna keep trying. I should, shouldn't I? Too many times I try to do something and I can't, so I throw it away. I'm not going to keep throwing it away. I can keep trying, even if it is silly. I know it is in there; I can see it, but I can't get it. I hope I get better."

I asked what was "in there" that she was looking for and she said sadly, but emphatically, "ME!"

"I can see you, Mammy. I know you are there and just the same inside."

She reached out tenderly, looking sorry for me and I felt myself pull together and say, "I'm okay! I'm a big girl now!"

Her concerned reaching out beckoned me, so I stood up and we had a good hug and cry.

"You are my precious one", she said, "and I'm proud of you."

Wow! Such comments are more precious than rare diamonds to me.

Then came the knock on the door and I told her it was the bus.

"Oh, no!" she pleaded, "Do I have to go?"

"Yes, Mammy! I need the space to do what I've got to do. I can't do it otherwise. I'll see you later."

She went away with some understanding, I hope.

I couldn't cope if she didn't attend the day centre.

* * *

We have completely abandoned baths now. After breakfast and a shower, when the boys had all gone their various ways, we rested a moment in the peace and quiet, and I asked Mum what she could remember of her wedding day. She replied, "Nothing at all!"

"But you haven't even thought about it yet!" I countered.

"I can't remember anything." She repeated. "We were too young."

I reminded her how Daddy seemed to suddenly change, when a new doctor in Orkney changed all of his medication. She couldn't remember, so I tried to remind her of the things she had told me, about him becoming "like a teenager again, smoking roll-ups" and starting to be sociable.

It was great that he had a couple of good years before he died, but it was a real shame that his medication wasn't reviewed much sooner.

I also suggested that it was good that he wasn't around to cope with her dementia. She agreed, but argued,

"I was always like this: getting everything wrong and forgetting everything. He used to hate it and get very angry with me."

"You were always scatty", I agreed, "but I don't think you had dementia. He wouldn't have known what to do with you now. He might have tried to drown you."

"He probably would." She nodded, not at all shocked by such an outrageous suggestion.

"How does it feel to have lived for thirty-two years with a man that you knew had tried to kill you and may do so again at any time?"

"I don't know. We were too young. He was hurting himself. And scared."

"I guess he was scared, but I don't think he had the right to terrorise his wife and children! Did you ever think you should have left him?"

"No! How could I?" she said incredulously.

"I suppose you thought it would be worse if you tried to leave him; that he would find you and kill you anyway?"

She nodded.

"Weren't you ever angry?"

She laughed. "I would never show it!"

"How do you feel about it now?"

"I don't know. Anyway I've blocked most of it."

I told her that I was angry about his treatment of her and of us. Although I know that he had his own baggage from his own terrible childhood, I believe that he had no right to inflict such cruelty on his family.

I think we have the right to be angry. I also loved Daddy and have forgiven him. I pray that he will now know true peace. The damage takes a lot of healing. It was not her fault. It was not our fault. Daddy was responsible for the damage he caused.

Mammy was also responsible for the damage she caused by her neglect and coldness, but it is too late to open that can now.

I don't know how much she followed, but she seemed more at ease after our chat.

In the shower she had such a lovely smile, she almost looked as if she was enjoying the water. I felt very protective towards her, willing her to feel safe and loved and okay. I washed her gently, so much desiring her well-being and healing.

I am feeling even more sensitive, with some guilt, because I am to meet our social worker tomorrow to discuss the possibility of NHS funding for long-term residential care.

* * *

CHAPTER 9

I have been thinking of painting a canvas for the dining room, and was saying how nervous I get when painting. Mum couldn't understand me, nor could she remember the many paintings, metal ornaments and gadgets that Dad had made during his life. Dad never liked what he had made and on completion would either destroy it immediately, or would present it to someone apologetically. Happily I have three things that Dad made for me during my life. He also made tractors, trailers and boats, always to his own unique design. He was particularly gifted with metal work and engines.

After I was disowned at seventeen, I had little to do with Mum and Dad for the next three years; although I did see them, when they allowed it and when I felt strong and safe enough.

Aged twenty, I went to live in Germany, and shortly afterwards, Mum and Dad moved up to live on Graemsay, in Orkney. My British home thereafter was Pa's house.

In the early days on Graemsay, Mum and Dad lived with no running water, no electricity nor any mod cons. They had both always enjoyed "The Good Life" series on the television, and having an old croft with lots of land, must have seemed like their good life was finally about to begin. In some ways it was. They only had each other to look out for.

Eventually they installed electricity and Dad put a system in to pump water from the well into the kitchen.

Every second Sunday, at 12:30, they would walk across to the phone-box in the middle of the island and wait for me or Debbie to phone. I wanted to visit them, but whenever I asked, Dad would say no.

Eventually, as a university student, I took the long bus ride from London Victoria to Thurso. Next came the sick-inducing ferry from Scrabster to Stromness, and the small boat from Stromness to Graemsay. The journey took two days. The views and the wind were breathtakingly beautiful on the sea at that time of the morning. I was very anxious, tired and excited. Dad didn't know I was coming.

After an awkward and difficult entrance, we had a lovely time. I adored the place. It was bleak, but not as barren as the picture that I had painted for myself. They had goats, sheep, chickens and geese, and Mum had a good crop of potatoes, onions, curly-kale and plenty of sea-weed to eat. It really was quite idyllic.

Dad made his fire breathing home-brews and even got in some wine and beers later to mark the occasion.

I was hoping to build bridges and bury the ghosts on this trip. In a sense, some of that happened, because Dad did apologise and I realised that he simply didn't think that his actions had been wrong. He thought I was just too young.

However, he also told me that he had read my letters (in which I had told them about God's grace, mercy and forgiveness) and he said that he had prayed the prayer I suggested and asked for salvation, but had not received anything. I told him to not rely on his feelings, but to go on seeking and believing.

I also asked Mum if I could be her daughter again. She said:

"I suppose so. I never really liked you, but you're okay now." Then she added, "But I'll be glad when you go again, because I've got a lot to do and you're upsetting my routine."

I certainly felt a great deal better leaving Graemsay, than I did going.

I didn't see Daddy again. He died of 'acute alcoholism', five years later at the tender age of forty-nine, during one of those evenings drinking the home-made fire.

God rest his soul.

I believe that God heard Daddy's prayer and did forgive him. When I reflect on his last five years on Graemsay and the positive, dramatic changes in his life, I know that God faithfully did a great work of grace in his life.

I went up for the funeral in Aberdeen and stayed a fortnight with Mum. She was bereft and devastated.

* * *

Before Mum went today, I decided to confront her about the day centre.

"I do like it!" she said.

When I explained how I saw her behaviour, she tried to explain how "it's the suddenness" of leaving that bothers her. That I do things "too quickly" and then I'm gone.

I suppose that with not having a memory backup, everything seems sudden and, simultaneously, everything goes on forever? Life must be very unpredictable for her.

She seemed better prepared today though, so maybe I should go back to telling her what's happening next, to give her more time to respond. I used to do that, but it seemed that I was just giving her more time to worry, but things change, so I will too.

At the carers' group last night, the St. Peter's Wing were doing their presentation. I felt slightly overwhelmed by the focus on drugs: drugs for the Alzheimer's disease, for sleep, for depression, for anxiety, for the bowels, drugs for this, that and everything, and also the emphasis on test scores. Mum scored nine on her test, but she was in a strange place, with a doctor whose English was not very clear; being watched and put under pressure to perform. As a teacher, I know that these conditions are not optimal for anyone.

I took the opportunity to ask the consultant again about therapy and why I thought that if I supplied some of the facts about Mum's past, perhaps a therapist could help Mum to "unblock" issues. I still didn't get a clear response.

I am making sure that with the help of a therapist and a God who heals, I will have no unresolved issues left in my heart or mind.

Our social worker came again today, to check how things are.

She said there is now a place available at Broad Glade and, if I were desperate, Mum would be considered. Believing that the place was full with a waiting-list, this news came as a sudden shock.

I don't feel I have the right to make this decision alone. I don't know who I'm supposed to put first. She won't rush me and she listened to all of my ramblings.

I have given her Debbie's phone number, as, having Welfare Power of Attorney, the decision of "where it is best for Mum to live" lies ultimately with her.

It's good to know that if I do get desperate, they can step in. Please God that I don't become desperate, but that things will fall naturally into place at the allotted time and I will know peace.

* * *

At Take-a-Break today, I witnessed more of Mum's attractiveness to men.

I was aware of two new people having joined the group some weeks ago, but I hadn't had the pleasure of speaking with them. The man was staring at Mum and asked if we were sisters. Mum didn't even acknowledge his remark, but sat there serenely smiling. Then he said to me,

"She is very pretty, I quite fancy her."

"And you are?" I asked, somewhat amused by his fixation.

He gave his name and I looked enquiringly at the lady, who smiled, "I'm his wife!"

We were celebrating another birthday. It makes me sad to see Mum, twenty-five years younger than the birthday girl, but so much less able to communicate or function sociably, yet somehow still enigmatic for the gentlemen.

I presumed that the gentleman flirting was the one being cared for by his wife and I wondered how much more difficult it must be to care for a spouse than a parent.

* * *

I arranged to visit the very local care-home, that our social worker told me is considering registering for dementia patients.

I had a good chat with the manager, who has been working there for fourteen years and who has her own mother-in-law living there (which is either a high recommendation or at least expedient). They have between twelve and fourteen residents, the youngest being already eighteen years older than Mum. They do seem very homely and to take pride in the place and love the residents.

I intend to ask our social worker to plan Mum's next respite there, to see how well she would fit in. It would be good if Debbie could come and look at these places too and discuss the options with me.

Mum says she wants a diary again.

Debbie and Mum always kept a diary. I think I'll get one for 2008 and we can fill it in together, at teatimes perhaps.

I think I'll also do a "This Is Your Life" style album for Mum. It could be very helpful for friends, volunteers and carers to see something more personal about her, and give them more of an anchor for chat and discussion.

* * *

This morning Mum had two of her funny turns. It prompted me to phone the Neurophysiology Dept. to find out when we can discuss the results of the sleep-deprived EEG that she had two months ago.

It seems I have slipped up somehow. Apparently Mum had missed an appointment on the third of November. It was not in my diary and they had not sent us a letter, but I did find it written in the notes I made when we visited earlier in the summer. Hopefully we will be able to reschedule.

These fits, or whatever they are, do add to my stress, because I feel nervous to leave her alone even for a few minutes, lest she hurts herself.

I saw the first one begin and was able to take the cup from her hand and hold her steady until it had finished, but I was then afraid to leave the room. After the second fit, I put her in the big armchair, with the TV for company and went to have my shower. It struck me again that the majority of fits have been directly after breakfast, and a couple have even been before breakfast. Is it the suddenness of going from horizontal to vertical that triggers them? Is it a change of blood sugar levels? I must ask the consultant.

I thought it best to stay indoors this morning, so we made a start on the "This is Your Life" booklet.

I found a pile of good photographs to illustrate the major stages of Mum's life, but I realised how patchy my own actual knowledge of specifics is, especially dates and place-names in her life. I hope I will be able to find out this information.

* * *

A new volunteer has taken Mum to a garden-centre for a couple of hours. She is superb with Mum. She is interesting and interested and manages to think of purposeful excursions. This week the purpose is for Mum to get some Christmas cards and to see the decorations. The volunteer friend always says that *she* has had a lovely day out too.

On Friday we go to Marbella, Spain, to stay with an old university friend of mine. I am so much looking forward to it, but as always I am dreading Mum's disappointment, when she realises that we are going away without her.

This morning when I went to wake Mum, she was clearly still in a distressing dream.

I barged in with my "Wakey, Wakey, rise and shine", but Mum was sobbing and shrinking under the quilt, crying, "No, please don't. Please! No!"

I was concerned and curious, as she obviously wasn't fully awake yet. I stroked her head and told her she was having a bad dream. She continued sobbing and crying, "Mum!"

Later, when she was more awake, I asked her about it and she remembered that her mum was very angry with her in the dream. Apparently she was never angry or nasty, "in real life". She couldn't recall why she had been angry with her in the dream, or how she was expressing it, but it was clearly causing her a lot of distress.

I suggested that maybe Mum was angry with herself, as she often pulls herself down with phrases like, "You stupid woman. You silly thing!"

She agreed that she *was* angry with herself and said "it's like having a big hole in my head".

I guess it might be just like that. I told her that I see the disease in her brain like a set of fairy lights. Every so often one blows and that bit goes dark. I think that maybe the little fits are manifestations, or causes, of those blown bulbs and there are dark patches in her brain where once there was clarity. She likes my analogy and says it feels just like that.

Anyway I thought it would be appropriate to go to the memorial garden today and take some flowers. We did get the engraved marble vase, but haven't been back there since we erected it in August.

On the way to the garden, I asked her to describe her mother and she kept repeating that she "was a lady – a gentle lady!"

We arranged the flowers, said "The Lord's Prayer" together and thanked her mum for being a gentle mum. She said she couldn't remember anything about her dad at all

* * *

CHAPTER 10

It's now nearly two months later. Christmas has been and gone and yesterday we celebrated the Epiphany. So much has happened over this interval.

Debbie came for a few days at the beginning of December, but I didn't really get a break. I did communicate my concerns about coming to the end of my ability to look after Mum at home. She says she will support me in any way she can, and she does understand that it has been very difficult for me.

Apart from Monica we have had few other visitors.

On Christmas Eve, Joshua had a burning fever and spent most of the day in bed. After mid-night Mass, Simon was also feverish, and the two of them spent the next few days with an appetite only for Paracetamol and water. Most of Christmas dinner went into the freezer.

Joshua, Simon and Mum are all still coughing badly. The boys had a virus, apparently, but Mum had a chest infection and is now on her second prescription of antibiotics. Unfortunately Mum's coughing has caused "stress incontinence", which has given me wet chairs, wet mattress and a whole heap of extra washing to do.

Sitting in the waiting room at the surgery, with the whole family, was a rather comical experience. Other service users were quite clearly avoiding sitting anywhere near us. Mammy was distressed, coughing and wheezing severely. Joshua looked mentally disabled with his ashen face poking out from under his long woolen hat, exploding into dramatic coughing fits; the doctor even asked me if he attends "regular school". Simon looked like a vacant, zany zombie and Conor, wearing gloves and a T-shirt with "Heavily Medicated for Your Safety" printed across the front, was acting the part, twitching and groaning, just for fun.

Lastly, I saw the doctor alone and, not surprisingly, she recommended anti-depressants for me (which I refused) and prescribed the pill, which Simon had suggested that I now take. I had hoped that we would have a baby, but perhaps I am too old. To take the pill would be to give up hope. I could carry on with the uncertainty, expectation and the disappointment and agony each month. It is another difficult dilemma.

* * *

Mum went into respite for a few days, and we went to welcome in the New Year with Simon's family.

The prospect of putting Mammy, against her wishes, into a home; the thought of there being no hope of a baby; the house full of sickness, and Simon's increased anxiety are all pulling me down very low.

Lord, give us wisdom.

School has begun again, but it's Conor's turn to be sick, so I'm tied to the house again. At least I went out into the garden for a tidy-up and felt a bit more enthusiasm creeping back into my spirit out there.

* * *

Tuesday today and finally I had an hour's solitude. I managed to have a chat with the garden, but I missed a phone call. It was Mum's dementia doctor and I now feel really agitated, because we have waited six months for this appointment and I missed it. January 8th was firmly printed on my mind, calendar and diary, but all I remembered was that Mum's befriender was coming this morning and the district nurse this afternoon. She left a message to say she would send another appointment. I hope it won't be another six month wait.

Out in the garden I was delighted to see deep-red wallflowers, emerging pink stocks and proud fresh-green shoots from last year's bulbs. I was feeling a sense of awe in the hardiness of nature. The mini-roses are still in bloom and the Sweet William has not stopped flowering since last March. In only the second week of January, the flora is waking up again to dazzle us for another year.

When I woke Mum she was lying curled up on top of the duvet. Being slow to learn, I asked her why she didn't get back under the quilt after she'd been to the toilet. It was a stupid question that she obviously couldn't answer and made her feel distressed and grumpy.

I have to dress Mum every morning now. The socks she can usually manage if I present them one at a time. This morning she put the left sock on and then sat looking quizzically from the sock in her hand to the socked foot and the bare foot, for what seemed like five minutes, so I put the sock on for her, to put us both out of our misery.

The inhalers are now used twice a day and she still does her happy piggy impression and asks, "What does it do?"

When Mum was last in Broad Glade, they suggested that we request incontinence pads from the NHS, as they are both free and effective. She came home wearing one as big as a nappy that day.

A nurse bought some pads with her last week and, after filling in copious forms, she left me with a urine chart, to fill in during the week, and a sample bottle, ready for her next visit.

Apparently all is well. The sample was good and the scan to see how well she empties her bladder is fine too. She's going to keep us supplied with big and small "nappies", so that should help my washing load. They are all valuable improvements and a real help.

Yesterday I went in Mum's room to find the commode upside down on the carpet. It really makes me heave! The urine soaks through the carpet and the poo gets flattened by the commode. To have to reassure Mum and get her ready, with a nostril full of it, is quite unbearable for me. I had to clear it away myself today.

Throughout the morning Mum was downcast and sniveling, despite my hugs and reassuring words.

* * *

We had an interesting discussion on Tuesday morning. We had been out walking and we were having a cuppa and listening to an inspirational piece of music, when she began to cry gently.

"Daddy is here!" She said.

During the course of the conversation I learned that she couldn't see him with her eyes, but that he was smiling and at peace. She was questioning why this happens to her, remembering that it used to happen a lot more, but that she didn't think he would still be coming to see her. I asked whether she believed in an afterlife and whether they would meet each other again. She didn't know quite what she believed, but added, if they did meet again, "I hope he doesn't hurt me".

Poor Mammy.

I shared my hope that, if we do meet again in the afterlife, "every tear will be washed away." (Rev 7:17) There will be no more pain and we will know the truth.

* * *

I received a new appointment to see the dementia doctor on April 22nd.

The epilepsy specialist has written to the GP, saying "These features [on the EEG] are suggestive of an increased disposition to epilepsy. Please let me know if I need to see her again."

The GP doesn't know what to do and has passed it back to the specialist to ask what, if any, medication she recommends.

The dementia doctor didn't want to "step on the toes" of the Neurology specialist, so, thus far, nothing has happened.

And I missed *both* appointments.

* * *

Mum is still coughing and it's causing her much distress.

The doctor said the chest infection has gone, so a new investigation into "reflux", is being tried with the intervention of an stomach-acid reducer, called Lansoprazole.

I also asked the GP about communication from Neurology, and she found a letter on the system saying that Mum should start taking medication for epilepsy.

So, now she has to chew some "Tegretol" after supper too.

* * *

Another Monday and we are back to the doctors with Mum's cough. This doctor wants to try steroids again, to see if it clears with them. If it does, he will deduce that it is asthma-related and we will move forward with that approach.

Today we had to stop halfway to school, because Mum was distressed and refusing to walk properly, but wouldn't say what the matter was. I sent Conor on ahead and Mum told me that she "keeps peeing and can't stop". She said her clothes weren't wet though, but she wanted to go home.

She isn't making much sense at all recently and is often wet. I'm so glad we got the pads.

I wonder if the Tegretol is making Mammy more dopey and confused, but it's hard to tell, as she has good and bad moments anyway.

I am so grateful for my garden. Several times a day I wander around that beautiful space, marveling at the new growth and constant miracles and change. I watch the birds still flocking and flying in fabulous formations. I speak to the garden too.

Mum talks to the plants too, and hugs the trees, so we must both be potty!

I have two lovely, orange crocuses in the front garden and bunches of bulbs waiting to flower all over the place.

We are eating lots of brussels now, so that I can get the vegetable patch cleared, to plant beetroot, red-onions, blueberry and blackcurrant. I'll do rocket, courgettes and beans later too.

* * *

I finished an email and went through to make some tea. Mum was sitting hugging herself tightly, which looked like she was cold.

"No, it's Roger" she sighed shakily, "He's dead!" Pause.

"He died last year, Mammy. We went to his funeral."

"No, he was here, we were talking…and then he had to go. He was there (points to the window) and a car came…it knocked him down…he's dead! We were talking here, just now. That lady was here too. I'm going mad! He came up here and I spoke to him. Is he alive? I'm going crazy."

"You're not going crazy, Mammy, you are just mixing up your memories. Roger used to come to see you a lot on Orkney and he came here to see us last Christmas, so you have seen him in this room. He did die in a car though. It was tragic! He mistakenly reversed his car off the pier on Graemsay, after picking up his groceries."

I wondered whether the visits from Daddy weren't also part of a confused memory process?

* * *

Mammy has now seemingly forgotten how to swallow tablets, but not food.

Yesterday she had to take her first dose of eight tiny, red, steroid tablets. She couldn't do it. The tablets kept lodging between tongue and teeth, as she gulped down several glasses of water. An hour and a half later they were finally gone.

We then had the same problem at bedtime with the ordinary tablets. She even tried to chew the capsule and splutter out all the gritty contents.

This morning's steroids got to me. After spending half an hour on the first two, I abandoned them and we took Conor to school. We had to come back and take the rest, before I could take her to the day centre. It was another hour before we left, with one still in her mouth.

On the way back, I spoke to the pharmacist who said that soluble steroids are available, but the doctor would have to prescribe them. So I spoke to the doctor's secretary and she wrote it all down. She was very empathetic and I felt tears welling up, so I thanked her and left.

What a difference soluble tablets make. And she likes the taste of them. She still can't do the bedtime tablets though.

* * *

Simon has gone to his uncle's funeral. I wanted to go. I would have liked to have gone in November too, for his aunt's funeral. This is one of the challenges of having Mammy here: that we can't do things as a family, because Mum's needs are so specific, and respite care needs to be booked long in advance.

When I went in this morning she was already awake, half dressed, with her quilt piled up behind her. She was on the edge of the bed, crying.

"Whatever is the matter?"

"I didn't know where you were!" she sniveled.

"I was asleep in the next bedroom. I'm here now. Come and get dressed before you freeze."

I tried to reassure her, but I was simultaneously irritated and upset for her.

She is needing ever more of me, but I don't feel I have more of myself to give.

It is now just after 14:00. The morning's blue sky and strong scents have covered over with dark grey, and a snow gale is blowing. The day centre bus has just made an early delivery of a very sorry looking Avril. They said she was very pale and unresponsive and that she wouldn't eat her lunch, but just sat miserably in the corner.

"I'm too fat, so I didn't want any dinner, but it didn't work. I'm just being mardy." She confessed.

She doesn't "want to be anywhere."

She's drinking tea now, and gazing into the snow rushing horizontally past the window, but she can't see it.

* * *

Mum's dementia doctor rang this morning to offer Mum an appointment for tomorrow at 09:00. We will take it.

I hope Conor and the traffic allow us to make it in time.

Simon has devised an easier way for Mum to take her evening tablets: he mixes them up in a Weetabix and spoon-feeds it rapidly into her. She still finds the tablets in the mixture, but does swallow them with less anxiety. It's a step forward for now.

I don't know how the respite home will do it next week.

* * *

This morning felt blessed. Conor was ready on time and, despite the traffic, we arrived at the hospital with five minutes to spare. The dementia doctor was supportive and very attentive to Mammy. She is happy to see us again in nine months.

Investigations into the type of dementia are no longer deemed necessary. Again she stressed that she is more concerned with how well we are coping with the day-to-day. Mammy cried twice during the consultation. The doctor said that the steroids can make one weepy and miserable. She also said that we should persevere with the Tegretol.

No matter what the name or cause of Mum's condition is, there is no medication or treatment that can help anyway.

It feels strange and a little disappointing that after a year of investigations we have come to an accepted state of no conclusions and no solutions.

Anyway, of all the descriptions and information I have read, I do think that Alzheimer's is the "best-fit" for Mum's symptoms.

It may be academic, but such things do affect prognosis for Mum and her daughters.

And what happens next?

PART 2

Accepting my Limitations – Mum in a Home

CHAPTER 11

I became very anxious taking Mum into Broad Glade for respite on Saturday.

I was to pick Ana up later, as she was staying for the half-term week to allow Simon and I to have Thursday to Saturday away together.

Conor felt Mum's sadness and disappointment. She really hates me leaving her, despite often enjoying herself when she's there.

I distracted Conor from his grief afterwards, by booking some induction sessions at the gym, before going to fetch Ana from the station.

* * *

Our social worker phoned on Monday morning to say that Broad Glade now have a permanent room available for Mum, if we want it?

Do we?

We have to take it.

My ears were humming and I felt like my head would explode with indecisiveness.

"Yes, please."

How do I tell Mammy? Will she ever forgive me?

The social worker said I must tell Mum before I go away, so I'll go with her on Wednesday morning.

I pondered silently until after the dentist, and then told Ana and the boys. Conor was very understanding. He feels that he has done his bit for Nana too, and she will be close enough to visit whenever we want to.

For the next two days my head was like a ping-pong ball: relief, guilt, relief; prayer, fear, prayer; emotion, reason, emotion. I felt like she had died. Like she was gone forever.

On Wednesday I felt sick. The boys made sure I kept busy. I took them with Ana to their first Gym induction, and went over to Broad

Glade. The social worker was waiting for me and as soon as I saw her, the tears started to well up. It might have helped if I had cried earlier, but I hadn't.

We talked and then went to find Mammy. She looked so beautiful. She had had her hair done and was wearing a pretty dress. She eyed us suspiciously as we led her back to her room.

The social worker began the conversation and reminded Mum how, when she first came down to Nottingham, we were planning to find her a place of her own, where she could be close to us. She said that Mum now needs help with washing, dressing and making cups of tea, and Mum looked surprised.

"No, I can do things like that"

We told her that they now had a place available for her to stay there, where she would be close by.

I could not have imagined a better response. She smiled with delight and said,

"That's great! So we will be close again at last."

As we talked, I realised she had forgotten that she had spent the last fourteen months living in my house.

I could not have engineered that response in all my dreams. I felt so grateful.

I explained to Mum that I would help her move into her new room and bring some more clothes and pictures. She was full of smiles and affirmations.

I took her through to lunch and went to collect the boys, with such a spring in my step and praise on my lips.

I had no trouble packing that evening and felt almost sad to be leaving the boys behind. They are in safe hands.

* * *

I feel strange.

There is a lot to tidy up: family to inform, name-tags to sew in, stuff to take to Mum, financial assessments to do, change of addresses to notify various institutions of and visiting routines to establish.

Plus, I have my own doubts and guilt to allay, and my own path to find.

We start with name-tags, deliveries and repeat prescriptions to order.

Today I also have to take Mum for her six-monthly check-up at the dentist.

She was not so positive today. I was greeted with a peeved, "*There you are!*"

In the car and waiting room she asked me repeatedly what we were doing. She only had to have her teeth cleaned. It's amazing how her teeth have survived so well.

She enjoyed the walk around and seemed happy when I mentioned getting back for lunch, but, seated at the table at Broad Glade, she looked surprised and disappointed when I said I'd see her "tomorrow or Wednesday".

I kissed her and left, but felt like I'd given the betrayer's kiss.

I doubt myself again. Am I doing the right thing?

Everyone I've told thinks it is the best thing and say I've done well to look after her for so long, but I'm not sure. I couldn't sleep last night. I just sobbed.

The phone keeps ringing today and I won't answer it. I feel very low and lost.

* * *

The social worker phoned yesterday to say that Broad Glade would be doing an assessment over six weeks, before offering Mum a permanent place.

They are saying that she has deteriorated considerably since they last saw her at Christmas. The social worker expressed concern that we may have to find somewhere else for Mum.

I took Conor to see Nana after school on Wednesday. He entertained her admirably and knew it. He made her laugh so much, repeating the same jokes about her looking like a marshmallow in her round pink coat and soft pink hat.

We walked and went for some hot chocolate. I noticed that Mum has special cutlery in the dining hall and a large bib/apron for mealtimes.

I took her CD player and a selection of her favourite music, and Conor and Mum had a jive before we left. I was very grateful for his support.

I do wonder how she is when we've gone again, and whether she gets more confused or anxious afterwards.

I don't know how often I should visit her at the moment.

* * *

On Saturday I asked Broad Glade about my visits and they said they will monitor Mum's mood to see whether there is any detrimental (or positive) impact from our visits.

I felt much better and arranged to pick her up and walk over to 18:30 Mass. It was a special Mass where Joshua made his initial vows as part of his Confirmation preparation. Mammy seemed very content and independently asked if she could come to Joshua's Confirmation day.

Back at Broad Glade, they brought Mum some tea and a sandwich for her supper. The tea was in a two-handled, toddler style beaker to avoid spillage. I wondered if she minded.

This is a waiting period.

My moods are all over the place. After only fourteen months in our home, I feel like a part of me is missing. Like I have lost or forgotten something. If only I was confident that Mammy was happy there.

There is so much happening for us as a family, which I can at least attend to with greater freedom.

What is my purpose, my role now?

After this six-week assessment period, what will happen?

If she can stay permanently in Broad Glade, what should I do next?

My carer's allowance has already been stopped and as soon as she's offered a permanent place, the DLA will stop. I will have to pay for these six weeks in Broad Glade too.

I have to find some means of contributing to the home finances, to balance the books and to get me back into the world of employment. I know that I have much to offer, but I don't have much strength or confidence at the moment.

* * *

Julia went to see Mum on Monday. She seemed shocked at Mum's deterioration, but she likes the home. She said that Mammy didn't recognise her, but guessed that Julia might be her "daughter". She hasn't seen her since last August, so that may explain some of it.

Apparently Mum kept saying that she was "so bored".

She repeatedly complained, "Dawn's not been to see me…not since she's been looking after that old lady".

How interesting. I wonder whether the "old lady" is herself or Pat?

I also phoned the home (Julia is the only other person to have visited Mum apparently) and they said that Mum had been crying, in frustration at not being able to do anything.

I took Mum out into town, past her old shop and recalled her Tuesday wholesalers' days, when we would traipse through town with Mum's big red suitcase and Mum would purchase things for her shop.

We dined in "Ye Olde Trip to Jerusalem", and then explored the castle grounds. Spring is delicately announcing her arrival up there, with discreet displays of snowdrops and crocuses. We took the opportunity to hug a few trees and Mum and I had to link arms to give a huge trunk a proper hug. She was impressed by the panoramic skyline and wonderful view of the city, but was afraid of the height at which we stood and panicked about "falling off".

It was beautiful up there with her. She enjoyed the atmosphere in Starbucks too, as I fed her with the ciabatta and coffee.

She seemed very alert today, but, getting back into the car, she became confused as to what we were doing and why.

* * *

Sunday was my birthday and, double whammy, Mothering Sunday.

I opened my cards and then fetched Mum to go out to Wollaton for the day. It has been thirty years since I was last at Wollaton Park. It is a beautiful place.

Mammy found the stairs difficult and didn't really see a lot in the Hall, although she did make the right noises when I pointed out the stuffed birds and animals.

Again she appreciated the full-scale panoramas, the trees, the lake and the deer. And the chocolate cake, of course.

* * *

Today I phoned Aunty Monica. I knew she was sad that the time had come to put Mum into a home. She said that I had to put my "husband and children first", but she seemed disappointed.

In her opinion, the carers at Broad Glade don't speak to the residents enough and the other residents doze all the time. I know she will visit her when she can.

I also wrote to inform Mum's friend, Tony. It is difficult to disappoint others who love Mammy.

* * *

How has my life been impacted, now that I'm not caring for Mum at home 24/7?

I still have lists of domestic chores that don't get done and so many extra tasks for Mum.

My mornings and evenings are much easier, and my need to keep a constant watch on her has obviously diminished, but my concern for her welfare has not.

That she is close by is a great consolation. I want to continue enjoying as many days out with her as possible.

I have been much more relaxed and available to support the boys too, which is great. They are both going through important transitional phases in their lives and are needing guidance and supervision. Conor also needs a lot of extra attention, now that he doesn't have his Nana to entertain.

*   *   *

Yesterday Mum's Gynaecology appointment was for 13:45.

I had to be back at Conor's school for a show at 15:30, followed by a performance at Joshua's school at 19:30.

I thought the Gynaecology appointment might be a waste of time, as the problem came and went about a month ago.

The waiting room was packed when we arrived and filled to overcrowded whilst we waited. Thankfully, Mum was called in first and sent for an ultrasound scan. They had to do the scan internally and she didn't like it at all, but she was very patient.

The waiting room was standing-room only by then. Again Mum was called almost straightaway.

The doctor thought that Mum did have a problem, but was more concerned that the scan had shown her womb lining to be much thicker than it should be. She tried to take a sample of the womb lining with a very long and very sharp instrument, but to no avail.

After consulting a higher power, she said that it is very important that Mum has this sample taken on 28th March. Apparently, she will need a local anaesthetic and will feel very uncomfortable afterwards.

I am supposed to be in Newcastle that day, but the doctor stressed that this is more important. Mammy was very jolly and compliant, but had no idea what was happening.

We were back too late for Conor's show, but he was very pleased to see his Nana and insisted that we brought her home for a while. It worked out perfectly as I was able to take her back to the home and still be on time for a brilliantly staged performance of "The Wizard Of Oz" at Josh's School. I felt grateful.

I was left feeling strange about Mum. I had only been looking at her dementia, as she is so strong physically. Suddenly I had become very aware of her mortality.

* * *

We now have a date for the Broad Glade Review - her six week assessment. It is a fortnight today: Wednesday 26th March.

More good news is that I can still go to Newcastle, as the Gynaecology appointment has been rescheduled for 20th March.

I had an unpleasant dream: all my family and friends were looking down and shaking their heads at me, as Mum sat depressed in the corner. They were blaming me for Mum's misery and trying to guilt-trip me into taking Mum out of Broad Glade. I knew that to bring her back to my house was not the answer, and so felt confused and upset in the dream.

I spent the morning sewing in name-labels and spring-cleaning. There is much sorting and reorganising to do, especially in what was Mum's room. I felt a reluctance to finally remove the room labels.

I wanted to do something different with Mum this week. The forecast was not for pleasant walking weather though, so I decided on another trip into town, where there are more diversions and shelter.

When I picked Mum up she was argumentative about putting shoes on, going to the toilet, etc.

We had fun in the elevators in town, looked around the shops for a sewing machine and went to Waterstones' irresistibly aromatic coffee shop.

Earlier Mum asked me "How are the boys?" and I was struck by how fully cognisant she seemed, about who I am.

As she laughed and we conversed, I thought about how much I really love this lady now.

Later, Mum said "I've missed you, Dawn!" as clear as that.

I asked her why and she replied, "All the things we did. It seems a long time ago", although she knew "it wasn't."

I asked if she likes it where she lives. She affirmed that she did, but... There was a hidden "but".

"Should I try to come more often, Mammy?"

"It would be very nice, but you are too busy. I only have me to think about."

I don't know what the future holds, but I do know that the past has gone. It is today that matters.

This is the day that the Lord has made. I want to make today count for something.

CHAPTER 12

Mum's appointment last week was for the Hysteroscopy, under a local anaesthetic, but now they are saying they need to give her a general anaesthetic to do it. So we await appointment number three.

We came back from the hospital via Isabelle's. Mum made a comment about how nice it was to be around ordinary family life, because otherwise it's just her alone. I think she is bored and lonely at Broad Glade, but she was bored at my house too.

Yesterday I took the boys, Mum and Monica out to Newstead Abbey. It was very cold again but Mum appreciated the arrays of daffodils and the entertainment from Conor and Monica. Monica had picked out lots of photographs. It was good to see them, especially the older ones of my Dad's family. Granddad looked so old at forty-three, and my Dad was not even born then.

Monica remarked how neglected Mum appeared. Her hair did look terribly greasy and her white beard has grown long again. Tweezers time.

We got back to Broad Glade about 17:30 and had missed tea, but a carer kindly said she'd get her something.

Mum was grumbling, unaware of my attention on her. She said it was "not a good idea to make a fuss," as "it would only make it worse," and that "some people are just not very nice."

I wonder what is going on for her now.

* * *

Mum's review at Broad Glade went well enough this afternoon. Although they acknowledge that Mum has deteriorated substantially, they do think that they have the resources to care for her.

The two senior representatives from Mum's unit were honest and positive. I was taken aback when one said that she loved Elvis too, that they were of the same era. I looked at her, fit and working, and again felt sad for Mum.

The constant coughing has been bothering them all. Apparently the GP has given Mum a prescription for more steroids, but did so over the phone without even seeing her. I shall take her to the GP myself next week. They also want me to insist that she has another X Ray.

Monica said that when she was living in Orkney, in 1995, Mum had had to go to Aberdeen for a Bronchoscopy, because they were investigating the cough then; that was thirteen years ago. Apparently they found nothing wrong and wondered whether it was a nervous condition/habit. Whatever it is, it sounds like she "smokes forty-a-day", according to the care-workers at Broad Glade.

They also said that there had been an incident last week, whereby Mum was found "standing facing another resident, wringing her hands and saying that she wanted to strangle the lady." They did say, that whilst this lady could be extremely irritating, it was totally out of character for Mum to behave like that, and that they had to write an incident report.

I felt overwhelmed by it all and looked at my list of dry, academic questions as I tried to engage. I asked instead about the activities that are provided and whether Mum joins in with anything.

They talked of coffee mornings, bar evenings, music and reminiscing. They said how they put her CDs on in her room, whilst she gets ready for bed. They said they have a new TV channel that has black and white films every afternoon and spoke of bingo and giant tennis. But I know that Mum doesn't enjoy TV anymore, that she never liked bingo and, as for tennis...

I know she likes her music, food and attention.

I asked if they keep note of her visitors. There was only one (her sister), who came during the first week. I suppose people think that if Mum is going to forget that she's had a visitor, it isn't worth making the effort? Personally I think, as Conor put it to me once, "at least she enjoys it at the time!"

I did mention the hair washing. It seems that the ladies do not get their hair washed as part of the daily routine, but only by the hairdresser on a Wednesday, which means they have to pay for it. I emphasised that Mum needs her hair washing more often than that, because it gets greasy and itchy, but that she is not used to having rollers, curlers or a fuss made. It seems that the carers have a problem with this. I'll have to work out how I can do it for her myself.

Anyway, she apparently became a permanent resident on 16th February 2008, so I now have to inform the DWP, DLA, and various other agencies, about her change of address.

The social worker will email Debbie with the update.

After the meeting, the social worker and I went to see Mum.

I took Mum into her room and plucked her beard, which someone must have trimmed this morning. She had also been to the hairdresser and smelled lovely. We danced to some Elvis songs and talked about his life. She spoke of Elvis's manager and blamed him for everything that ever went wrong for Elvis. I suggested that perhaps fame itself was a challenge and she looked knowingly, with a coquettish grin and said,

"Fame has it's good side *and* not so good. I should know."

"What were you famous for?" I enquired.

"For my dancing. It was wonderful" she reminisced dreamily.

"And the bad side to fame?" I dared

"It's all over so soon!" she sighed.

She has always loved dancing, but has never been famous as far as I know. I dare say she created a bit of a stir on the dance floor though.

* * *

It is a real treat to enjoy the garden in the hazy sunshine. There are shoots coming through from plants I thought had gone – the Agapanthus, the garden mint and orange lilies. I now have "Scarborough Fair" amongst the spring blooms: parsley, sage, rosemary and thyme, along with bleeding hearts, wallflowers and diverse varieties of tulips and daffodils. The rhubarb and strawberry plants are growing and I've just put some trailing fuchsias in baskets. Even the well-pruned apple-tree has green, pink and white buds all over it. I am beginning to breathe again.

The hospital just rang to say I have to take Mum for a pre-operation assessment on Wednesday morning and then in for the operation at 07:30 on Friday.

Debbie has already booked her ticket to come on Monday 14th April, the day after Mum's birthday. I shall organise a party of Mum's friends for the following day, so that Debbie can take part.

Someone said today that it wasn't fair that I've been left to do all the work for Mum. In a sense that is true, but had it all happened to Mum whilst I was teaching in London, I wouldn't have been able to do anything for her either. I have had to take a career break, it's true, but I was in the fortunate position of being able to do so and, as a result, I have got to know and love my mum again. I have been able to care for and tend her in a way not possible before. I consider it now such a privilege and a very special blessing.

*   *   *

Getting up at 05:45 didn't feel like such a special blessing today, but it was so beautiful outside. There was a strong, fresh, thin-misty smell and the sun was behind an ivory veil, but very much awake and smiling. The birds were loud and clear and the roads all but empty.

Mum was ready when I arrived, so we set off and sailed through a dozy Nottingham and arrived half-an-hour early at the Hospital. As we sat at the reception desk, a man kissed his wife goodbye, having been told that she could keep her mobile on and phone him when she was ready to go home again. He went skipping out of the unit, laughing, "I thought I'd have to stay all day in this place!"

I knew they would need me to stay with Mum.

I recognised the unit and the ward sister, and realised that Mum was going into the room next to the one where I had had my "surgical evacuation" of the first miscarriage. That gave me a strong flash-back, as did all the repeated questioning:

"Any caps, crowns or loose teeth?"

"Any known allergies?"

"Name and date of birth?"

As I answered the questions for Mum, she had her lines to say too:

"I'm a pest, aren't I?"

"Will it go away now?"

I told her that I do believe in miracles and that she might wake up well again. The Lord does work in mysterious ways and I like to expect the unexpected.

I got Mum into her gown and the stream of form fillers gave way to the porter. I went down with her to the theatre, to answer any remaining questions and go through the consent form again. The doctor let Mum sign her consent, because "she seems to understand the explanation as it is given". She squiggled her signature and said,

"I hope we get it sorted this time!"

"What do you hope they do, Mammy?"

"I don't know. Whatever it is they're doing!"

The doctor explained to me that there is a slight risk of the camera puncturing the womb, in which case they would have to look in through the navel, to check it hadn't punctured other organs as well. This is "unlikely", but I had to give my consent in case of that too. Big responsibility for little me.

There were so many men in this part of the hospital, all hiding in green tunics. They caused Mum to behave in a very animated manner.

"All these young men around." I commented.

"Not for long though." she sighed.

"No, no staying power, eh?"

Mum laughed.

The men found me some fetching shoes, gown and a lovely mop-cap, so I could go to the anaesthetist's room and watch her go. It was a very psychedelic room, meant for children, I think, but I enjoyed it.

It wasn't as bad as watching my little boy go under, but it was still a strange experience.

In half-an-hour I was called back into the recovery room. The nurses there were discussing their bets for the Grand National the following day. I began to think about Dad and the thirteen years of Mum's life since he died. I thought of all of our lives since his death, and of that day when Mum phoned to tell me the shocking news. We had friends at our house to watch the Grand National, but as soon as I got the call, the party was abandoned and baby Josh, his dad and I, set off to Orkney.

When Debbie heard that Dad had died, she went into labour and gave birth to her third child, Olivia.

Back in the ward, we were brought some tea. Mum was amazingly alert. I wanted to sleep, but she was rearing to go.

"Has it worked?" she mumbled to herself under the oxygen mask.

She wasn't aware of me at her side. She lay quite still, humming and dozing and whispering her thoughts.

"I've just realised…I'm not coughing!" she smiled benignly, almost smug. "I can sing again!"

I realised that she thought that this operation was to solve the problem of the residual cough. We ordered some breakfast and she continued with an expansive look of glee and gratitude,

"Yes, it's better. I can dance and sing again… I can try anyway. Nobody knows though." She laughed gently and closed her eyes to hum, "Walking in the winter wonderland".

"Nobody knows, but I do. I can do them, I think. I can sing again…but they don't know…but it doesn't matter. BUT, will I do it?"

She put her hands together, rapt and whispering her thanksgiving and petitions over again. I joined her in prayer and in thanksgiving that the doctors had found nothing at all wrong with her womb.

The tea was cool enough, so I took off her oxygen mask and fed her jam on toast and tea, whilst Mum was smiling and dancing a tune to herself. The lady came back to collect the plates and asked Mum what she had had done.

"Nothing much." She replied, then she coughed.

"It's come back again," she whispered with an air of desperation. "Oh, no. It hasn't worked! Please no! What do I do now? Please let it be right. It's still there, isn't it?"

I intervened to say that she was in hospital to have her womb checked and that the doctors say her womb is fine.

I fed her lunch, took her to the toilet, dressed her and she was discharged. It would have been very different for her and the doctors if I had not been there today.

* * *

Only four days later, but a lifetime has passed since then. I feel like the inside of me is opening up into a giant chasm, that any moment will have to explode or implode; it cannot keep getting hotter and more vast and intense.

Today is April 8th. It would be Pa's birthday today. Pa died two years ago and I really miss him. Thirteen years ago, on the same night, my father died. This Friday night, the day Mum and I were in the hospital, Pat also passed away. Isabelle lost her mum on the eve of the Grand National, as I lost my Dad, suddenly and painlessly.

I can't believe she has gone. I was drinking tea with her last Monday morning. She was recovering from what we thought was a tummy bug. The following day she was taken into hospital and I haven't seen her again.

Dad, Pa and Pat – all linked in dates as much as in my heart and life. My poor Isabelle, Bruno and Violet have lost Grandpa and Gran-Gran in two short years. It's times like this that the strengths and weaknesses of all the family and friends come to surface. And there's a flood of memories to enjoy and to deal with.

I am grateful that I still have my mum. I will take her up to the remembrance garden today and then to Pa's grave to remember Pa on his birthday and Dad on his anniversary.

* * *

It is now two months later. Life is very different without Pat to visit and Mum to care for daily. I see Mum roughly twice a week now and we either go out or come to the house and enjoy the garden. Conor enjoys Nana's visits. He is always reluctant to let her go home again at the end of the day. She is equally reluctant to leave.

I had a party for Mum's birthday whilst Debbie was here, so that family and friends could see them both. Mum's sister and one of her daughters came, as did Mum's faithful friends from school days. It was hard to know whether Mum recognised anyone or not. She is still very good at pretending that she knows what's going on. Debbie last saw her in November, but Mum has deteriorated quite a lot since then.

Last week when I got to Broad Glade, she looked so happy to see me. We hugged, prayed and wept together. Broad Glade had phoned the doctors again about the cough and they had refused to come out apparently.

She was in much distress, crying and shouting at her cough, "Stop it! Please, stop it!" and, after an hour at my house, I had two wet chairs.

I took her to the GP and was surprised that they have resolved to stop looking for the cause of the chronic cough. I think Mum aggravates it by not actually coughing anything up, because it disgusts her. They have referred her for some physiotherapy, which I will go along to, and which will hopefully release the phlegm and get it out. I expect it will be similar to the massage I used to do, for a boy at school with cystic fibrosis.

I gave Mum a shower, washed and blow-dried her hair and plucked her beard. She was enjoying the pampering and seemed to need it. Fortunately I had some clean clothes for her at my house still and I will keep the ones I changed, for next time.

It was noticeably much more difficult for Mum to climb the stairs. Her co-ordination was as wobbly as her confidence. Half way up the stairs, I had one of those "Why?" moments, with a "never again" trailing closely behind. We did get upstairs, with great rejoicing. Coming down again was even scarier. I was out of my depth and trusting in God alone to accomplish this.

I have to feed her all of her drinks and food now. She can hold the cup, if she has drunk half of it already and I balance it properly in her hands. If I give her a sandwich or cake, she cannot eat it without constant prompts, but still has difficulty getting it to her mouth. When I feed her, I am like a mother with a baby, coaxing her with my mouth open, saying "Aaahh…" Mammy giggles, opens and eats, looking surprised at the food.

She is not losing any weight though.

* * *

I am going to fetch her again now and go for a good walk.

Well, her cough is a little better, but the staff at Broad Glade are still very disturbed by it and reckon that "more residents than ever" are suffering from chest infections. They clearly think it's Mum's fault. They don't hold out much hope for the physiotherapy either. I continue to hope.

She started to cry again when she saw me (can't blame her there) and hugged me very tight. As we reversed into my drive, she said, "Home again. At last!"

We walked down to a new local café for a coffee and muffin. I don't know how many times she said, "Oh, this is lovely!" in response to the fresh breeze. She also kept smiling at my face and said how lovely I am. Of course, I replied, I am your daughter. In the café she initiated a conversation by asking me if I get bored. I never do, but she does.

We then took Conor to a large, local park area, which Mum seemed to be enjoying so much, that I decided to leave Conor to play with his friends, whilst Mum and I went exploring.

It was a bad idea. I was not familiar with the route and, at one point, the path was very narrow and steep, and Mum couldn't stay on the path. I decided to continue, rather than go back, but the route became even trickier.

We crossed a disused railway and after walking what seemed like a full circle, Mum started to get distracted and confused. She was looking at the wild flowers on the path, saying that they were all hers and that someone had stolen them from her. She was becoming cross and stubborn and we had come to what looked like a dead end.

I tried to explain that the wild flowers belonged to the countryside and that nobody had stolen her flowers, but she didn't believe me.

I all but dragged her through the overgrown hedgerows back into the field. She was in a really bad mood by then.

I was relieved to see the car park again and Mum seemed glad to be back in the car. I left Conor to play and took Mum straight back to Broad Glade.

She was very red-cheeked and sullen, but gave me a big hug and told me to be good.

* * *

Life is about to change again for me.

I have been offered a job-share in a Year One class in a school. I know it is the right job, but am a bit nervous about all the work involved again.

The staff seem great though and I'm glad I've got time to do plans, meet the children and get to know the ropes in relative ease before the Summer holidays.

* * *

Today I went to meet the manager at Broad Glade, mainly to discuss finance.

She made the suggestion that I change Mum's doctor to a city council GP, so she can have access to some new dementia support, which looks rather good. I'm sure the county council will catch on to it in time, but, as she said, much of the provision depends on a post-code lottery. I'll definitely look into it, because my doctors here are great for us, but they don't like doing home-visits.

I saw Mum too. I took the lid off her beaker and let her enjoy her coffee properly (she hates the toddler-beaker). Then we put raincoats on and went walking. She was so happy to be out and was squeezing my hand to say thank you.

She walked well today, with power and good balance and pace. Her face registers immense pleasure as the wind blows over her and wipes the cobwebs and cares away. She repeatedly asked after the boys and we were able to converse well.

I hadn't learned my lesson from Tuesday though and took Mum down two unfamiliar alleyways, simply out of curiosity. I thought Mum was going to get into a strop again, but she was happy to touch the plants, say that she knew them and that this is the way that she usually comes.

I am thankful that she was more lucid and aware today. She didn't like me leaving though. I know she loves the visits, but I still don't know whether it makes her worse when I go away again.

The garden is looking fantastic. The climbing angel-rose is full and heavy, and the two cuttings I took have flowered beautifully. My grapes, blueberry and blackcurrant are all looking good. The raspberry is ahead of itself and has four fruits coming already. Keep off birds, there's one for each of us. Yummy! Strawberries and rhubarb are making progress finally, and the tree is full of tiny apples. My "Turkish delight" roses are out in full splendour and the ornamental poppies' short and delicate lives are being enjoyed daily. Even the Agapanthus, that I brought back from Jersey, is getting ready to flower. I'm excited about the Physalis too, as I'd only seen it in its autumn glory as "Chinese lanterns", but it now has gorgeous, white, fairy-dress flowers, and the foliage is exquisite. I have a new crop of vegetables too: onions, beetroot, carrots, parsnips, sugar-snap peas and spuds.

* * *

I phoned the proposed new surgery, but they had already received an application form, so I bowed out gratefully and went to get Mum.

I found her in her room today, which is unusual. Her music was on and she was sitting sobbing in the chair. I watched her for a moment and then said, "I thought the music made you happy?"

"NO!" she grunted, "Not now!" She grumbled some words about, "nasty… no nice people any more… always following…"

I went over to her and squat down, but she didn't recognise me.

"Go away and just leave me alone." she snapped.

I found a member of staff, who was clearly baffled and a bit irritated by Mum's behaviour. Apparently Mum had woken up crying and had been telling everyone to leave her alone all morning.

Then a male care-worker came on duty and, within minutes, he had Mum out of her room and smiling. He told her I was there, so I got the big-squeeze hugs and the tearful *where* have you been?"

She admitted that she had "just been mardy", and she laughed, amused and scandalised, when I told her how she had behaved.

We had a lovely, event free afternoon and Conor helped me to escort her home again in the evening.

But something strange and unpleasant seems to be happening for Mum.

* * *

Yesterday before fetching Mum, a senior member of staff from Broad Glade phoned. She had contacted the new GP with an urgent request for a referral to the "Dementia Support Outreach team". She used the word "violent" to describe Mum, saying that she has been crying all the time, throwing things and pushing staff away.

It sounds like she is rebelling.

When I arrived, they were still trying to contact the GP for some support. They are obviously doing all they can.

The manager said that Mum had thrown her bowl of cornflakes over the table, so they have moved her to a new table, to dine alone. I hope that is a temporary solution rather than a permanent precaution. On reflection it seems rather severe.

They had told her I was coming and I found her in one of the lounges.

As they announced my arrival, I had no opportunity to see if she recognised me today or not.

I get ever-tighter hugs. This time she cried, "I didn't think you were ever coming back again. Where have you been?"

We walked back to my house together, earning ourselves a refreshing cuppa.

Many times she asked, "How are the boys?" and "so what have you been up to?" I answered every time.

I tried to find out what Mum has been experiencing to cause such a change in behaviour.

She said that she "does this and that and then it's all gone, nothing happened. I can't do anything. I think I've done it, but I haven't."

She said "yes" to feelings of frustration and anger. Frustration about the above and anger at herself, "because it's me that does it".

I told her that being mardy makes everyone else miserable too, because they want to cheer her up and help, but they cannot if she's being mardy.

I said she is doing her best. I wish I knew how to help.

I think she would prefer to live here with us, but it was too difficult. I wonder if I should have forced myself to keep going for her. Sometimes I think she's so sweet and defenceless. I feel I've not been fair to her.

When I took her back yesterday, the evening staff were standing in a corner chatting and told me to "put her in a chair somewhere." I am very grateful to them, but I do wish they would try to interact more, as they do in the day-centre, with conversation, activities and games.

She is safe there and I don't have to do all the work now, so I must not complain. I'm sure she feels that I've abandoned her. I have to remind myself that she was often frustrated and bored living with us.

I am trying not to think about what would happen if her defences and mask fall altogether, and she decides to rebel against all the fear, pride and pain that held her for so many years. If she finally lashes back, what will she do, or what will happen to her?

I need to speak to the dementia doctor, or to the outreach team.

We talked about family and Daddy. I had Mum's brass tankard downstairs, which still contains some of Dad's ashes. Mum had it inscribed with:

Malcolm T. Haynes
(Dick)
Dec. 1945 – April 1995
A Very Special Brew
&
no half measures.

It's supposed to be funny. Special Brew was his favourite beer. Clearly he had a very full measure that night. It killed him!

He was definitely not a man for moderation.

All or nothing.

CHAPTER 13

It seems that all the carers' services are compiling surveys at the moment. It was strange to think back to the volunteers and befrienders we had, and to how much I valued them for what they offered to Mum in terms of their friendship. Mum could speak with them in a way she would never speak to me, as her daughter. They each took Mum out walking and would have a good laugh and "put the world to rights".

I did mention, on one form, that I had been disappointed, when Mum went into Broad Glade, because none of her volunteer friends were allowed to visit her. Even though Mum didn't like going to the day centres, she still had a variety of activities on those days too. Now she only has me to visit and take her out. The rest of the time she is stuck in that warm, enclosed environment, surrounded by "old people".

I asked Age Concern whether volunteers could provide some company to the lonely residents in these places too? Perhaps I need to go more regularly and be satisfied with just taking her for a walk, rather than a whole day out.

* * *

This morning I got another call from the unit manager at Broad Glade, saying that Mum has refused drink, food and medication and is pushing everyone away. She had "gone off to another unit and walked into someone else's bedroom." The unit manager asked me to come and calm her down and get her to take a drink.

Mammy was in her room, door closed, music on and she was crying. We had a long hug and she apologised for being mardy again.

Her general complaint is still that there's "nothing to do". And she hates that beaker with the spout.

I said that these people make meals and cups of tea for her and help her with washing and dressing, but she said,

"Oh, I don't want that. I do all that for myself!"

She let me put her walking shoes on, glad to get out for a while. As always she transformed the moment she hit the fresh air and soaked it all up. We had a brisk forty-minute walk, up hill and down dale, and got back to Broad Glade in time for lunch.

I wanted to defy the system and restore her to her place at table with the others. So I sat with her through lunch and dessert, helping and encouraging her in a way that they cannot (not because they don't want to, but because they are too busy).

The other two ladies on the table thought I had come to visit them.

Mammy did well independently with the main course and I fed her the dessert, at which she melted into raptures of giggles and delight at each mouth-full.

Mammy looked suspicious when we first sat down at table and her expression told me that her thoughts were not good. She laughed when I reminded her that I'd known her all my life and I knew when there was something awry. What she expressed was that she didn't trust the people around. She thought they were taking her things from her, as some triggers from the unconscious mind were in fear and mistrust. It reminded me of when she thought that the wild flowers were hers and that someone had stolen them. I reasoned that the people there were too busy cooking her tasty dinners to be stealing cardigans.

The noises in the dining room were disturbing. The TV and a radio were *both* on high volume. There was additional noise from the carers, who had to shout to find out what the residents' wishes were:

"Do you want ice cream or custard with that, Avril?"

There were involuntary and more unpleasant noises from some of the residents too.

Mammy was not the only one disturbed by the cacophony. It seemed to make them all a little fractious and jumpy.

I spoke to the carers for a while before I left. They are all working very hard, but are obviously severely understaffed and are unable to provide the level of care that they feel the residents deserve. They pointed out that, as the residents in their care get older, their needs increase and for some residents their needs change substantially, as Mum's have done. There are only two carers for fifteen residents, which, at peak times is nowhere near enough. It is a residential care home, rather than a nursing home, but they *are* registered for dementia and many of the residents do need high maintenance.

I have decided to write some letters, to the Council and to Age Concern, to make a few observations and suggestions. They cannot form policies and make changes without ideas for outcomes and solutions from others. So I'll give them some of mine concerning staffing and volunteers and see what comes of it.

Debbie rang, so I told her about Mum's change of behaviour and how she is.

Something I remember my mum saying when I was young was, "They shoot horses, don't they?" I think it was from a film, but I remember her explaining to me the meaning of the title. Now, when I see her so lost in distress, confusion and frustration, I think of her comments and wonder.

I think that she really does not like her life.

* * *

I got to Mum's about 11:00 yesterday to meet the Physiotherapist. The staff didn't know that the Physiotherapist was coming.

There have been complications with the GP situation. Mammy is no longer registered with our GP, but the surgery to which her medical records were sent have changed their mind about accepting new patients. So Mum doesn't have a GP at all.

The home is desperate to get her seen by a specialist. A CPN (Community Psychiatric Nurse) from St Peter's Wing is expected to visit soon.

I was informed that Mum had had nothing to eat or drink and no medication again that morning.

I found Mum marching down a corridor towards me, being herded along by one of the friendly carers. She approached with her head down, eyes up, face like a charging bull in thunder.

I said something like, "What's up, Misery?" and thought she would kill me. She dodged defensively until I said, "Mammy?"

She gave a desperate cry and rushed into my arms, sobbing and grabbing so tight as if terrified, but relieved. "I thought I'd never see you again!" she sobbed.

I'd only seen her two days before, but of course she doesn't know that. When we were hugged out and wet with tears, I took her to her room. She kept saying how she was daft, stupid, and that she tries to do this and that, but can't. Unfortunately she doesn't know why she can't do it, or even what it is that she can't do. She knows she keeps crying and "being loony", but doesn't know that she's being aggressive to others.

She is scared. She thought I'd gone forever. She said that she keeps seeing Dad and that he wants to take her somewhere. She wanted to go, but it didn't happen. She said she doesn't want to hurt me.

I poured out all the reassurance and love possible.

When the Physiotherapist came, Mum was red-eyed but calm. I was surprised to learn that she'd already seen Mum last week and had shown one of the carers some exercises to do. They were fairly straight forward breathing exercises and I'm not sure how effective they will be. But we did them.

Then I checked out Mum's medication to make sure there were no more surprises. She has had codeine for the cough (and now needs something to loosen the bowels, because of the codeine), and she is on another dose of antibiotics.

I gave her the medication and we played music in her room and had lunch there. We were listening to Willie Nelson, so she was maudlin rather than eating.

"Stop sobbing and eat, or I'll turn the music off", I laughed.

"Yes, Mammy!" she replied, taking another mouthful.

Mammy was staring at me again with a soppy look, put her arms towards me and said, "You're lovely!" She kissed me.

It's strange but a blessed treasure, finally having the warm hugs and kisses that I'd been desperate for as a child.

* * *

There was a message left for me this morning from the County Councillor. He got my letter about staffing in care homes and responded immediately. He thanked me for bringing it to his attention and promised to take the matter up with the Strategic Director before giving a proper response.

I phoned Broad Glade to see how Mum was before I went in. Apparently she was compliant this morning. The CPN had been yesterday (I'm disappointed that I missed her, having asked especially to see her) and she has prescribed a new medication.

I arrived just before lunch. She didn't hug me quite so tightly and said she was "All right now!"

She seemed settled and happy having lunch. Getting ready to go out, she suddenly looked up and scowled at her reflection, saying, "Does *she* always have to come?"

I realised that she was being serious, so I asked, "Do you mean that gorgeous lady in the mirror?"

She grunted, "I don't like her. She's always there!"

I had to laugh, but it was so difficult to show her that it was her own reflection that followed her into the bathroom. She understood eventually and laughed with me, but I expect she'll forget again. Maybe she expects to see a younger, brown-haired lady in the mirror?

We went off to shake collection boxes at Tesco. She wore a rose hat and a smile and we filled our boxes and met a few lovely people. We did a good stretch of walking afterwards and Mum and Conor had the chance to chat and play.

Mum is concerned about her eyesight again.

When we got back to Broad Glade, they took her to do her night routine and Mum expressed some anxiety about not having much money. I reassured her that she had already paid for it all and she seemed satisfied.

* * *

I saw Mum on Monday and we went for a very long walk. We took flowers to Pat and Pa's graves and enjoyed each other's company.

She still seems more settled, and again mentioned needing "new eyes". She even said she'd like to take up the guitar again, which I've not heard her consider for a long time.

* * *

Yesterday I got home to find a message from a new social worker, saying that he had "been asked to do an assessment of Avril's needs, as Broad Glade were having problems providing her care".

Broad Glade had contacted Social Services because, Avril had become "verbally and physically aggressive" and had, at one point, "pulled a resident out of her chair".

I was shocked to get such a message from a stranger. Fortunately, he wanted to inform family and get me involved from the beginning of his new case. I do not understand why Broad Glade did not tell me. I do understand that they have to be proactive, but they could at least communicate their intentions with me.

Interestingly, he said that he'd gone to Broad Glade on Monday, but that they were "all too busy to see him", so had left again without meeting Mum or talking with anyone. He said they "must have been a bit short-staffed".

After I'd recollected myself, I phoned the unit manager at Broad Glade. I wanted answers about GP, medication, CPN input and anything else they were considering doing, or that I might need to know.

I did get some answers: Mum is now prescribed Trazodone twice a day (apparently the CPN said that was "all they could do for her"). Mum is also registered with a new GP.

The unit manager said they had contacted Social Services to reassess Mum "as backup", so that they can provide the best care for her.

She described Mum as "quite threatening, although she hasn't actually hit anyone".

She also described a situation last night, where they had provided entertainment, and Mum, although enjoying the music, got distressed because of the noise volume. They then sat her just outside the door and Mum enjoyed it fully, she said. To me it just shows how a little flexibility and understanding enables Mum to fully participate in something she enjoys.

She agreed to involve me when Social Services do the assessment, and said I must always go and ask, if I have questions.

I think that everyone is doing their best, but that priorities and resources vary.

Trazodone is a *serotonin modulator* used as a sleep aid and for depression/ anxiety/ schizophrenia.

* * *

The social worker did an assessment of Mum yesterday, but is waiting for the nurse to do an assessment too.

He said that Mum was clearly very distressed and that he felt sorry for her. He doesn't think that Broad Glade is a suitable place for Mum, in that they don't have the staff, or the time, to give Mum what she needs. His concern is that the sort of environment better suited to Mum's needs tends to be much more severe in terms of the behaviour of residents. It could be quite a scary environment for Mum, he said, if we don't look carefully.

I was minding Isabelle's children this morning, but at 10:00 Broad Glade phoned to say that Mammy was very distressed and could I go and calm her down. Fortunately, Simon was here and able to fetch her instead.

Mammy was in a bad way and cried a lot. What follows are snippets of what she expressed between sobs and tissues. In brackets are some questions or clarifications added by me:

"Silly, silly man! He's gone! He didn't have to do that!"

(Do you think he did it on purpose?)

"I know he did! I've said my goodbyes. He knew he was going. He said so, but I didn't believe him. He said, 'I'm going to bed'…and he killed himself."

(How?)

"A knife. I don't know what sort. Then he threw it away and I couldn't get it back. Don't tell the kids will you? He looked lovely when he went. Don't tell the boys. Silly, silly man! He knew that we loved him. I think he was happy…I'd never seen him like that…dying."

(I thought Daddy died at Jimmy's house after too much whiskey?)

"Yes, he was there and then he came back. He came in HERE (she was pointing around the table) and he said he was going somewhere…I didn't know he…YOU STUPID man! Don't tell the kids, will you?"

(When did this happen, Mammy?)

"It was round about here…about this time. He said, 'I'm going now' and then I found him. Don't tell the kids…I don't know what they'll do."

(I explained that Josh and Conor had never met Daddy, that he had died thirteen years ago, before Conor was even born. I said that Daddy had never been to this house.)

Mum frowned for some time, looking very confused.

"No, he WAS here. I know it sounds silly, but he *was* here."

I made us all some more tea and came back to find her grinning like the proverbial Cheshire cat.

"He's just come…he's smiling. He looks lovely…BIG HUG FOR ALL!"

Isabelle collected her children after lunch and Conor took Mum to watch a DVD, whilst we waited for her sister.

Today it is twenty-six years since their mum died. When Julia came, we took some flowers up to the remembrance garden. Julia approves of the remembrance vase. We weren't there long, then we dropped Julia off and I took Mum back to her 'home'.

She always asks me why I'm going and when I'm coming back. "See you soon", is never enough.

* * *

Today Mum and I came back from the TAB Summer picnic, expecting Debbie at any moment.

"What are you feeling, Mammy?" I asked, because she was clearly distressed.

"You don't want to know!" she growled, giving another of her very suspicious, shifty looks.

"I really *do* want to know what you are feeling, Mammy."

"Horrible! If you want to know…I want to kill myself. I know it's wrong, but I can't go on…I can't live any more. I've felt a long time… I'm sorry. It's stupid. It's wrong. I know that I can't do it though…kill myself…I'm a coward. I'd better clean up. The boys will be coming home…I'm sorry I'm a coward…I can't."

"I'm glad you are a coward, Mammy. I don't want you to kill yourself. Did you think about *how* you would kill yourself?"

"I can't even do that!" she sobbed.

"Do you think you should kill yourself because of Daddy?"

""I can't though…"

"Good. I'm glad. Do you think Daddy is waiting for you to follow him to death?"

"Probably…" she drifted away.

"If Daddy's in heaven, I'm convinced he'll be praying for you to have the grace to live a full life, not to die."

"I can't do it. And I don't want to. I'm sorry…" she reached out for a touch.

"I forgive you, Mammy."

"Thank you." she smiled, as we embraced.

Eventually Debbie phoned to say that she was visiting a sick relative-in-law and wouldn't be in till late, so I took Mum home again.

As we got near to Broad Glade, she asked, "Where are we going?"

"I'm bringing you home." I answered. "See you later."

"Are you going?" she sighed sadly.

"I'll be back soon and Debbie is coming too. Be good."

"There's nothing else." She added with an evident disappointment that stabs my heart.

I went home, sad and disappointed that Debbie hadn't managed to see Mum today. Still, it was lovely to see her and her son James when they did turn up. They had very good reasons for not being there earlier. They were on a different, but equally important mission with a dying lady. Debbie and James promised to spend the following day with Mum and we were all happy to share the evening together.

On Tuesday evening we said farewell to Debbie and James, and then it was Conor's 'Farewell to Year 6' - an evening of drama, song and tears – lots of them, like a dam bursting and sending a domino wave over the whole line-up of year six children.

Mammy has no idea that Debbie has been to see her and there's no point trying to contradict her. In her reality, she is right. She always has been. She is a strange contradiction of the stubborn "I'm right and I know it" and the other ever-present "I'm useless/I can't do it/I've got it wrong again."

She does speak conflicting messages to herself. I am not dissimilar.

This is a busy week getting ready for a trip to Germany and then for Faith Camp straight afterwards. So much to look forward to and so many friends to be grateful for.

I have asked Isabelle, Julia and Monica to visit Mum and look out for her whilst I am away. I know that Monica will see her as often as she can. I feel much reassured by that.

* * *

It was great to be back in Nussloch, where I was an Au-pair for two years. I felt very conscious of the time that had passed by. We enjoyed a satisfying balance of sightseeing, walking, eating and relaxing with good friends. It was great to spend time with my special friend 'Little John' too.

Now I'm home and unpacking, washing and repacking for camp tomorrow. It's also Josh's fourteenth birthday today.

Isabelle's crew had all visited Mum on the Tuesday and Monica had been to see her on the Wednesday. Apparently Julia had planned to go on the Friday, but had phoned in advance and was told that Mum had gone out with the relatives of another resident? I must investigate that, as I know that Monica had trouble getting Mum into the car, when she took her out for a picnic.

That was quite a surreal experience for me: I was on the top of "Holy Mountain" in Heidelberg and answered my phone to Monica, who wanted me to tell Mum that it was okay for her to go out for a picnic with herself and Alf. She was fine then, but apparently, bringing Mum home again was a different story completely. It seems that they could not get Mum back into the van. Monica presented an amusing image of several people chasing Mum around the car park – which I thought would have made them think twice about letting her go off with strangers.

Monica, who saw her own mum behaving badly with dementia, saw a side of Mum that shocked even her.

* * *

After church on Sunday, I walked to Broad Glade with Conor and Violet, intending to make Isabelle's house our walking destination for Mum, for tea and cakes and then a good walk back.

She appeared very miserable when we arrived and had been sobbing all day, apparently. She didn't seem particularly pleased to see us, but was glad to be invited out for a walk.

Walking up the steep hill to Isabelle's house is challenging for most of us, so Mum did really well, stopping only twice to catch her breath. Walking down the other side felt very dangerous, because she didn't seem to know how to control her balance and not run into the walls or topple forward. She wouldn't be able to go home again that way.

Mum was no better at Isabelle's and seemed to be physically very hunched up. Walking or sitting her head was bowed low to the ground. I tried to get her to sit upright, to drink her tea or eat biscuits, but she couldn't do it. She seemed to be closing up.

Isabelle offered to give us all a lift home.

Mammy was just so heavy and weighed down with grief/depression/drugs? I carried some of it back home with me.

* * *

Today I called Mum's CPN. She explained her role in Mum's care in terms of psychiatry/medication. The Trazodone is to help control Mum's agitation and depression. She is now on 250mg per day. The CPN will be going to see her this morning and will speak to me later.

Broad Glade then phoned me. They said that Mum has been "swearing at and hitting staff", has been refusing help with dressing, eating and drinking; she hasn't slept for two nights, has been pacing around and now won't come out of her room.

They are having a meeting on Friday, for the nursing assessment (NHS review), as they feel that Mum now needs a higher level of care.

I thought Broad Glade were exaggerating, so I decided to continue with my plans to go with Conor and Isabelle's crew to the Ice Stadium and take Josh for his eye-test.

Then I began to think about Mammy again.

PART 3

Sectioned. Hallucinations, Drugs and Laundry

CHAPTER 14

I had a call from the social worker this morning, to say that Mum "attacked the CPN" yesterday.

The same CPN went with the social worker again this morning and Mum "attacked them both".

I should have gone up there yesterday. Mum has still not drunk anything and has refused medication and food.

She has physically attacked one of the carers too.

They think that she needs to be "sectioned", in a secure hospital unit, until she can be sorted out.

I went straight there. Conor had to come with me as I couldn't leave him home alone – not knowing how long I'd be. I warned him that he might have to play quietly outside and might not be able to see Nana straight away.

They didn't want me to see Mum first. They wanted me to wait until they were all there – dementia doctor, social worker and GP - as the social worker required both of their signatures to get Mum sectioned. They are meeting at 11:30.

I wanted to go and calm Mum down. She sounded scared and like she felt cornered. I didn't expect this. It all sounded so serious and I didn't know what I was supposed to do.

Mum's whole unit had been cleared of residents.

I could feel my heart beating. It all felt very over dramatic – almost comical somehow.

I knocked on Mum's door and heard her growl an emphatic "GO AWAY!"

As I opened the door she lunged towards me with manic movements and scary eyes.

"Mammy," I pleaded. "It's me, Dawn, your daughter…"

"GO AWAY!" she hissed.

I pleaded again and she rushed towards me, hands grasping, teeth clenched and growling,

"...Or I'll kill you!"

I snatched her hands and tried to look her in the eyes. She fought back viciously and tried to bite my hands, but fortunately I am physically strong too. She slammed the door into me as I tried to squeeze through. She seemed to have a room full of invisible guests and they were all in a rage.

She really seemed like a person 'possessed'.

I came away, because I was not helping and because Conor had followed me down and was becoming very distressed at this hideous sight.

* * *

The doctor explained that Mum would be taken to the St Peter's Wing at the hospital and be properly assessed there. She gave me all the contact details and sent us away, before the ambulance people and police could restrain my poor little Mammy and take her away.

We were quite shaken up by the time we got home.

Conor knew "it wasn't Nana", but it was like a bad spirit that had made her ill.

Broad Glade was no longer adequate for Mum's needs, so something better would come of this.

All shall be well.

* * *

A nurse from St Peter's Wing kindly phoned to give me an update. They expect Mum to be there for six - eight weeks, during which time they will investigate her responses to different treatments, drugs and environments to see what will work best for her.

She said she expects me to visit regularly and to do Mum's laundry. Mum had no belongings with her, so I need to take her some clothes and toiletries urgently. She advised me not to bring the children, as the ward "can be quite distressing," with "unpredictable behaviour, screaming and some violent outbursts".

Visiting hours are quite strictly 14:00 – 16:00 and 18:00 – 20:00. Mum has two key nurses assigned to her.

'One Flew Over the Cuckoos Nest' springs to mind. But I haven't been yet, so I cannot judge.

I am still in shock, I think.

The social worker then phoned, to say that Mum had "put up a good fight" to stay in her room at Broad Glade, but when she arrived at St Peter's Wing "she changed completely".

Apparently she welcomed tea and biscuits and tried to communicate that she knew they were doing their best to help her, but that she didn't understand what was happening.

She asked where I was and he told her that I had been there this morning. She wanted to know why I wasn't with her then.

It was good of him to phone me. I felt a bit better.

I am down in their paperwork as 'nearest relative' and Debbie as 'next of kin'.

The social worker did phone Debbie, before they 'took her away'. I recalled my dad singing, "They're coming to take you away; ha, ha!"

I'd better tell Monica and Julia too.

Isabelle took me back down to Broad Glade to pick up some things for Mum, but I'll take them tomorrow, as I'm completely drained now.

I was surprised that Broad Glade seemed to be in a hurry to clear her room and give me *all* her stuff. I wasn't prepared for that and said I had come only for immediate supplies, but that I would be in touch after speaking to St Peter's Wing.

As far as I know, no decision has yet been made for her *not* to go back to Broad Glade, even if it is not the most suitable place for her. Still, they will have to wait for me to take a larger hold-all to clear it properly, but I will check with the social worker first.

* * *

Today as I set off to see Mum at the hospital, I felt a great peace. All shall be well.

I had a chat with the lady in charge, then booked in Mum's belongings and labelled the CDs and 'This Is Your life' book, that I'd brought.

Mum had had food, drinks and medication during those twenty-four hours and allowed herself to be washed and changed. She seemed much less angry today.

There seemed to be a lot of staff around, who showed an interest in hearing about Mum and were very accommodating, particularly considering that I was there out of visiting hours. The general environment is much more volatile than Mum is used to, with lots of sudden, dramatic incidents, screams and mini emergencies.

I went nervously into the dining area where Mum was and said, "Hello Mammy", and went to hug her. I got the old response of tears and hugs, so I took her away to a quieter room, where I could help her with her food and pray with her. We did both successfully.

She seems to be hearing many voices and conversing with them all simultaneously. She keeps mentioning having a baby and being too old, and she seems to be seeing and hearing Daddy all the time. Sometimes 'Daddy' was distressing her and she started giving me shifty looks again, but she would switch from fretting, to giggling, to smiling, to laughing outright and back to panicking again, all in the space of a what outwardly appeared to be a complex monologue.

I found some of the residents a little alarming, but a quiet male resident came to join us after dinner and we put on an Elvis CD. Mum and I danced through the whole album.

Mum intuitively knew when I was about to go and asked would I come again. Of course I will. I feel very positive about all this now, although I've no idea what is next.

* * *

On Sunday evening I went to Broad Glade, with Conor, to get more of Mum's things and then on to the hospital.

Unfortunately, it was the sad and angry Mum we encountered this time, hissing at us to "go away" and turning mine and Conor's legs to jelly again.

I didn't know who to talk to or what to do, so we exchanged clean for dirty clothes and came away. Conor was very disappointed and I felt sorry that I had taken him. I had taken him to reassure him that Nana had been happier again, but it might take time for her to settle.

Julia is planning to go and see Mum tomorrow, so I'd better warn her, as I'd told her that Mum was better again.

* * *

Julia went anyway and was "devastated" to see how much she'd deteriorated.

She described Mum wearing a "granny apron" that was open down the middle.

Apparently the conversation went something like:

"Hello Avril. It's your sister."

"No, you're not!"

"I am, I'm your sister, Julia."

"NO. You're not!" said with such a look of anger and contempt (not like Avril at all).

Apparently Julia was on her way out again, when Mum called out to her, "Who are you?"

"I'm your sister."

What's your name?"

"Julia."

Mum then sneered at her and Julia turned and left, without looking back. She wished she hadn't been to see her there.

Julia thinks it's worse for us than it is for Mum; but I don't think that we can know how it is for Mum. As far as I can see, Mammy is in a very bad way at the moment and she is finding life quite unbearable.

* * *

Today I spent about five hours planning for my teaching job in September.

I had horrible dreams last night about being in my new class, with uncontrollable children and unsympathetic teaching assistants.

There is so much happening in my life that I have no control over, so I guess the dreams are not surprising.

The house and garden are a mess. The hot-water immersion doesn't work and the shower switch has broken, so Conor and I had to wash in the hand basin this morning. The cooker and the microwave are on-the-blink too, but we won't let it all get us down.

I really want to speak to a doctor at the hospital and get a realistic prognosis for Mammy.

I spoke to a nurse who said that it is difficult to discuss these things over the phone and that I should ask to speak to a qualified nurse when I'm there next. He also suggested that I speak to Mum's *new* dementia consultant. I'm not sure why they have swapped consultants. All he could say is that Mum "sometimes needs restraining, when she invades the personal space of others". Also, he said it is difficult to get near her to wash her, or give her food and medication, and that they are having to give her space to observe her.

When Simon returned with the car, I went with Mum's clean clothes, not knowing how I might find her.

I was met by a friendly nurse, who invited me to a carers' meeting tomorrow at 14:30. I passed the lounge and saw Mum smiling and relaxed on the couch. Great.

I sorted out the laundry and came back to sit with her. I could see that she was doped up, but she was quite lucid, 'chilled out' and lovely. Several times she asked me if I wanted something to drink or eat.

She referred to Dawn a couple of times and then laughed at herself when she realised that Dawn was there.

She also said, with a smile, "he's still up there!"

I guessed she was referring to Daddy 'upstairs still', as he was often in bed for days. We shared some memories of the cats, goats and of some of the things that Dad cleverly made over the years.

I then said I needed to go fetch the boys and she asked if she could come with me, but I suggested that they needed her help there and she agreed.

I don't know what it was, but I could have enjoyed a dose of that 'chilling juice' too.

* * *

Last night I felt so incredibly tired, that I could hardly stay awake for the boys' bedtime and prayers. I couldn't get up easily this morning either. I was 'babysitting' and had errands to do before the carers' group meeting, at the hospital.

On arrival, I hadn't a clue where to go, but I saw Mum and went to say hello. She smiled as I went and hugged her, but when I called her 'Mammy', she stiffened up and said,

"You're not my Mammy!"

"No, I know," I laughed, "You're my Mammy and I'm Dawn!"

Her eyes narrowed and she pulled away again, doing the "No, you're not…"

"Look at me, Mammy," I said shrinking myself down to be face-to-face with her, "Don't I look like Dawn to you?"

"You look like her, but you're not!" she insisted.

I made a sarcastic retort and excused myself to find the group.

It consisted of three professionals, four 'relatives' and me. The nurse that I'd met yesterday gave me coffee and looked after me, as I was a bit tearful. The group were mainly coming to terms with Power of Attorney issues, hospital visiting conditions and stuff. The staff spoke about "memory boxes", and one qualified nurse commented on how useful our 'This is your Life' book had already been for her to connect with Mum.

I just wanted to know about the "What's next?" issues, and what I need to be doing to support Mum. The nurse explained to me that under Section Two of the Mental Health Act, Mum being sectioned means that she cannot leave the ward for twenty-eight days. It also gives the hospital authority to calm Mum with drugs if necessary. That was what they did yesterday – injected a dose of Lorazepam (which is addictive, so they don't do it often).

It is too soon for them to know what is best for Mum, but they will do the NHS "continuing care checklist" themselves and that will then be sent to social services for approval.

I asked about Mum's room at Broad Glade and she suggested that I speak to the social worker about this.

It was good to speak to the nurse. She said that I must always find someone to speak to before I leave, rather than bottling up questions and issues.

I feel a bit less lost now.

*　*　*

On Friday night I was at the hospital again. Mum had had another shot of Lorazepam and was 'chilled out' on the bed. I found happy ways to keep a conversation going and wished I'd brought Conor with me. I took a photo of her smiling, to show him.

She seems to be becoming racist. She told me last week that she can't stand the staff nurse and today she was negative and unresponsive towards the carer offering tea and sandwiches – both of these ladies were friendly, gentle and brown-skinned. When the 'tea-lady' left, I asked Mum if she wanted some tea.

"Coffee please. And a sandwich if there is one," she replied.

I went out and told the lady that Mum had changed her mind.

Mum was huggy and sweet to me and she seemed to remember a lot from early days again today.

*　*　*

Today I spoke to the social worker and to the manager at Broad Glade. The room has been left available for Mum, until a decision can be made. The social worker will see me at the hospital review tomorrow.

Monica went to see Mum today. She took with her a pile of photos, but she didn't stay long. Mum was hiding in the loo and wouldn't come out, so Monica went in. Mum didn't acknowledge Monica, wouldn't look at the photos, was cantankerous and insisted that the photos all belonged to her. Monica could understand her own mother becoming aggressive with dementia, because, she said, she had always been a horrible lady, but she didn't expect my mum to go nasty.

I suggested that because so many horrible things had happened that Mum couldn't control, that maybe all her hidden fear and anger was now expressing itself, free from inhibitions.

Monica also fears that visiting the angry Mum makes her more distressed, confused and angry. It seems to do no one any good. It's difficult to know.

When she's relaxed and happy Mum gets so much out of the visits, even if they are immediately forgotten, but the good moments must add to her general store of well-being.

* * *

It is Tuesday morning and I'm feeling strong and positive. Joshua is looking after Conor and I'm going to ask more questions.

When I arrived at the review, they were still discussing someone else, so I sorted Mum's laundry. We nearly made a mistake though – the nurse took me to Mum's room and opened the wardrobe. I noticed how empty it seemed and started to hang up her clean trousers and tops, when I realised that the clothes in the wardrobe belonged to a man. Eventually we discovered that Mum has been moved into a women's ward, sleeping six, and I finally got the laundry sorted.

Mum was lovely and not particularly dopey. She was giggling and chatting with herself, asking and answering her own questions, but aware of my presence.

She asked me if I'm "better now" and interrogated me with her eyes, when I said I was, to check that I wasn't lying. I remember that expression.

"Are you sure you're okay? I'm not out of the woods yet." She added.

"No? But there's light ahead and you're getting better." I offered.

Mum giggled again. "I'm bored. Can I come home with you? What are you here for?"

"I've come to see the doctor." I was happy to say truthfully.

"Me too." She added.

"I haven't seen you for so long; I thought you were never coming back."

I had brought the tweezers, aware that Mum's beard was growing furiously. I began to pull the wires out, trying desperately to distract her from the sensation, but she seemed to feel the pain of the plucking more than ever. Then the nurse called me.

"My turn", I announced cheerfully, "See you later."

The review was a bit formidable. There were six of us: the dementia doctor and her shadow, the social worker and his shadow, the staff nurse and little me. They tried to reassure me that they were all working to find the best solutions for Mum. I trust that they are.

They don't think that Broad Glade is suitable for Mum any more, but they can't say what *is* suitable "at this early stage".

I asked about the medication and put my case for giving Mum more of the Lorazepam. The doctor was adamant that Mum would stay on the Trazodone, that there isn't much else on the market and that Trazodone is very effective. She added that Lorazepam should be used "as needed" when Mum is particularly difficult or violent. She argued that because one can become tolerant of Lorazepam, it should be used sparingly if it is to remain effective.

The staff nurse said that Mum likes to be alone and seems content wandering about all day. She said that problems only occur when the staff need to get Mum to do something like wash, eat, get dressed, take her medicine, etc; only then does she become difficult and aggressive.

They said there is no way of knowing how Mum would progress with the disease, whether she would become more aggressive or more benign as time passed. They would be looking to place her where she would not have to be moved again as she deteriorates.

I wanted to say that I am looking for a miracle, but tears came instead. It isn't easy to believe in miracles when folk around are throwing pessimistic circumstance and prognoses at you.

They said they'd involve me in their decisions, gave me a tissue, and showed me out.

Mum was still in good form.

A man was sharing the two-seater settee with her, with his arm around her waist. I sat in the adjacent chair and tried to talk to her, but the man leaned forward, glared at me and said,

"Go away! I'm warning you, go away!"

"Don't you start!" I said, feeling both amused and ruffled that he was spoiling my quality time.

Mum looked at him and smiled, chuntering to herself and then kissed him on the shoulder. I sat back and took out some paper to make notes. The man again leaned forward and growled,

"Go away! I mean it. She's my wife!"

"And she's my mother," I retorted, heartbeat quickening. "So who does that make you?"

I laughed at the whole situation and at myself, and settled back to look with love.

A nurse came in with a ball and a target. Mum and her new man-friend chose to play. Mum aimed sideways and shook her head saying how she's "no good at it". The man then threw and scored, so Mum had another go with renewed vigour and concentration, and scored too.

When he had the ball, Mum thought it was still in her hand and was trying to throw nothing.

"I need something a bit heavier," she complained, looking at her cupped, empty hand.

I noticed that Mum responds to all the conversations around, but doesn't expect a response herself.

So, when the nurse said, "I'm going to fetch you some tea. Are you warm enough, Ivy?"

Mum replies, "That'll be nice. I think I'm alright…Oh, there you are."

She seemed to be enjoying the man's attention and lunchtime was looming, so I made to leave. She asked if I will come back. Of course. She made me smile today.

* * *

We are going away tomorrow, so I want to see Mum before I go. Conor wants me to phone first in case he can come too. We prayed on the way and found her brimming with tears of joy and hugs for Conor and I. We had the old "where have you been?" Conor had a smile from ear to ear as he led Nana to a comfy place to sit. Unfortunately, he kept opening his mouth and putting his foot straight in it unwittingly with concepts that were no longer part of Mum's reality. I did not fare much better. She kept saying how bored she was, with nothing to do. I reminded her that hospitals can be boring, but you just have to wait until they give you the "all clear".

She didn't want to hear that she was in hospital.

"Nobody told me." She complained.

We changed the subject and said, unwisely, that we were going away for the weekend.

"Can I come?" she asked.

"You have to wait for the doctors to finish your assessment, Mammy. They won't let you leave the hospital until your test results are through."

"They didn't tell me. Why? There's nothing wrong with me!"

It was like treading on eggshells and trying to avoid breakage, so I suggested some music. Conor led Mum to the music room and was a bit confused when Nana insisted that (my) Daddy was there. Fortunately there was no one else in the music room, so we closed the door. There was a Patsy Cline cassette there, so I suggested that. Mum agreed and we danced and sang ourselves silly.

"You look different?" she said after dancing and staring quizzically for some time.

"Do I? Just greyer around the edges, I expect." I answered, but thinking "I feel different, dancing around like this is the best music I've ever heard. I feel zany myself, but very thankful too and sort of content."

Mum was enjoying the dancing and she looked great. She was much less podgy and was standing up straight and dancing well.

"No, you're different…It's Daddy!"

Oh, that makes sense then?

When it was time to leave she was disappointed that she couldn't come. It felt like all the fun had been undone and forgotten and only the pain of separation remained for her. It was heart breaking.

* * *

We've just come back from our weekend away. I have really missed Mammy and look forward to seeing her later. Seeing others with their mums makes all this seem so much more tragic and makes me feel protective of her.

I couldn't find her at first. Nor any staff.

Then I heard someone saying, "Your daughter is here, Avril".

So I retraced my steps and found her lurking in the shadows of a doorway.

"Don't *do* that!" she began, with a bit of a smile, "You're trying to trick me. I thought you'd gone. But you look different… That's why, isn't it? Have you seen him? Well you should… Yes, I thought you had! Is that why you are here? Me too! I don't know what it is. Yes, I saw Dawn there with him… She does! You can tell by her face. So why don't you ask?…No, it doesn't look good. Did they send for you? I'm just waiting. I'm scared!… No, I know there isn't, but they don't tell you."

"Mammy, who are you talking to?" I asked, fascinated by this new dimension and eloquence.

"I wasn't talking to anyone! Yes, you were, it was her." she answered herself.

"Who is 'she' Mammy?"

"Daddy! Yes, Daddy."

"Daddy isn't a 'she'." I said, stupidly.

"No, you're right. He's not good... Why, what's the matter... A bit of this and that! He's grumbling... I know, but he's not good today."

We sat down in a quiet place and she continued in her 'Gollum' style speech;

"I want to go home... Yes, I'm frightened. You have to stay, that's why they called you... Yes I know, but I want to go home. There! Did you see him? Daddy..."

A lady walked in and came over to the window next to us. Mum glared at her. The lady said, "Do you mind if I close this?" (Curtains)

"Yes, I do mind. Go away!" said Mammy, beginning to rise aggressively towards the woman.

"She's only trying to close the curtains, Mammy." I pleaded, whilst trying to hold her down. "It's a good idea, because it's dark outside now."

"No, she's not! They do that, if they can get away with it. And then it's gone. You know it's them. There are some horrible people and they take them. I know you don't believe me. You have to watch them."

At this moment a man came in, noisily dragging a chair.

"Oy, stop that! Get out!" Mum shouted.

Fortunately this man's relatives helped him with the chair and Mum grumbled on about how it was him, them, all those others...

"Why do they do that? Maybe I got it wrong. They will think I'm a loony! Did you get it?... You did? It came? And what did it say?... He's clear? Oh, thank God! Oh, that's great." She turned to me again with a look of sheer relief and joy.

"So it came? He's clear?" I asked, trying to muscle in on this conversation.

"What do you mean? Oh, I've forgotten now." She added, clearly distracted by my interruption.

"Who are you talking to, Mammy?"

"A man."

"A man?"

"Don't say it like that!"

"Sorry Mammy, but I can't see the man. Who is he?"

"Can I go home now? No? Why not?... Do I have to? I'm scared... He's all right! I want to go home... Can't I? What did they say? Was *she* there?"

I became aware of the bell ringing indicating that visiting time was over. I kissed her and said, "I'm going to do the laundry now."

I got the key and sorted her laundry. Boy, how it ponged! I looked over to her still chuntering, so I left without interrupting her again. Every day is such a different experience. Today she seemed to be two distinctly different people talking to each other and quite unaware of my presence for most of it.

CHAPTER 15

My visit to Mum started well today with a big smile, hugs and tears. The nurses said that it was her first smile all day. Apparently she had only consumed one small glass of squash and two biscuits, so I got her a drink and we sat down in the empty dining room.

I had spoken yesterday to Debbie and Mum's friend, Wendy, and I told Mum all about it. She was responsive and drank her juice, so I ordered a second one.

"We were coming to see you today," Mum began, "but we were busy chasing the boys around and doing this and that…Daddy was… but we wanted to come. How are the boys?"

I explained that Josh was in London to see the new Batman movie and that Conor was at home having a saxophone lesson. A few sentences later, she asked after the boys again and I repeated my story.

"No," she argued, "she's here!"

"Sorry, I meant that JOSH is in London."

"No, she's *there*!" she emphasised, pointing to a blank wall.

Clearly she was hallucinating and beginning to get cross with me. Then she was distracted by 'someone' under the table. Looking down, she smiled sarcastically and began remonstrating,

"What are *you* doing there? You should be in bed! Go on. Back to bed now!"

"Who was that?" I asked stupidly.

"Dawn! You know what *she's* like!"

Then she addressed me, "Well, what are you waiting for? Who *are* you?"

A black cloud had come over her again. She hung her head and asked, "Do you want something?"

I said I wanted nothing. That I'd just come to say Hello.

"I said '*who are you?*' she repeated with agitation.

"I'm Dawn, Mammy."

"No, you're not."

"Who am I then?" I challenged.

"You ask me? You look like him, but…"

"I'm your daughter, like it or not!" I said, getting up. "I've got some laundry to do now."

I did the laundry, found her again and kissed her goodbye. I'm too tired for this today.

* * *

Mum's friend, Wendy had apparently gone to see Mum on Friday, but Mum didn't acknowledge her, so she didn't stay long. Julia and her daughter went on Sunday and had a similar experience.

I took Conor with me to see Mum today – our last daytime trip before the Autumn term starts.

I start my teaching job tomorrow. We are all a bit apprehensive, especially Conor and I, with new schools and unknown challenges ahead.

It's also the end of Mum's twenty-eight day section tomorrow and I've heard nothing about the hospital's intentions or plans for her.

We took fresh doughnuts with us, hoping to tempt Mum into eating something. It's good that she is losing some weight, but she does need to eat and drink *something*.

As we arrived, a nurse was reassuring a very distressed Mum. She saw Conor and I and rushed over with tears and grabbed me for a big hug. Conor joined in too and Mum seemed so relieved and happy.

Then the nurse said, "See, Dawn did come!" and Mum stiffened up.

Then Conor added, "It's nice to see you, Grandma!" (Why he called her 'Grandma' and not 'Nana', we don't know)

Mum panicked and pulled herself away from us, stammering, "No. No, you're not…Go away! You're lying…No!"

We got nothing else from her. She wouldn't eat the doughnut, wouldn't speak to either of us; she had such a look of hatred towards us. Conor was upset again and Mum marched up and down the corridor chuntering to herself and growling whenever she passed us.

A nurse was concerned and said that Mum had had no medication, food or drinks for two days. Her mouth was dry. She said that obviously they wouldn't be sending Mum out like this. They would need to see her condition stabilised.

She said that they wouldn't give Lorazepam because Mum was not being 'physically aggressive'. I argued that she *was* being verbally aggressive and was pushing everyone away. More importantly, she was in danger of *self*-harm by not drinking anything, and surely they must be able to do something, or she would die. She said they would address all this at the review tomorrow.

* * *

Well, I am back at work, doing a job-share in a year one class. On my second day, (yesterday) I had a missed call from the social worker to say that, at Mum's review, they had decided on a 'Section Three' for a further six months at the hospital.

After an exciting day in my new class, I went to see Mum.

She is oblivious to what is happening and to where she is, it seems. Mum greeted me with the old smile, hugs and tears of relief, or joy, or whatever it is she feels when she recognises something.

Immediately she began to talk fluently about Avril and Dawn, about how unfair it was that Dawn always got more of something. I don't know who she was talking to.

Suddenly, she seemed to sense someone tugging on her trouser leg and became irritated, saying,

"What are you doing here again? Who are you? Avril!"

Her thoughts were interrupted by some visitors leaving the ward and she turned suspiciously to me.

"Who's that?" she enquired.

"I've no idea!" I replied, still squatting down on the floor, where her eyes were fixed.

"Yes you do! Who is it?" she demanded.

I fumbled an explanation about them visiting people staying there, but suddenly another lady, brandishing a 'zimmer frame', emerged from a door beside Mum, only to attack me with,

"Why did you say that? Why did you say you would…"

I backed swiftly away from the frame and Mum pulled away from me saying,

"Why are you here?"

"I came to see you." I replied feebly.

"No you didn't. You don't know me!" she accused.

I began, stupidly, to argue with her, feeling stressed and fed up with these difficult games. I said something about her not getting rid of me this time and threatening to tell her everything I knew about her. She didn't want that either. I knew I was being unhelpful and speaking out of frazzled emotions. I fired some memories of names and places at her deaf ears and walked away to sort her laundry.

I was shaking and upset when a kind nurse offered me a cuppa, a listening ear and some words of comfort. I calmed myself and found Mum in the same spot in the corridor on my way back. I kissed the back of her head cowardly and she said,

"You leaving now? Goodbye!"

"How did you know I was going?" I asked incredulously.

"Go on. Get on with it!" she spat.

"Goodbye, Mammy." I sighed.

I never know what to expect when I visit Mum.

* * *

On Tuesday she wouldn't allow me anywhere near her. She was saying, "Go away. No!" the moment she saw me.

I couldn't be bothered to argue, but I'm not giving up hope.

* * *

On Saturday she was pleasant again, a bit dopey, but relaxed. She must have asked me over thirty times, "Where've you been?" "What are you doing now?" "Where is it?"

For my own sanity I tried using identical responses, then tried varying my replies, but her questions remained the same. At least I got to hug her.

It's the days when she fights that are the most difficult for me. I want to shake her out of it.

* * *

It's Wednesday 17th September today. I've been trying to tie up some loose ends with regards to Mum's affairs.

I spoke to Broad Glade, who have emptied Mum's room and put all her remaining belongings in storage, so after school I drove by to collect them. They asked kindly after Mum. I was surprised to see such a large sack full of her belongings still.

It felt strangely like the end of another era; as if she had died and I was clearing her estate. I found myself in a bit of a trance, but glad to be getting on with inevitable tasks.

I came home for a drink and to collect Mum's clean clothes. Simon offered to look after the boys' dinners, homework, showers etc.

My head was throbbing - not the best frame of mind to go to see Mum, but it was all I had.

I found her alone in the lounge listening to some country music.

She seemed disturbed by voices, hallucinations and questions, and threw it all at me. If I could have taken it all away from her, I wouldn't have minded, but she became increasingly agitated.

"Where've you been? No, it's not.... You haven't! Who are you? You look like her, but you're not! Go away."

"I am Dawn and I won't go away. I love you. And I'm staying here!" I challenged.

"You still here? Go away! You're not her!"

"Lord give me strength", I screamed inside.

I told her I wouldn't go, that I'd come to see her and I wanted her to stop acting like a mad woman.

Then she told me that I was dead. That they'd had my "thingy" (funeral?) already. She didn't seem to think it incongruous telling me I was dead, so I don't know why I argued, but I wanted to 'snap her out of it'.

I hated feeling so ineffectual and useless, unable to reach her or comfort her.

"Why are you still there?" she moaned.

"I'll be back!" I said and went home.

* * *

I'm finding it tough being back at work. Two days a week are taking up more than half of my week in real time and much more in head-space. It will settle I'm sure, but I do seem to be running behind myself and catching myself coming in the opposite direction.

I still haven't spoken to the social worker and have heard nothing from the consultant since the first review, over six weeks ago. I know it's up to me to do the chasing.

Julia calls me from time to time to ask after Mum, but she won't go again herself. Debbie is moving back to England this week, for good. Actually, not England, but a large cottage on mainland Orkney. I wonder how she'll find it seeing Mum now? I hope Mum is having a good day when Debbie goes.

Mum had a good day on Sunday. Well, good from my perspective. I managed to get her to take two and a half glasses of water and her medication. She said the coffee "tasted like poo" and the nurse made a funny comment in relation to NHS services in general, but she liked the water.

She also let me accompany her to the toilet, which felt like quite an honour after all her recent behaviour. She had a long wee, which I thought was a good sign of a certain hydration level, but it looked more like 'cola' in the bowl when I went to flush it.

We talked a lot of nonsense about the boys, my job and the sunshine. Round we went with pleasantries, but then her body language changed and a deep frown set in. She looked frightened and confirmed it:

"I'm scared!" she confided.

I asked her what she was scared of, guessing the answer.

"You know what! Daddy." She whispered, exasperated.

I didn't know what to say for the best, but I hugged her tight and tried to reassure her that Daddy couldn't physically hurt any of us any more. We went over this theme for some time and she tossed and turned and wavered in her understanding of the reality that I was presenting. She seemed to understand that Daddy had died and that she had his ashes in a brass case, but she still believed that he could and would hurt her.

Having been married to this formidable, abusive and broken man for thirty-two years, her fear is understandable.

We prayed together until she seemed visibly less anxious.

It was long after visiting hours, but I clung on to the moments, feeling happy to be of some use this time.

* * *

The social worker came round to see me last Tuesday and made me more determined to speak up at the next review. The hospital have been observing Mum for over eight weeks, watching her deteriorate. She isn't eating, drinking or taking her medication, but they don't seem to be trying new drugs or doing anything proactive.

Mammy seems to be becoming more and more obsessed by the hallucinations and monsters in her head and is angry, frightened and miserable - *tormented* really is the best word. They can't send her to any other place in this state.

I want to know what the plan is.

Personally I think Mum is suffering from more than dementia, but I don't *know* that. She appears psychotic or schizophrenic, but I know that these behaviours are also manifest in dementia. The nurses are very concerned for her and do not seem happy with the care plan themselves.

We have to trust that the consultant does know more about dementia and available drugs than the rest of us, but I know more about Mum than they do. I feel that she is in too much distress.

* * *

I was pleased to hear that an article I wrote over the Summer has been published in the October edition of the 'Curate's Diary'. It is the first thing I've ever had published, except school policies.

Also, some bad news: Ofsted have announced they are coming next Tuesday for a one-day inspection. Obviously I have offered to be there to support my colleague.

I then realised that I was expecting Debbie and family over that weekend and that Mum's long-awaited review is the same day as the inspection.

* * *

Debbie came over and went to see Mum, but didn't get a good reception. She went with her daughter, Olivia, on Saturday and found Mum quite monstrous. Mum scratched Debbie. Despite my warnings, I think they were still shocked to see the way Mum has deteriorated these last two months.

On Monday I decided to do a job application before going to school. As it is a temporary contract, I have to now apply formally for a permanent post.

I also had to prepare for Mum's review. Debbie and Monica are coming, so we are going as a team.

* * *

Tuesday all went to plan: the Inspector came into our Year One class and, as she left at 10:15, so did I. Apart from the buzz of nerves, there was a very positive and warm atmosphere throughout the school. I felt proud to be a part of it. We expect a good report.

Mum's review was positive in that the consultant does have something that she wants to try. It is Haloperidol, a drug often used for schizophrenia. One of the difficulties at the moment is that Mum won't take medication orally so that limits them to drugs that are available for intravenous injection. Hopefully, if this one calms the monsters in her head, then they might be able to get her eating and drinking again and she might consent to taking medication orally. She does not consent to the injections, but part of having a 'section' means that they *can* force an injection. It isn't really possible to force someone to swallow.

It's not ideal, but it is a move forward. So I am satisfied for now and will keep monitoring the situation. Monica and Debbie also made their thoughts and wishes known, so it was positive in that respect too. Sitting discussing Mum in this way got to me again and I couldn't restrain the tears.

I had attempted to see Mum before the review, but she saw me coming and screamed at me to go away, so I did the laundry. Monica had a more successful attempt later. When Monica's mum finally went into a home, they prescribed what she describes as a 'Happy Pill', which calmed her angry, malicious behaviour. Monica hopes that the Haloperidol will be a 'Happy Pill' for Avril.

Anyhow, more anxiety over for this week, but I now await the interview for my job.

* * *

Three weeks later, the Haloperidol seems to be having a beneficial effect. Gradually Mum is mellowing again. They have found that she will take tablets orally if administered just as she is waking up.

She is still different every time I see her, but each time a little more settled. I am so grateful for the positive changes in Mum.

Last time I saw her she was much calmer, but it was nearly impossible to understand anything. She seems to have renamed everybody and everything. She was "Aferbabby", I was "Ackally", and I really cannot remember it all.

Today she was laughing and giggling and busy trying to "sort things out". I don't tell her who I am any more, but I tell her what the boys have been up to and she tells me about "the to-do with the people upstairs" and all the things going on in her busy head.

She seemed so relaxed today. They said she'd had a cuppa just before I came and I persuaded her to drink a glass of water. She was talking to the water and trying to play the glass like a trumpet. Of course she got wet, but we were both in stitches.

She still has conversations with people in her head and is clearly very confused, but she doesn't argue with me or attack me any more.

It is great to enjoy each other's company again.

I finished a tough half term at my school: the inspections both went very well and last week was a whole day of interviews for my job. There were four applicants including myself. I know my nerves got the better of me doing the teaching task and I bodged it terribly. I didn't get the job.

For now I'm just thrilled for Mammy.

Chapter 16

We enjoyed a peaceful half-term, but this weekend was full of activity and celebration, including Conor's birthday, parties and fireworks.

On Friday afternoon Mum was still in good form. Her clothes showed evidence of custard and I watched her drink tea and eat a chocolate bar. She also drank water and sang to the cup again. She seemed calm and less bothered by imaginary worlds. She played and laughed, let me hug her and enjoyed me massaging her back. It was great. I didn't want to leave her this time, but I had to get the car back for Simon.

Today I got a call from another doctor, who described a seizure-type manifestation that Mum was having this morning, and she asked me about the seizures that she had experienced in the past. It doesn't compare at all. Apparently the top part of her body just trembled violently for as long as you might wave, but it was occurring every twenty seconds this morning, so they called a doctor to watch her. By this afternoon, the 'shakes' were happening roughly every twenty minutes. I asked if this was perhaps a side effect of the Haloperidol, but she said not. I took the opportunity to ask about the dosage. They are being cautious with the new drug and started her on 0.5mg. They have now increased it to 1.5mg.

Apparently they all cheered as Mum ate a proper lunch today and she was sitting laughing with some ladies this afternoon.

Then the doctor asked a sobering question that took me aback: If she gets very sick, do I want them to resuscitate her? I had to ask what this means in reality, because if she gets poorly I want them to treat her as they would anybody else. What she meant was, if her heart stops of its own accord, do I want them to give her shock treatment or resuscitate in any other way? She made it clear that they wouldn't advise resuscitation and that, although they like to consider the wishes of family, legally it is a medical decision that would be made by the doctors anyway.

It is a scary thought, that the doctors carry such power, particularly when you hear of cases of abuse of that power and the growing sympathy for 'euthanasia'. But, on the other hand, if it *was* her time to go, I wouldn't want to hold her back to suffer any more, when she could be set free and enjoying heaven. To deny her death, when it called, would be much more cruel.

I have not actually thought about her dying yet. I have been more concerned with the quality of her living.

Still, at sixty-two, I can't see her leaving yet. I must speak to Debbie about it and phone Monica to give her an update. She might fancy coming with me tomorrow.

* * *

Monica did come and was delighted to see her back in her happy and 'naughty' mood. Mum has such a cheeky laugh.

Monica had received some poems from a good friend. The poems convey such sweet fondness of memory. They tell a beautiful story of Mum and life on Graemsay.

I read the poems twice out loud and we talked about the images and memories: of Mum building walls from stones off the beach, to protect her shrubs from the incessant wind. I'm not sure how much sense Mum actually made of the poems, or how much she does remember.

Monica enjoyed talking about her memories of her two years living with Mum at 'Clett', and talked for all of us in her very entertaining way. Mammy was able to respond with independent comments and contributions though, just like her old self.

As we were leaving, Monica asked if we could come again. Mum's response reminded me of the time I first visited Mum and Dad in Orkney: that she would be glad when I left, because I disturbed her routines.

The junior doctor, with whom I had only spoken on the phone, came in and introduced herself. Fortunately she didn't ask again about the resuscitation issue.

* * *

This morning I had a funny memory: years ago, my friend, Little John, used to tease me for always saying, "I can't remember". Today I remembered that as a young child at the caravan, my mum made me write one hundred lines, stating, "I must never say 'I forgot'." After that I tried very hard instead to admit that "I can't remember". I wonder if there's a faulty memory gene in the family.

I was also musing over the changes in Mum's life since Dad died. In the space of a few years, Mum did so many new things with her life. She began driving again – something she'd never done since passing her test in Nottingham twenty years before. She did a motor-mechanics course in Kirkwall. She ran the Post Office on Graemsay and did a computer course. She worked voluntarily for the 'Red Cross' in Stromness, bought a guitar, took lessons and began to play guitar at church.

When applying for the job as 'Sub-postmaster', Mum listed her hobbies as "Designing; Knitting; Gardening; Music; Watching boxing, ice-skating and gymnastics; Languages; Science and Computers."

It seems so sad that Mum had the chance of an independent life at forty-nine, but within ten years she was completely incapacitated with this dementia.

I wonder what made Mum's brain deteriorate so quickly? Did the brain rebel against having choice and freedom? Did she miss the routine, challenge and suspense of living with Dad? Was it a lack of stimulation? Do infections, strokes or knocks on the head cause its onset? Is it a genetic predisposition? Do I carry those same genes? Or is dementia simply no respecter of persons and comes to devour whomever it wills?

Does anybody know?

* * *

On Sunday Mum stood motionless in the corridor with tears wet on her cheeks and droplets falling from her nose. She seemed so totally dependent and vulnerable. She had no idea why she was crying and said that she didn't want to live any more. She probably feels totally alone in her world.

She asked after the boys again and soon we were singing and dancing to Roy Orbison. I left her smiling and dancing, but again I feel like I have abandoned her.

One of Mum's key workers phoned yesterday to ask permission to give Mum the flu jab. I took the opportunity to ask questions in general. She told me that the consultant had wanted to reduce Mum's medication now that she is doing so well, but that the staff had argued (and won) to keep her medication as it is, *because* she is doing so well. They are all very pleased with her progress.

In terms of her future placement, reading between the lines, it looks like it will be after Christmas before they attempt to place her. They want to see her properly settled and stable first.

I think it will be better for Mum to be in a more homely environment where she can perhaps make friends and have her personal belongings around her again. Maybe she still likes going out walking. I do hope that there will be a suitable home for her within Nottinghamshire. I will contact the social worker soon to see what recommendations and time-scale he is considering.

I think I have been very well guided by the social services and support teams throughout these two years caring for Mum. I could not have managed alone and they have truly provided where I could not. It has been an invaluable support and I take this opportunity to say a big *"thank you"* to everyone involved in helping to care for Avril.

We are so blessed to have the NHS in this country. Of course they cannot work miracles and are not perfect, but they provide a wonderful service to so many needy people, who otherwise would be suffering alone.

* * *

I'm just back from seeing Mum again tonight. I felt that she needed a hug and am so glad I went.

I thank God for these precious moments. If she were still in Orkney and in good health I would probably still not have seen her since my wedding. I may never have had the opportunity to know her. But it seems a tragic price to pay for closeness.

She seemed down-in-the-dumps when I arrived. I began to chat and recognised the song, 'Are You Lonesome Tonight' playing somewhere near. We located it in the big, empty lounge and began to dance. It was so good to sing, smooch and jive our way through eighteen fabulous Elvis tracks around the big room. At one point I looked up to see two nurses smiling at us through the window. I felt like a goldfish in a bowl, but very proud. I was even offered a cup of tea today.

Again Mum's key worker reiterated (in a whisper) that, although she was handing me the Care Homes Directory, they were "not in a hurry to send her away".

I wonder whether I might be allowed to bring Mum out at all? I think she would like to be involved in some carols and Christmas events. I could always take some Christmas spirit to them instead. Maybe Conor could bring his flute and play some carols. They would all enjoy that I'm sure.

* * *

I am continually surprised at how much happens in a week. Ana was with us for the weekend and, after taking her back to the train station yesterday, I went to see Mum.

The staff were singing her praises and saying how she'd eaten six slices of jam on toast for breakfast. Mum seemed very lucid, but then began the conversations with herself again.

"So how do you like it here? It's okay I guess, but there's not a lot to do. Is it Cocker? I don't really know. I just sit and watch. Oh, that's good though, isn't it? I suppose so."

"I've got a fella!" she suddenly confessed.

"Oh, another one? Where is he?"

"He's here and there...but it's like that. She came up and you know... DAWN?" she suddenly shouted, looking behind her, "Are they all right in there? Yes, it's Tatty and Blatty. They're okay then, the bobbies? Yes. That's good then. Tee hee!"

A couple of times she had these conversations with 'Dawn', about the "babbies".

Then she squashed her fore-finger and thumb like a mouth and said to it, "Isn't that right babby-wabbies? Are you not going to answer me then? No, 'cos we're not really here!"

Then she exploded into hysterical laughter at the fun of it.

I was hard pressed to follow her today. But she was in good form and most of her soliloquies were positive. She enjoyed a back massage and took part in ordinary conversation too.

She asked about the boys and the second time she added, "but I've asked that already, haven't I?"

I wish I could record all her words accurately, because I do find it fascinating. Her speech follows no normal, logical syntax or semantic pattern. She also said something about being "ready to come out of her mind and be normal again", but I forget the exact phrase.

I wanted to tell her my news, but didn't. I'm pregnant again.

Today I was busy making appointments for doctor/midwife and my annual haircut.

I'm waiting to hear from Debbie too, because she's finally gone over to Graemsay to show a prospective tenant around 'Clett'. It will be good for the property to have someone living there, especially over the winter.

* * *

I took Conor on Sunday. Mum was in a gorgeous mood. She seems like the only sane one there now.

There was a man wandering with his pants around his ankles, another kicking and fighting the nurses, another trying to grab hold of Conor – he was very brave, but his face told a different story.

Mum just kept smiling through it all. I do want to get her settled somewhere a bit calmer.

On Tuesday I spent a leisurely morning preparing to go for my eight-week scan. I enjoyed a luxurious shower, admiring my firmly rounded abdominal shape and my breasts like huge ripe lychees. I felt beautifully pregnant.

I decided to go alone for the scan, because Simon was nervous and I wanted to stay positive. Entering the ward I encountered the nurse who had talked us through our last bereavement, sixteen months ago.

The scan was the same as the first, almost exactly two years ago to the day.

I went for a hot drink, devastated, sent Simon a text and drove home. I told the boys and tried not to feel anything.

I feel very blessed in my Spirit. Part of me, emotionally and physically, is scared about going through another miscarriage. The last one was almost unbearable.

Isabelle came over to support me whilst I made arrangements with the hospital and phoned school with my apologies.

I shed my first tears of mourning for the baby I will never know.

Isabelle accompanied me for the pre-op tests and forms. The operation was scheduled for Friday morning. I appreciated her company. Spending over three hours in the hospital is never a pleasant experience.

* * *

On Friday, I was there for eight and a half hours, but I drifted through most of that in anaesthetised, semi-consciousness.

And now it's all over again. I still look and feel physically the same as I did on Tuesday morning. Emotionally I feel quite different, but I am still blessed.

I've not been to see Mum for a whole week. I hope to go tomorrow, because, if nothing else, she will be needing her laundry.

And I need a 'Mammy hug'.

* * *

Mammy intuitively knew that something was wrong, so I told her and enjoyed a proper cuddle.

I had brought Christmas cards for her to send, as promised. I reminded her of people and as she approved, I spoke and wrote... "To Debbie..." and she added "and all", which I wrote and then "with lots of love from Mum?" and she nodded and added again, "and all!" And so we continued for seven cards.

She was dressed in a pretty, sparkly jumper, which I didn't recognise, but took a photo of her looking so lovely – the first I've taken since she went into hospital nearly five months ago.

I am trying to imagine the transition, which has to happen, from hospital to some new place. After all of her previously active outdoor life she has been in the hospital with not one walk outside for all of that time. I don't know how it will be for her, exhilarating or unpleasant? Last week I told her about Tony, who is moving house yet again and she shuddered, saying she was glad that she didn't have to move. But she does.

* * *

Today I spoke at last to the social worker. He apologised for being so busy and said that he has seen Mum twice since.

He observed her today, singing happily, but then she became fixated on some thought or hallucination that distressed her for some time. He said that the ward staff had given a generally positive account of her mood, improvement and well-being.

Apparently we are waiting on an overworked somebody who has to do another assessment, before we can look for a placement. It was hoped that it would be done before Christmas, but this is not looking promising.

I aired my concerns about taking Mum outside after so long indoors. I would need to request a 'consent for leave', (as she is still under Section Three) but it might be possible to take her out with a member of staff into the secure courtyard for a time, he said, and maybe another day take her for a walk around the grounds.

This next stage feels scary for me. I want to make sure that I get it right for her. I don't think I did last time. I'm sure they will give me sound professional guidance. I am praying for wisdom.

It is nearly Christmas. This time last year, Mum was at home with us and Pat was living around the corner. We just do not know what is around the corner. We really have to live the best of each day and be grateful for every blessing.

* * *

Today is the Epiphany 2009. Ana shared Christmas with us and has returned to London. Little John has been too, and Catalena is with us now. Friends are priceless.

My priority now is to do some thorough research of care homes, so that I can find the perfect place for Mum to move in to.

I took the boys to play carols at the hospital on Christmas Eve. Josh was very worried. He hadn't been to see Nana since she was sectioned back in August and he very nearly bottled out of performing in 'a mad-house'. As the boys began to play the carols, Josh on guitar and Conor on flute, residents began to gather and join in the sing-along. Mum was right beside us, singing and blubbering happily. Before long the carers had brought half the ward along and we had to keep repeating our rather limited repertoire.

It was a wonderful atmosphere. I distributed chocolate biscuits and really felt that Christmas had finally arrived. It was amazing how these dear people, many of whom have forgotten their own names, can sing all three verses of 'Away in a Manger', word perfect.

The power of music on the soul never ceases to strike me as remarkable.

Josh actually enjoyed the experience in the end. I am sure he will perform in alternative 'mad-houses' with his band. He did get a bit worried when one of the patients wanted to tidy his music book away whilst he was playing. "Who is this guy?" Josh's eyes mused. He was pleased to have overcome his fear and done something good for his Nana and for others.

I was very proud of them both.

When we first arrived at the hospital Mum was looking more miserable than I've seen her for a long time. As I sat her down she was able to say that she "just wanted to go away, completely, and not come back". She took pains to assure me that it wasn't the place or anybody else's fault, just her "being mardy".

The carols made her forget again and she opened her presents and cards with child-like anticipation.

It was a jolly Mum that we left behind.

* * *

Yesterday Mum was sleeping in the chair, so I sorted her laundry and went back to wake her up, but I couldn't. She was smiling and twitching and occasionally saying "yes...", but her eyes remained closed.

She managed to drink coffee, eat custard creams and enjoy a massage, all with her eyes shut. There was going to be no other meaningful interaction, other than stroking her hand and kisses, and I felt that she might prefer to be undisturbed, so after an hour I went to speak to the nurse.

I had long since meant to ask about her medication, since the time I pretended to drink the 'orange medicine' and they looked a bit worried when I acted dopey afterwards.

I wondered why she was so dozy now. The orange medicine was the Trazodone (100mg, three times a day). No wonder she is sleepy. The Haloperidol is just once a day and she also takes Carbomazapine twice a day. Apparently these are all to control her mood.

There is still no date for the Continuing Healthcare Assessment, which needs to be done before we know what can happen next.

* * *

CHAPTER 17

Yesterday I hit a major low. I have been finding communication with Simon a cause of immense frustration since the end of November (when I told him I was pregnant). I have been trying to change this, but fear I have just pushed him further away. I am finding it difficult to sleep with ear-ache, blocked, streaming nose and racing mind.

I think about these last two years: I have lost three pregnancies, two friends, a job, struggled with my Mum and feel I'm losing control of her care.

Last, but by no means least, my Isabelle's recent challenge has also rocked my boat. She has had breast cancer, has had a mastectomy and is now, thanks be to God, on the road to recovery. I love her so much. Again I feel so grateful to live in the UK with a great NHS provision available.

Taking an inventory of all this was illuminating. I think I need to be a little kinder on myself and on Simon. We both need to learn to have a little more fun together and enjoy what we have, whilst we still have it.

I am grateful too that I do have this opportunity to love my Mum now.

Anyway, Mum was in much better form on Sunday, and was contentedly gabbling away, making up what sounds like fun little rhymes with sounds.

Haloperidol is an old-style anti psychotic, commonly used in hospitals to control agitation and hallucinations – symptoms of schizophrenia. It has a sedative quality. Apparently care homes usually take their clients off Haloperidol as soon as possible. It is thought to produce a severe stoop and a general comatosed, dependent state.

Mum's mood has definitely improved since she began to take the Haloperidol and she appears to be much less tormented by hallucinations and psychotic behaviour. But yes, she also appears stooped and pretty well comatosed much of the time.

I felt nearly human enough to venture back to see Mum today.

She was sleeping when I arrived, so I sorted the laundry before waking her. She was quite disoriented and kept dropping the biscuit that she'd been given, whilst I held the cup of tea. She was also very jerky – huge sudden involuntary 'starts' that she seemed completely unaware of. It was alarming.

The cup of tea went down very well though and then she started singing. It was hilarious. There is no way I can convey the experience as I beheld it. She was talking to someone invisible to me and then began to chant, "Wee lee dee baba kaka da, wee dee wee dee dada moko daba, POP!" Then she would laugh and say "What was that? I'm being silly. You dabada!. Shall I go again? All right then – Wee la ba da ba..."

I said, "I think you've gone daft!"

And she whooped and clapped with delight, "Yeah!"

To the annoyance of a frail old lady next to me, Mum continued for the whole hour, but was clearly having such a wonderful time herself. Eventually she stood up to entertain more fully and began to sing even louder, but this time the sounds came to the vague tunes of "Old MacDonald" and "Jingle bells". It is difficult for me to do justice to the poetry, but she clearly knew what she was singing. Once she stumbled over the flow and started shouting, "Bugger, Bugger..." until I said, "Mother!?" and she laughed, saying that she had forgotten.

"Am I stupid?" she asked.

"No, but daft as a brush and twice as hairy!" I replied, to which again she rejoiced with cheers and laughter. She looked and sounded happily tipsy.

It must have been quite a surreal sight, me alternating between massaging Mum's back and plucking the beard out of her chin; Mum laughing ecstatically and chanting her funny rhymes; and another lady leaning over me, kissing my head and telling the wall that I was her grandson.

* * *

I'm having one of those mornings of morbid thoughts: If it's all down to genes, I'll either have a heart-attack, cancer or dementia.

Where is my faith?

But as Josh once said, "We have to die of something. These health freaks will feel a bit daft in hospital when they are old and dying of nothing!"

I am trying to justify my existence again, busy with various projects and people, but because I am not earning an income, I feel wrong, restless and my confidence and self-esteem are very low.

An important project for me at the moment is to sort Mum out, but I get impatient and am finding this waiting process very frustrating.

* * *

I feel a bit more cheerful now, after a call from my lovely Isabelle. Her dressing is removed and her wound is healing well. She also has permission to drive again, which will be a great relief.

Meanwhile the sun is beaming out through the January rain and a little snow-drop has appeared in the garden.

I've been doing some digging recently and I am so much looking forward to the delight of Spring splendour, and itching to get some fruit and vegetables planted.

* * *

I got a call from the social worker on Wednesday morning, to invite me to the multi-disciplinary meeting (MDM), which was to take place *that* morning at 11:00. I wished they had given me more notice, as I had already arranged to spend our anniversary with my husband.

I told the social worker that I was nervous about what would happen to Mum if the home she goes to should take her off the Haloperidol and her hallucinations and torment should return.

He said that he'd seen her on Tuesday and she was looking very dishevelled and distressed. She had looked greasy and unkempt on

Monday too, but I didn't ask anybody why, as she had been in such good humour.

The social worker phoned me back later with feedback from the meeting. It was much more inconclusive than I had hoped. Apparently two nurses had done the Continuing Care Assessment and had agreed that Mum was not at all ready to be discharged.

They felt that the only place suitable to meet Mum's needs would be Gold Acre, which I remember being mentioned to me last Summer. What I hadn't realised was that Mum's dementia doctor had put in a recommendation for Mum to go to Gold Acre several weeks ago, but that the staff at Gold Acre had refused her on the grounds that they didn't agree that she needed their level of care.

The nursing team recommended that Mum's medication be reconsidered and that Mum's doctor should reapply to Gold Acre for a place.

Apparently, Gold Acre is a brand new NHS unit, offering "excellent care", but their budget is restricted and so are unable to employ enough qualified staff to run to capacity.

It also seems that they do their own independent assessments of applicants and, strangely, do not consult with any other professionals or interested parties. The nurses doing the assessment on Wednesday, on the other hand, are of the opinion that Mum will continue to need at least the same level of care that she has had in hospital, and that any other care home would not be able to cope with her needs and possibly end up being readmitted to hospital. That is my concern too.

I was surprised to learn that Mum's dementia doctor was not at the MDM either, so we will now have to wait whilst she reads the report and makes her response.

The social worker said that Mum was even more distressed and "vocal" (shouting and angry) on Wednesday and that she seemed to be in a very tormented state again. He said that she was still unwashed, because apparently she is being very uncooperative with the staff in the mornings.

I have arranged to see Mum's dementia doctor at her earliest convenience to discuss these issues properly, but that meeting may not be for another four weeks.

Anyway, I'm going to see Mum again myself and see if I can make any more sense of the situation.

* * *

Mum was fine with me, albeit a little dopey again. She was smiling, singing her own version of 'Daisy, Daisy' and copying some of the voices and sounds around her. She was laid back on the sofa and still very twitchy. Occasionally she would lift herself up to a sitting position and then lower herself back down again, like a version of 'sit-ups'.

She relished some chocolate and we managed a sort of a conversation. I asked many questions and she made various responses. She thinks that Wendy has been to visit her, but not Julia or Monica. She can't be bothered to do the gardening any more and doesn't miss Orkney. She cannot remember much about her mum or dad, but thinks that Julia was bossy. Being a mum was sometimes really lovely, but sometimes "Brrrrr!" She'd like to go and look at the Spring flowers when they're out in bloom, but she is a "big baby", even though she thinks she is not big.

I asked a member of staff about the greasy hair. Apparently this week, Mum has been distressed, difficult to handle and shouting in the mornings, but she would ask the night staff if they'll bathe her this evening.

She was unsure, but believes that the doctor may have already made some changes to her medication.

* * *

The dementia doctor has accepted that Mum will need fully-funded health care and that Gold Acre is the best place for her. She has agreed to apply again to Gold Acre. That means that I can go and have a look around. Hopefully, seeing the place will reassure me and at least some progress is occurring.

I've updated Debbie and she has spoken to Julia, who is feeling guilty for not visiting Mum.

At the hospital today, Mum was pacing the corridors and had a face like thunder. She was clearly distressed and angry, but I got her to sit down with me. She was quite unintelligible and was asking and answering her own questions with great belligerence. I got the impression that she thought she had had a fight and someone had taken something that belonged to her, but I don't know.

I got her to drink a glass of water, then began to massage her back and shoulders again. That did the trick. She loves the massage and her scattered words indicated that she wanted to be massaged like that forever. She smiled at me then and asked who I was. I said, "Dawn" and she acknowledged that she has "got a Dawn". I laughed, daring to say that I was Dawn and she was Avril, and she seemed to accept it and be happy. Whatever had distracted her before had now been replaced with a feeling of well-being and she was warm and responsive again.

I kept up the massage as much as possible, whilst she soliloquised, "Who are you? Avril... Oh, I see...and Kaka? I don't know. It's mine though... Over there...I'll get it back." The rest I couldn't follow.

On Thursday evening I was at a girls' night. One lady asked how I know Isabelle and I was telling her about being disowned and Isabelle and her dad taking me in. The lady was horrified that my mum could have disowned me and, like many people, couldn't understand why I then chose to take her in and care for her when she was in need. Immediately two Bible scriptures came to mind: "Honour your father and your mother" (Exodus 20:12) NIV and "Father forgive them, for they do not know what they are doing." (Luke 23:34) NIV I noted that the fifth commandment did not say, "Honour your father and your mother, only if you think they deserve it".

No matter what she did or does, she is still my mother, who brought me into the world. She did what she could, and it is for me to do the best with what I have and give all the love and support that I can.

* * *

The electric light outside makes the snow flurries dance and swirl like those beautiful fireworks. This fabulous display lasts so much longer though.

This winter has been so much colder than the last. Apart from my one 'snow-drop' there are only a few buds, no flowers at all, and it is already February. Today the garden is hiding underneath a thick blanket of snow. The path looks like a giant hop-scotch, marked out by thick white lines.

It's like Narnia, but without the white witch and with hope.

* * *

Today is day three of settled snow, but the sun has been shining and most of the roads are clear, although the pavements are still treacherous. The rooftops are dripping and all is beautiful.

Yesterday Isabelle went to the hospital for her test results. I thank God she no longer has breast cancer. It has not spread. She has chosen a difficult path of chemotherapy and several other drugs, which will continue over the next five years, to improve her chances of a long life with no recurrence of the cancer.

We are going to celebrate tomorrow with a day of luxury at Eden Hall Spa.

More snow is forecast, so I went to Mum again this afternoon.

She looked disgruntled and lost.

I approached with a "Hi there, you! Can I have a hug?"

She allowed the hug, but began, "No, it can't...I've got to stay here forever...I think. And Cacker and Tatter and Mammer...so they do!"

She looked as if she was going to cry, so I led her to a chair and we had another long hug. She indicated that something hurt in her body. I think it was her lower abdomen, so I told the nurse and tried to reassure Mum that maybe she is constipated again. With hugs, kisses and soothing words she soon cheered up.

They gave her a banana flavoured 'Fortisip' shake, which I helped her with. She loved it. "What is that?" she kept repeating with sweet smiles. The smiles turned into rapturous giggles, as I started to massage her back and shoulders again.

Meanwhile, a lady with pink rimmed eyes and lilac eyelids sat smiling over at me, bemused by Mum's changing expressions.

Another lady, who has been there nearly as long as Mum (I've never seen her with a visitor) hurries along the corridors, whimpering "Nobody wants me...nobody wants me!" Sometimes she will say that to a resident, but most of them do not know how to respond, so she rushes away again with a pouting, sad bottom lip and runs into the toilet. Then she starts again. She needs a hug too, I'm sure.

Two of the men there walk around trying to fix things and straighten it all out. They think that they are in charge. (Nothing new there!) A different lady was clutching a baby-sized dolly. She asked me some questions and I did my best to agree with her as I had witnessed her, moments before, having a shouting match with another resident. At least we were not in the room with the lady that always screams, "HELLLLLP!"

Suddenly Mum jerked and made as if to jump up. "I'd better get on with it!" she announced.

"What have you got to do?" I asked.

"I've got chores to do... and the babbers!" she smiled.

I went to get the laundry and then left a more positive Mum to get on with her chores.

* * *

I'm glad I saw Mum yesterday. It looks like Nottinghamshire has closed down today due to snow. Most schools have closed, as have lots of roads, so our day at the Spa has also had to be cancelled. Of course, Simon has gone to work. He will probably be the only one in the office.

Last night I watched a TV Programme about Terry Pratchett and his fight against Alzheimer's. (See Notes 3) He said that he wants to "make Alzheimer's sorry that it ever caught [him]." It is fascinating for me now to see someone in the very early stages of the disease, observing the first signs of deterioration. I was also interested to note that he was diagnosed as having the symptoms of a 'variant' of Alzheimer's, known as PCA, where the back of the brain (normally associated with vision) is most affected. Listening to him describing his difficulties with hand-eye coordination, I was reminded of Mum's earlier problems, although she was suffering memory loss too. Researchers on the programme were saying how close they were to a breakthrough in finding a cure, but even Mr. Pratchett, in the early stages of the disease, admitted that he cannot wait that long.

He had heard of a possible cure - an LED light helmet - which he asked to trial. Subsequent tests revealed no further deterioration, but no improvement either. However, no deterioration is very positive, given the nature of the disease. I wonder whether he continues to use it.

A doctor commented that he had probably had the disease for ten years before it was noticed. I don't know whether that means that you either have it in you anyway (genetically), or that you somehow 'get' it and it takes a long time to manifest. It means that there must be a lot of people out there with Alzheimer's that don't yet know it.

* * *

Now the heating has broken completely. Conor lost his mobile phone whilst sledging in the thick snow and he was raw cheeked, cold and soaked through.

But we had lots of fun and he is now outside building a very tall snowman.

I didn't go to see Mum yesterday, as the trouble with the heating has meant that Mum's clothes were not dry. Happily I could go today.

Mum is still only sixty-two, but looks ninety-two. She appears to have shrunk even more – head bowed pitifully low, shaking, and shuffling along in green slippers, with the pockets of her cardigan scrunched between grubby, fumbling fingers.

As I approached I watched her snap at someone, her greasy hair flat and wispy over her eyes. Despite her protests, I hugged her, her head buried in my shoulder bone.

Her speech is becoming more unintelligible, but I knew she was distressed. We found a place to sit and I gave her some more banana milk-shake, lots of kisses and words of reassurance until she had melted again.

She said she had five daughters and had lost them all. She was looking for Avril, Kacker, Tater, Acklewer and Wallerker. I told her that her daughters were safe and well and that she is Avril.

Sometimes she smiles at me with a warm love and gratitude that is so beautiful. She is very receptive to hugs and affection at those moments. Other times she looks at me like I have three heads and horns.

I spoke briefly to one of the carers to ask him what he knows about Gold Acre. Unfortunately, it is another hospital ward, so she will only stay there until her mood and behaviour are stable. Then she will have to be moved again. I thought that she was being kept at St Peter's Wing until she was stable, and then they would find her a permanent placement. He said Gold Acre is about two miles from the East Hospital. I don't see the point in moving her twice.

When I returned from sorting her laundry, Mum was standing singing to a table full of people.

* * *

This week has been busy and different, fun even. As a school governor, I have been eagerly involved in the exciting and daunting responsibility of headship interviews.

Yesterday I enjoyed Mum's company too. In herself she seemed content and playful. She was all clean, sitting alone in the silent music room.

"So, what have you got to tell me?" I chirped, holding her hands.

"Dabberdaberdada, batterbatter...Cacker a mama... and some food!"

"Right! That's me told!" I laughed.

Mum was smiling, eyes closed.

"The babbers? They okay?" she asked me. I said they were.

"Not much clucks, no! I just make 'em up as I do it." She began to giggle. "The babbers are going off and badadaba...daft things!" Mum hooted with laughter and began to giggle hysterically.

"What is it, Mum? Come on, share the joke!"

"It wasn't me; it's Callus. I can't remember now." She flung her head back and pretended to snore, a wide grin across her cheeky face.

"Somebody else a popper da babasee plos...Yes!" she said, gesticulating knowingly.

I asked her whether what comes out of her mouth is what she had expected.

"No!" she admitted, but didn't seem too concerned. Then she took a big breath and began an operatic piece, "Day, day, wee, lie twee lie tay lie... Bubbles!" She laughed..."Plopalopa tapatapa weeleelee..." And then to the tune of 'Jingle bells', "Da da da, da da da, an da way la day..."

"Mama, Mama" she suddenly whimpered in a sweet baby voice. And she answered herself, "I thought you were carrying on?...okay!... Wye ly wye ly and I lay day lay way and go go go to bed. Plop!" She made as if to snore again. "And they say - 'Goodnight'."

I began to laugh at Mum's entertainment and make some equally meaningless, but encouraging comments myself. She was clearly having fun.

"Why, is it a man?...Because I like babbies! That's all right then. I want to go to bed and I want to stay on. Well, you have to 'Eeny meeny, tatty tatty, catter catter...Then you say, 'How are you today!"

She giggled again for some time..."Eh? Mister Matter Mat? Are they fighting? Little bits, yeah."

"You're playing, aren't you?" I laughed.

"Yes, we are!"

I put a CD on – The Everly Brothers – and immediately Mum began to 'da, da' the tune, but used no words and all the wrong phonemes. She was enjoying the music though.

After collecting her very smelly washing, I took my leave, smiling too.

It is a year ago since Mum left my home to live at Broad Glade. I feel sad remembering her having to go, still doubting whether I did the best thing for her.

* * *

I have just dropped Isabelle and Brian off at the hospital for Isabelle's first Chemotherapy. I am looking forward to taking them home again later and knowing that she is fine. I want to see Mum as well, but Isabelle comes first today.

On Tuesday Mum seemed content and lucid, hardly babbling at all. I took her into the music room and we sang, danced and had a laugh. Her nails were ripped and jagged, so I pampered them. Then she showed signs of discomfort and agreed to let me take her to the toilet, change her pad and wash her hands and face.

I had been told that there were some student nurses doing studies on the ward and that one student had chosen my mum. I took my leave of Mammy and went to speak to the student, who was a fourth year medical student with many questions. He had already spoken to Mum and was wondering who "Cacker" was, but I have no idea.

Mum was wandering when I came out, but she was angry and distressed again. I tried to calm her, but she shouted, "Just GO, if you're going then!"

So I stole a hug and left.

* * *

On Saturday she was clean, smiley and trying to converse in her light-hearted babbling. I helped with her tea and biscuits as she no longer uses her hands or eyes very effectively. I can put a biscuit to her mouth and she won't think to tell her hands to hold or catch the biscuit once she has bitten into it. I asked her what she could see. She didn't know. I asked if she could see her hands, so she held them up and looked at them.

"Can you see your wedding ring?"

She couldn't, so I swiveled it around her finger, marveling on how it has been there for forty-five years. I asked if she could see me. She looked and smiled, "You look lovely".

* * *

In the week, I got a call from St Peter's Unit to say that I should not visit at the weekend as they are decorating the corridors, so I went to see Mum on Friday night instead. I haven't done an evening visit for some time.

Mum was in a gentle mood, clearly tired and wanting to go to bed. Her body seemed to be twitching in spasms, but not bothering her at all. She was hallucinating and talking to the babies. 'Cacker' was there it seems, but 'Cacker' is apparently not one of the babies. She seemed to enjoy my company and the back rub as always.

Yesterday I got another call from St Peter's Unit, to say that a place has now come up at Gold Acre.

I have been to see Gold Acre. It is spacious, pretty, peaceful and strangely unpopulated. A nurse showed me around and I am very impressed. I think Mum will be very comfortable there. There is a separate unit for severely challenging behaviour. Opening hours for visitors is much more flexible (simply avoid arriving at meal times) so I hope Mum might get more visitors there.

She will be taken there on Wednesday morning in a black cab. I think it will be better if I go up to see her when she's arrived and settled a little, because too much fuss stresses her out.

I wonder how she is going to experience the move, having not been outside the ward since last August? I'm sure the nurses are experienced in handling these situations and they will ease her transition gently.

It is all moving once again into the unknown and another new era is beginning for my mum and for me.

* * *

CHAPTER 18

Today I saw Mum in her new 'home'. The staff at St Peter's Unit had escorted her with her belongings to Gold Acre.

I found her in the large dining room dozing on a two-seater settee. Nearby was a familiar face from St Peter's Unit, strapped into a comfy chair and demanding a lot of attention. I engaged with the other lady a little, finding she had a mischievous but agreeable nature. There were three members of staff sitting drinking tea, probably having a breather after lunch; they said that Mum had "settled well and eaten her lunch".

I sat next to Mum and gently woke her, but it was a cross face that looked back at me.

"Who are you? What do you want?"

She seemed irritated and unsettled by the unusual morning and journey, but looked all clean and fresh. I gave her some tea, then suggested that we have a walk around as the loud lady was annoying Mum considerably. I could see a door to a pretty garden, but Mum said she couldn't be bothered to go outside today. All the names of Cacker, Caller and Avril came up with the 'babbies' again as she spoke to them, but she soon began to cheer up.

We looked at her room, which was not yet ready; there was a blow up mattress and sets of tools and cleaning equipment in the en suite bathroom. The wardrobe was still empty. Mum kept walking towards the window and bumping into the radiator. Then she would turn, walk and bump into the bed, turn, walk and bump into the door. She didn't seem to be seeing anything at all and was walking with a strangely tilted gait.

I managed to steal a few hugs, but she just leaned against me, quite still and resigned. Still, she seemed to understand later, when I explained that I would need to go to fetch *my* babies, and she let me kiss her goodbye.

The nurses assured me that Mum would be well looked after.

On my way home I went to see Monica, to explain where Mum now resides and to update her generally. I find it hard to believe that Monica will be seventy this month.

It just remains to phone Mum's sister and her friend Wendy, who both expressed a wish to see Mum when she was no longer in St Peter's Unit. I wonder whether they will visit her now?

Today Isabelle phoned to say that her hair is malting so much from the 'Chemo', that her husband has given her a close 'number 1' crew cut.

* * *

On Monday I found an easier route to Mum's new sojourn.

She seemed more settled, but was wearing hospital clothes as they still need to tag her clothes with Gold Acre labels and name tags. She was in her room listening to Buddy Holly, as apparently she had been disturbed by some noises earlier.

Her flesh was pale and peaky, but we spent a pleasant hour together before she began looking restless and lurched forward several times, looking fretful, so I asked if she was wanting to get up. She was, but I was unable to coax or lift her out of the chair, partly because I was afraid to further strain my back.

I asked for assistance and two nurses came and hoisted her out of the chair. I realised that it was the chair that was to blame for the struggle, as it was designed for the sitter to be wedged in the valley of a deep triangle. Once out and standing she seemed very disoriented and unstable. She was swearing, which is so out of character, and kept banging into everything despite her cautious footing.

We went for a brief walk around, but she was pulling against me and chose to go back to her room. I tried sitting her on a normal chair from which she pulled herself back up and indicated that she 'should' be back in the wedge chair. I helped her back into that and she calmed again.

The doctor came to introduce himself and asked me why Mum was still on a 'section'. I couldn't answer that fully and felt that such information should surely have come with Mum in the transfer; certainly the assessment that his own staff had done should have been available to him. He seemed very amiable though and had a slightly playful demeanor.

A senior nurse came to give me the paperwork and forms to fill in. She asked me to supply Mum's toiletries, and I promised to bring a better selection of Mum's music.

I was concerned about Mum's general health and let the nurses know that as I left. They assured me that they would look after her. I believe they will.

* * *

Our house is still very cold and full of brick dust and mess. The new stove is still being piped in and we have suffered leaks and floods this week.

Josh is taking over the task of digging my vegetable patch over and enjoyed the pleasure of having a robin sit beside him to sing for his supper, as he worked at picking out the weeds. It was a beautiful moment for him and it gave me joy to see them both.

I took in the CDs and toiletries. Mum was in her own clothes and seemed much more content. She was sunk into the chair in her room again and we played one of the CDs. My new routine is to cream her face with 'Oil of Ulay', which for me is Mum's special scent. She enjoys the sensation and the contact.

I noticed that her face seems very flaccid and dopey; her mouth seems to hang half open in a 'gormless' expression as her eyes flicker and stare at nothing in particular. But she didn't look as pale as before, and a nurse commented on how well she had settled in.

It was a curtailed visit, as Isabelle's second dose of Chemotherapy went much quicker than anticipated, and I was to taxi them home again. As I left, Mum smiled and admonished me to be good.

* * *

On Mothering Sunday she was in her room again, with Buddy Holly still playing.

I seemed to make her jump as I came into the room. She appeared very jittery and agitated. She was unwashed and greasy too, so I feared she might be experiencing problems again.

I switched the music off, which she seemed to appreciate. She kept saying that she wants to go home and wants to go to bed. She was crying and moaning, then apologising for "being silly".

She did seem to be tired, but it didn't seem like a good idea to indulge her in sleep at three in the afternoon. I fed her a 'Fry's Turkish Delight', which relaxed her enough to talk and laugh again.

The nurse had only praise for her progress and anticipates that they will take her off the 'section' at the next review. That will mean she's able to go out again.

I really enjoyed my time with Mum today.

* * *

On Thursday she was still in her room, but was looking much better.

Another dose of 'Turkish Delight', Oil of Ulay and much talk about something and nothing.

I called in on Monica on my way back, to take her a birthday card and some chocolates. She wants me to take her to Mum's next time.

It's great not having to do Mum's washing; it actually frees me to go more often, as I don't have to wait till all the laundry is dry.

Meanwhile I've been chopping up lots of wood, as the boiler stove is finally in place and burning as much rubbish and wood as we can feed it. It keeps the dining room particularly cosy, but also heats all the radiators and the hot-water tank.

* * *

Sunday was beautiful, a clear blue sky, warm and still. The nurses had brought Mum out of her room to meet me, so I took the opportunity to take her outside into the sheltered garden area.

Mum was very shivery and unsteady on her feet as I almost dragged her out. We sat in the sunshine, Mum wrapped in scarfs, as we began to sing, laugh and make jokes. She seemed to get 'You are my sunshine' into her brain and couldn't get it out again. It made us both laugh and we tried to find alternative songs. We had a fantastic time for about an hour, until Mum began to feel the cold again. She looked so pretty out in the fresh air and I took a few photos.

It felt like a real milestone had been reached and I'm now looking forward to more trips out with her. Again I left her happy and went out with a joyful spring in my step.

* * *

I've been thinking for a while that Mum's face is looking different. It is difficult to discern as she is losing weight and has developed some peculiar mannerisms and twitches, and will sometimes hold her head in a tilted position for no apparent reason. Anyway, she is beginning to look as if she has a wedge of chewing gum under her top lip. Debbie also noticed that she had a "monkey-mouth".

Finally on Easter Sunday, when I took Monica, I lifted Mum's lip to find a large white swelling and filthy brown teeth. I was shocked. Surely if her teeth had been cleaned, anyone would have seen the swelling, which I presumed was an abscess.

I called the nurse and asked her to make sure that Mum is seen by a doctor or dentist as soon as possible. She wrote it all down in the book reassuringly.

I prodded Mum's lip, but there was no sign of any flinching or pain.

We both had a lot of laughter with Monica.

* * *

Debbie took Olivia and James to see their Nana on this visit, for her birthday, and Olivia made several short videos of them all dancing. It was a much more positive experience for them than the last time.

Mum had six birthday cards altogether, from Monica, Julia, Debbie, me, Wendy and Tony.

* * *

A week later, back from Ireland, I learned that the ward dentist had referred Mum to the Maxillofacial Unit at the West Hospital. I asked Gold Acre to inform me of the date, so that I can hear for myself what the doctors have to say.

I finally took Monica out for her birthday treat, then Monica came with me to see Mum.

We decided to hoist her out of her bucket chair with a view to a stroll in the sunshine. There is no way she can get out of that chair alone. It took time and a large dollop of encouragement to keep her standing without wobbling.

I was horrified at how unstable Mum seemed to have become. We all but dragged her to the garden, but once outdoors she was off like one of those squash balls in slow motion, bouncing into all the walls.

Apart from toppling the bird table, she had fun and enjoyed the sunshine and the breeze.

I do need to ask why Mum spends so much time in that chair.

* * *

Today I phoned Gold Acre and found the ward manager very calming and sympathetic. He asked me if I had any concerns, to which

I replied that I would welcome an opportunity to discuss Mum's care-plan, as I do have some questions. I imagine he was groaning inwardly, but he remained very encouraging. He said that Mum's consultant was on holiday, but that on his return I would be invited to the weekly review.

I did express some concerns about her mouth, hygiene and her 'triangular bucket' chair.

* * *

This Friday, three weeks after the ward dentist saw Mum, I have been given an appointment for the Maxillofacial Unit on May 20th. That is satisfyingly sooner than I had anticipated.

Before a trip to London, I finally contacted Mum's friend Wendy. When I next went to Mum's I spotted a bag of large chocolate buttons and said, "has Wendy been to see you?"

She said "Yes, yes she did."

It is unusual now for Mum to actually say a complete sentence, even one as short as that.

After getting Mum suitably animated with Gene Vincent and Kenny Rogers, I took her hands and, with a "shall we dance, Madam?" managed to coax her out of the bucket chair.

Dancing was a bit strange – more like a clumsy smooch around, but Mum seemed happy to be up. She does bump into everything when left to her own devices, so maybe that is why they prefer to keep her sitting - for health and safety reasons.

Julia has decided that she does not want to see her sister again. She wants to "remember the old Av". She admitted that her choice might seem selfish and I did try to give her a different perspective.

* * *

I think that some of my concerns were heard, because on Friday the 'bucket-chair' was gone and an ordinary chair in its place. Of course that meant that Mum was wandering around the corridors, getting lost and bumping into everything. But I don't want her to lose the use of her legs.

I must write down some questions for tomorrow's meeting with the new consultant. Care Plan? Medications? Section? Daily routine/ hygiene? Meals? Behaviour? Exercise and Stimulation?

* * *

So I got my list of questions out:

Medication was a straightforward one. She's still on the epilepsy control (Tegretol), the anti-depressant (Trazodone) and the anti-psychotic (Haloperidol). The latter he has already reduced from 3mg to 1mg daily and intends to drop that one altogether. If the hallucinations and distress come back, he plans to try ordinary anti-dementia type drugs like the Aricept. He said it all so matter-of-fact. I was sort of anticipating that this would happen with the Haloperidol, but I didn't expect the hospital to do it after spending all this time finding drugs to stabilise her. But I didn't say any of that.

I don't want her to deteriorate again now she's finally content (-ish).

He said that her progress is reviewed daily by the staff nurse and three times a week more officially. He does the rounds weekly, but has been away for a month. He mentioned the growth in her mouth, and that he had noticed some cellulite on her leg, for which he'd just started her on antibiotics. (I didn't know cellulite was an infection.)

He asked if Mum had ever had a firm diagnosis and, as I tried to explain, he too said how it was "all just academic". We discussed Mum's deterioration since 1997 and he asked whether any of us offspring would like to be tested for that specific gene that causes early onset Alzheimer's.

He thinks that Mum has both Alzheimer's and a type of vascular dementia, because she presents such big mood swings and the psychosis. He said that Mum has been taken off the 'section', so I asked whether I could now take her out?

"You could always have taken her out. You only needed the doctor's permission!" was his astonishing reply.

I don't know where I could take her now though. It is a scary prospect and I couldn't do it alone. She is a bit more mobile again though, now that she is not perched in the 'bucket' for hours.

He also said that Gold Acre is "a hospital unit for complex needs and behaviour issues" and that their job is to stabilise patients ready to send them into more permanent home settings. This I did know, but I had put it to the back of my mind, as the last assessment concluded that Mum would continue to "need at least the same level of care as at St Peter's Unit".

He said that he would expect Mum to be able to move on in a few months, and asked me if I had somewhere in mind? I do not have a clue. She isn't ready for an ordinary nursing home, even one dementia-registered. He reassured me that a social worker would get involved again, when the hospital decide to discharge her, and that they would all help to place her appropriately.

I asked about daily routines, stimulation and care-plan, but that clearly was not his area of expertise, so he referred me to Mum's key-worker. I must find out who it is and run the rest by him/her. The consultant has given me plenty to think about.

* * *

Mum is becoming tearful and unstable again; possibly the result of a reduction in medication?

Today I met her shuffling the corridor with a look of confusion and rage that she'd had before.

The nurse said "Look, here's your daughter, come to see you!"

Mum glowered and said "Who are you?"

She looked angry and started to scream, mimicking Betty (another resident). I took her back to her room away from the noise and closed the door. I asked if I could have a hug and she said that she didn't have any.

"No hugs for me?" I questioned

"Well I suppose..."

I forced her arms around me and cooed and encouraged. She started to cry and said,

"I want to die. Well, you can't! I want to kill myself...No, you can't."

I just held her, prayed and told her how loved she was. Then I creamed her face, so she would smell like Mammy again and we both sang and laughed, whilst I fed her lunch.

Someone had tied her hair back in double ponytails and she looked very pretty.

When I made to leave, she playfully said, "No, don't go!" We were both smiling and bouncy when I left.

* * *

I was concerned about them taking her off the Haloperidol, but this time she seemed fine.

She had had her nails painted and was wandering the corridors, singing to herself. She was playful with her gabbling and entertaining the 'babbies'. The hallucinations were much stronger again, but seemed positive.

She is often questioning the babbies and telling them off. "I'll kill you!" was a more extreme reaction, but the babbies are never far away. She was making creepy sounds and faces to a rhyme and then building it up to a scary finale to make them jump.

She was clearly enjoying herself. She seems to understand the majority of what I say, but unfortunately I no longer understand most of her replies. It doesn't trouble me, though I would love to know what she is trying to say.

Before leaving I went to check about Wednesday's Maxillofacial appointment. We discussed how to transport Mum and concluded that a wheelchair and taxi would be easiest all round. I will meet them there.

* * *

Today I got a message from the boss at Gold Acre, saying not to worry, (although you do wonder) but would I please call her.

She said she was completing a check-list for Mum, "for future care" needs, of which I will get a copy. She reiterated what the consultant had said: that she has settled well and that when she does become agitated it is predictable – with noise, for example. She was informing me, she said, because Gold Acre is "a challenging behaviour unit" and Mum apparently does not qualify as challenging.

I mentioned my anxiety about taking Mum off the Haloperidol and she agreed. She said that they had taken her off and within twenty-four hours had noticed such a change that they had put her straight back on it.

She said that Mum is one who can join in with activities and does. They have activities two mornings a week apparently. I must always come on the wrong mornings.

* * *

I arrived a little early at the West Hospital, realising that I was nervous for my little Mammy venturing out into the unknown today. I got myself a coffee and observed my environment, feeling quite transparent myself and somewhat spaced out.

I spotted a big taxi with a little Mammy in it, and a carer, who used to work at West Hospital, began pushing the wheelchair. Mum had a face like drugged thunder. He said that she had been difficult and "quite vocal this morning", but I learned later that she had been aggressive and had been given a shot of Lorazepam to make her more compliant.

In the Maxillofacial Unit I worked hard to cheer Mum up. By the time the nurse came she was smiling sweetly. They sent us to their x-ray department with a doubt in all our minds as to whether they would be able to do it. The team were so friendly and good humoured, it was a delight to be there. They were able to do the x-ray with Mum sitting, so I fled. I didn't want to be around those rays myself.

They took her back in for a second x-ray, then we went back to see the doctor.

He was from Ghana and spoke almost exclusively to the chap that had brought Mum from Gold Acre, rather than to Mum or me. He said the 'growth' was a cyst and that he would want to completely remove it, under general anaesthetic, as soon as possible.

He used the x-ray to show how the cyst had pushed back the bones and parted the front teeth. It is incredible how a growth could move the teeth so much, in such a short time span, especially when you consider how long kids have to wear a brace.

He went on to say that, because Mum was not in a position to give her own consent, he would need the approval of one other doctor before he could go ahead. I asked whether the person with welfare power of attorney could make that decision, but apparently not. He said that if two doctors made a decision that was contested by the person with welfare power of attorney, the latter would *not* win. It is not worth the paper it is written on in court, he says.

I was shocked and fascinated. Not that I would want to take a doctor to court.

I am sure that medical predisposition is to preserve life, but I *can* imagine issues about the quality of a person's life, versus medical intervention, arising.

* * *

CHAPTER 19

I took the boys to see Mum on Wednesday, as they had not seen her since Christmas. She was wet and smelly when I got her out of the reinstated bucket chair.

The boys were bored, but that can't be helped. We dropped in on Monica on the way home too; they were certainly not bored there.

* * *

Mum's cousin Mike and his wife, Val came with their daughter. We had lunch, then they followed me in their car to Gold Acre.

Mum was a bit grumpy initially, but we soon had her laughing. We sat outside and baked in the sun together, enjoying one another's company.

I received a copy of that 'NHS Continuing Healthcare Needs Checklist' yesterday. I was surprised by some of the assessments that they have made. For example, they have three descriptors of need: "A - meets the described need. B- borderline. C- clearly does not meet the described need". One category of need reads, "Continence care is problematic and requires timely intervention." They scored that 'C' (no need), but she wears pads all the time and is often wet even with them. The other contentious one for me reads, "mood disturbances or anxiety symptoms or periods of distress that have a severe impact on the individual's health and/or well being." They gave that one a 'C' too. We all know that Mum has huge periods of distress. Maybe they think they have her under control now? I don't. She got 'C's for 'mobility', 'nutrition', 'skin integrity', 'breathing' and 'Altered States of Consciousness'. Mobility and the latter I would also question. She only got 'A' for two categories of need: Cognition and Communication, the latter which reads, "unable to reliably communicate their needs at any time and in any way, even when all practical steps to do so have been taken." That made me feel very tearful.

The person sending the checklist did write, "when we get involved with a community nurse assessor and social worker we will meet with yourself and go through a more in-depth checklist." So it's not all set in stone yet.

I am concerned that they are anxious to discharge her before she is ready.

* * *

Last visit to Mum was very interesting. She was in her room after lunch, chatting and crying with another resident. A nurse then came to remove the other chap and put Mum's music on.

Mum continued talking and I was struck by how much more alert she seemed to be. Several times she looked directly at me, making good eye contact and smiling. There were also more English words expressed and the hummed tunes were recognisable. She was entertaining 'the babbies' again with Frere Jacques, Jingle Bells and some with 'make you jump' endings.

I realised that she has not looked like Avril for a long time; like 'the lights are on, but there's nobody home'. This time there *was* somebody home.

I passed a comment to a nurse, who said that Mum's medication had been increased (the Carbomazapine) because she had been becoming more shaky. I think that might explain the improvement in Mum's alertness too. That medication is to keep the epilepsy under control, but it is also used against bipolar disorders and schizophrenia.

* * *

The last couple of weeks I've been finding the visits more difficult. Most of the time she is talking to herself in a way which makes me completely redundant. She doesn't even answer me with the same degree of clarity that she does herself.

"Avril? Yes? Diddle dee da bee her? No, I don't think so. Oh, I see..."

But with me, there is no such level of conversation. I will have to be content to just be an observer.

Some days she is more shaky, others more alert. She is still very emotional, but not as angry or depressed.

In my recent dreams Mum is constantly with me, and I am aware that others do not think that she has any needs. I awake feeling even more protective of her than usual. I have been thinking about all the issues a lot: her past, present and future and how best to meet her needs.

Today, as I was getting ready to go, the hospital phoned to say that she had fallen.

She seemed more dozy than usual when I arrived, but she livened up throughout the visit. They had boxed her into the chair by putting her feet up to prevent her falling again.

She has a large swelling over her left eye and a big bruise down the side of the right cheek and on her right upper jaw. They said that no-one saw what happened, they just found her on the floor.

I wondered whether she had one of her 'fainting fits' again, but they have not been mentioned. The doctors gave her a thorough check over and are satisfied. I think she is going to have two real shiners over the next couple of days.

We enjoyed one another today and, as we listened to Elvis, she kept clapping and telling him how much she loved him.

* * *

Isabelle has endured her final chemotherapy at last. It has been horrendous for her, but she has carried it brilliantly well. She always looks beautiful and doesn't moan at all. I think she will bounce back quickly. Her head doesn't look like a tennis ball any more.

Tomorrow Joshua has his first 'gig' at an open-air festival. He has been busy revising for exams, whilst doing lots of band-practices for this special occasion. I'm sure I'll feel proud to see him performing live on stage with his own music and lyrics.

* * *

Mum has two yellow and purple eyes, but is much the same in her general state.

Nowadays, I usually find her sitting in her ordinary chair with her legs propped up on the bed; I suppose they are nervous that she might fall again.

I have been taking her outside for a walk, as the weather has been quite glorious. Yesterday she was very wobbly though; it took her a long time to find her balance as she can't see what she is doing and mistakes patterns on the floor for obstacles.

It makes me smile that the sort of words that she still speaks clearly are almost instinctive responses. So, if I say how soft and velvety the petals look, she says "Yes, I know!" Or if she receives a strong taste or sound sensation, it will be, "Oh, that's lovely/horrible..." Sometimes she will choose the opposite adjective, so yesterday, when I gave her a cool drink, she said "Oh, that's nice and hot."

* * *

Simon has been made redundant, which could well be a blessing, as his work has been all-consuming since Christmas. Hopefully now he will be able to focus more on his exciting projects and innovations and get a business going. We might all need to tighten our belts for a while first though.

* * *

Today I found Mum dozing in a bucket chair in the dining room, but was first given some forms to fill in about Mum's qualifications, employment history and such things, which did seem strange under the circumstances.

The staff have been concerned again about Mum's shaking and have referred her back to Neurology at the West Hospital. The appointment is for next Tuesday.

Two nurses took Mum back to her room and she sat smiling, eyes closed, doing her new sit-up movements. Heaving herself upright she would chant, then would slouch and be immediately asleep, mouth open and completely relaxed. It shocked me at first as it looked like she'd died. She is also very pale. I could not wake her with words or strokes, so I squeezed her knees and she jumped, chanting a few more jingles and again out-for-the-count.

I was given a hot meal, dessert, cup of tea and medication to feed her with. It took over an hour until the plates were empty, and all the time her eyes were closed. She would open her mouth to eat and then be asleep again. Every time I squeezed her knee she would playfully growl like a tiger and giggle, but her sleeping was not fake. The staff reasoned that they had given her a bath this morning and it had made her tired. When she'd finished eating, she stood up, eyes still shut and began to shuffle away.

We had good fun today though; I really enjoyed her playfulness and having something to do.

The nurse recounted a recent occasion, when a doctor asked Mum to open her mouth and she snapped at him like a crocodile and made him jump. She is funny.

* * *

I have been made a director of Simon's new business. That is new, exciting and equally daunting. I need to make some wise decisions.

I wrote down a list of things for which I feel myself responsible. It seems endless, but we do need to earn an income too.

I was at the West Hospital today for Mum's appointment in Neurology. She was with two members of staff and looked very dopey.

The Neurologist was most impressive. Whilst we were there he read through the salient parts of Mum's two years in Neurology:

the diagnosis of frontal lobe epilepsy, the EEG, etc, and asked me to describe exactly the sort of seizures that I had witnessed. Then he took Mum's hands, spoke to her, and touched her face and hands very gently.

He then offered his diagnosis very clearly and confidently:

He doesn't think Mum has epilepsy, rather that she is exhibiting 'Cortical Mioclonus', which is very common with sufferers of CJD and Alzheimer's. Frontal Lobe seizures usually happen in the night, in deep sleep, not during waking hours, he said, but that Mum's faints, sound like 'complex partial seizures', followed by Mioclonus as she comes out of the faint. ('Complex' because her brain is so caked with plaque.)

We all experience some 'Mioclonus' – it is that feeling as you fall asleep, you dream you are falling and jerk yourself awake. That, he believes, is what Mum is doing. Apparently the Tegretol would need to be at least 600mg, twice a day, to keep epilepsy under control, but Mum is on 100mg twice a day, so it would not stop her having epileptic seizures anyway.

The point is that Tegretol does not control Mioclonus either. We could stop the Tegretol and put Mum on 'Cepra', which would control the epilepsy and the Mioclonus, but it could be very disruptive to her mood.

The Mioclonus does not damage the brain, so we must consider whether it's worth taking the risk of changing her medication. If the Mioclonus were causing Mum distress, or she began having seizures, then it might be worth trying the 'Cepra'.

The other question he posed was about the dementia: now that Mum is so far gone in her dementia, the symptoms are pretty much indistinguishable, but it could be 'Fronto Temporal' dementia, he thought, rather than Alzheimer's.

He said it might be worth doing another MRI scan, if we wanted to know for sure. Do we want to put Mum through that to satisfy our own curiosity, or not?

So, they are the two questions: MRI? Change to 'Cepra'?

I still question whether I have done the right thing for Mum. I see her pretty face warm to life with affection and interaction and I wonder how different her quality of life might be if she had remained living with family around her. I know that the physical environment would also be too challenging here now, with stairs and corners, and showering was already dangerous before. Plus the complete incontinence. But these are not insurmountable challenges.

* * *

Mum is still much the same. She has been sad/weepy/fed-up when I find her, but cheers up and is happy by the time I leave.

Sometimes she just bursts into laughter for no apparent reason.

Last time I went, the traffic was bad and I arrived at noon. I know they have 'protected mealtimes', but often I arrive before lunch and am able to feed her myself.

When the nurse came to answer the door she looked at her watch and said that I could not come in, because it was a minute after twelve. I apologised for being a bit late and said that I liked to feed Mum, as she always eats in her room. Eventually they let me in and I was able to feed a very tearful Mammy.

We managed to get out into the garden for fresh air and a walk about too. I put her hair into two pretty plaits as I followed her around and fed her Turkish Delight and tea.

* * *

A friend told me about the RCN's (Royal College of Nursing) decision to be neutral about new laws on 'assisted suicides'. I also read that the new Mental Capacity Act states that "doctors must now starve and dehydrate patients to death in some cases. And if they refuse to do this doctors – and nurses too – can be dismissed and treated as criminals." "'Euthanasia by neglect for mentally incapacitated people", was how it was described.

It could be just scare-mongering journalism, but I must investigate. Shocking thoughts. The article from RCN (on the BBC website) states,

"The move comes as a survey for a newspaper suggests 74% of people want doctors to be able to help people to end their lives. According to the survey..., support for assisted suicide was especially strong among those aged between 55 and 64. The poll also suggests that six out of 10 people want friends and relatives to be able to help loved ones to die without fear of prosecution."

[See Notes 4]

Clearly the issues are very complex. Funding and quality of life being just just two aspects of that complexity. As with the question of 'they shoot horses, don't they?' We consider it 'humane' to put a suffering animal 'out of its misery', if it has no prospect of recovery.

And how many people can our NHS support on it's over-stretched resources? Allowing a person to die 'with dignity' – is this 'playing God'? Or is keeping somebody alive on a machine, with no hope of recovery, also 'playing God'.

There are questions about responsibility, morality, equality (who champions the cause of the poor) - issues that we all need to address realistically.

I find the possibility of abuse of such powers disturbing.

I believe in the sanctity of life, but I admit to respecting conflicting perspectives here.

* * *

I had a heavy wave of depression on Thursday, which I can still taste. It was as if all the disappointments, fear and pain of my life was on me – from my dad, disastrous relationships, mental illness of others, miscarriages, deaths, sickness and my mum's suffering.

I am not depressed now, but still feel bruised.

Today I was advised of a multi-disciplinary meeting, to be held on 22nd September, and warned that they will be sending Mammy out "into the community", as there is nothing more that they can do for her there, as "her needs are not too severe".

I am expected, meanwhile, to find a suitable home for her.

I will need to contact the social worker for some direction in all of this, as I don't know what sort of places are available or suitable.

I stayed some time with Mum, who was very concerned about 'the babbies' again. I kept reassuring her that the babies were all sorted and happy, and that she had done it all.

She kept shouting for 'Help!' and 'Stop it!' but was unable to explain.

Suddenly I realised that it was after 17:00 and tea-time. I fed Mum, but was reminded twice about 'protected mealtimes', implying that I should not be there at mealtimes. I said that if I am not allowed to stay and feed her, that they should let me know for definite.

* * *

This morning I had a message from the Maxillofacial Unit, saying Mum's operation is next Monday. It said that she would also be required to attend tomorrow for a "pre-clerking" and I was to phone back, if we could attend. I rang Gold Acre, but they had not yet been informed.

It has finally been confirmed, but I will have to take Mum in myself, as Gold Acre "do not have the staff to spare at short notice". I cannot get Mum into my car, so I'll have to order us a big taxi.

* * *

Mum was washed and ready and the taxi came swiftly.

In the waiting room at Maxillofacial, she started to make sudden involuntary noises and to sing, coming across quite loud in that environment. The other people waiting seemed bemused and slightly disturbed by her presentation, but Josh (who I'd asked to accompany me) and I were amused, knowing that she was happy and enjoying herself. She even shared Josh's earphones and listened to some of his 'noise-music'.

We waited nearly two hours, until the whole waiting room had emptied, before we were called through to see two nurses. Mum had to be weighed and measured, have blood taken, blood-pressure measured, swabs taken and ECG done, and I had forms to fill in.

Getting Mum on to the scales was a comical palaver involving Josh lifting Mum's feet one at a time and me heaving her forward, whilst the nurses stood watching. Because she was coming from a hospital setting, the rules were much tighter on hygiene, with a long list of questions about infections, medications, etc that I was not able to fully answer.

They have given Mum some 'antimicrobial wash', which will have to be used from now until the operation on Monday. They also gave instructions about food starvation from midnight before the operation. Their biggest concern was that Mum should have an escort with her all day, otherwise they would not go ahead, because they themselves do not have 'specialist' staff. I assured them that Gold Acre would be sending someone, as a week is not 'short notice'. They did say that they would endeavour to give Mum the first operation of the day, to lessen the risk of her needing to stay in over night.

Doing the bloods was stressful as the needles made her jump, but we got through the experience with the promise of some chocolate. The last call was for the ECG. By the end, Mum's mood was turning sour, so she didn't enjoy the hot chocolate or the sandwich.

The taxi came very swiftly, but it was half past rush hour and took forty-five minutes to get a very grumpy Mum back to Gold Acre. I gave the papers to the nurse in charge and explained all the instructions. I told her that I would be at the hospital at some point during the day, but that I had other commitments on Monday.

* * *

On Wednesday Gold Acre phoned to say that they were not prepared to send anyone with Mum on Monday. They knew the hospital's rules and therefore, that if she is to have the operation, I will have to go and stay with her all day.

Mental-health practitioners apparently do not stay with patients in ordinary hospitals and ordinary hospitals don't admit mental-health patients without a full escort. The obvious conclusion: mental-health patients do not get the treatments that they need, unless someone else is there to accompany them.

The ward manager seemed to imply that it was my "fault" for arranging the operation, when in fact the doctor, two months ago, said that Mum needed to have the cyst removed as soon as possible. I cannot leave Mum with an untreated cyst growing in her mouth, displacing her teeth and nostrils. They still don't even know whether the cyst is cancerous or not.

This must have been a recent policy shift, as Mum has twice been fully escorted to hospital by Gold Acre staff.

I am disappointed that the system is allowing the most vulnerable to be neglected, as if they do not deserve to live in comfort or dignity. I cannot understand a healthy person not wanting to offer unconditional care to anyone in need.

I realise I am the one responsible for Mum's care, not the 'system'. At least she has somebody.

* * *

My garden is now completely overgrown. I have harvested a feast of garden produce – garlic, onions, potatoes, beetroot and peas, but I spent too long bending, pulling and definitely not looking after my back or pacing the work.

* * *

Gold Acre staff finally agreed to escort Mum to hospital, so I met them there at 08:30. The nurses had managed to get Mum first on the list, thankfully.

We dressed Mum in the backless gown and then the escort left. Mum perked up a bit then and responded positively to my conversation, tickles and jokes. Wheeling along the corridors in the flat-tyred wheelchair, Mum was clearly enjoying the rides. "Wheee..." she giggled around each corner.

The tiny anaesthetist's room felt over-crowded by Mum, me and the two nurses. They needed to shuffle her up the bed, so two male nurses squeezed in too. To reassure or hold her still, I was useful, and to answer the questions of course. Despite the warning, the needle still hurt her; then on with the sticky monitors, oxygen mask and sleepy juice. She'll be fine.

Less than an hour later, I was recalled to the recovery room. Mammy was screaming and throwing her legs all over the place, with blood seeping from her nose and mouth. She was clearly in great distress, but whether it was pain or not I couldn't say. The monitors did not show anything obviously wrong. The anaesthetic should have been making the operated area numb, but as Mum didn't calm down they gave her 6mg of Morphine, then a shot of Lorazepam, but Mum continued howling and writhing around the bed.

Her glazed yellow eyes were swollen and bulging, looking manic. They wheeled her back to the ward, where I tried to calm her.

Sometimes I whispered, "Mammy, Mammy, it's alright." Then her screams would settle more quickly, but I didn't seem able to improve her overall discomfort.

Was she hallucinating or speaking to us as she shouted "Go away! No! Go home!"?

When they straightened her up in the bed they used a slide mat and four nurses, so it's no wonder that I struggled trying to do it alone.

Back on the ward after a short cafe break, Mum was still in great distress. She wouldn't even let me moisten her dry, bloody lips. As the afternoon faded I was resigning myself to having to stay overnight, as

I supposed that they would require her to be stable and to have eaten before sending her home.

She was slightly less volatile by 16:00, but still contorting her face and shouting, "Kacker, you're my mother...Avril, I love you...No! No! Tell me why...Go away!"

I would have to wait for the doctor to do his rounds, so I tried to get Mum to drink some water, but I couldn't even get her to sit up.

Amazingly, an hour later I was told that Mum could go home. Getting her up and dressed was a fiasco, but I have to admit to being highly motivated to getting her back to Gold Acre, where she could begin to recover in peace and I could go home.

Then the doctor came and said that Mum's cyst had been very substantial and that she must use the mouth-wash regularly. He would like to see her again in a couple of weeks.

It was becoming obvious that Mum's teeth and nose were already going back into place. She looks like she'll have another black eye though.

In the taxi, Mum objected to bends and speed bumps and suddenly she yelped and heaved. The driver administered tissues and bowls just in time, as Mum vomited up copious amounts of thin, brown bloody fluid. He drove on and we were using the second bowl as we pulled up outside Gold Acre. The smell had long since turned my stomach, but the driver was completely non-phased by it all. The special taxis have been superb.

After depositing Mum, medication and paperwork, I got a taxi to Isabelle's and was soon relaxing with a beer in her garden.

* * *

I still have done little about finding a new home for Mum. I phoned the social worker, to see if he could steer me in the right direction before the MDM, but his advice is for me to do nothing. He said that Gold Acre had been wrong to make such a demand before a decision has been made. Apparently we will all discuss the NHS assessment and the social worker's assessment at the review. He seems to be very cross at the way they are going about this.

I am relieved not to have to find Mum a home by the end of next month, but I hope it doesn't jeopardize Mum's chances of the best care.

Mum has recovered from her ordeal, but still has yellow bruising around her face.

The weather is still fine enough for us to stroll in the garden area and, despite finding Mum rendered immobile in her room when I visit, (either in the bucket chair or with her feet up on the bed) I always manage to get her up.

On Saturday I got her out of a soggy, smelly chair and took her into the bathroom to change her. She was quite lucid and in much better form when she was clean and up and about.

* * *

CHAPTER 20

The boys are now back at school for Conor's year eight and Joshua's final GCSE year. I am progressing with the decorating and Simon and I are busy setting up our new business. I wonder what other exciting challenges we have in store.

The check-up at the West Hospital was not so good.

The doctor began by explaining that it had been a Kerotocyst, formed from the cells that make enamel for teeth. Good that it is not a cancerous cyst, but it does mean that it could grow back again.

When he checked inside her mouth his disgusted expression told the story before his words did. Apparently the wound was completely infected and full of puss. He did say it is difficult to keep such a wound clean, but I don't think he expected it to be so bad. He requested a sharp pink needle, unsure as to whether Mum would allow him to proceed, but did so armed with a bowl to catch the fluid. It was satisfyingly gross as he injected a needle full of Corsodyl to force out an equal amount of puss and gunge into the waiting receptacle. Poor Mum, the unpleasant sensation must have tasted foul.

The doctor prescribed a dose of antibiotics and rescheduled the checkup for next Thursday. Waiting for the prescription, Mum was saying again how she wants to kill herself and then arguing that she shouldn't.

I do wonder how old that notion of wanting to die really is. Or is it a new thought? Is she capable of new thought? There is so little that she says intelligibly. "Where are the babbies?" "Who are you?" "I want to kill myself." - These seem to be all I hear nowadays. It is terribly sad, but fascinating nevertheless.

* * *

They have decided to take Mum off the Tegretol and put her on the Cepra to control the Cortical Mioclonus. It has certainly stopped the jerks already.

I find her very 'low' though, but that may just be a reflection of my own mood. On Sunday her head was so stooped, that as she shuffled around her room it was the top of her head that made first contact with each wall. I found myself following her around with my hand in front of her to cushion her head, just like you do when toddlers' heads come level with all the table-tops.

She has started asking me who I am again too. Occasionally she finds my answer reassuring, but just as often she cannot believe me and is distressed by it. I think she likes the hugs, kisses and human contact, but there's not much else I can do.

* * *

The second check-up went much better. The infection was gone and the hole was beginning to heal. The doctor showed me the extensive, gaping hole in her mouth. He requested some 'BIP', which smelled like a fabric soaked in pungent, yellow 'germalene'-type stuff. The purpose was to block food going into the hole and stop reinfection. It also allows the wound to heal inside out so that it can heal completely clean. Courageously he tried to poke a strip of this antiseptic 'BIP' into the hole, using tweezers, but she wouldn't let him. She was outraged.

She left the clinic stressed and man-handled, but soon forgot and seemed happy in the taxi.

Mum's review, or MDM, is tomorrow. I feel anxious, as I think Gold Acre will say that Mum has to leave them, but I expect there to be a dispute, between the NHS and the Council, about the level of Mum's needs, suitable alternative care and, of course, funding.

* * *

I read again through the 'NHS Continuing Healthcare Needs Checklist' that Gold Acre completed in May this year, and I have highlighted areas I consider inaccurate. I took it with me to the meeting where five of us were present: the social worker, Mum's key nurse, two other specialist nurses and myself.

Firstly one of the specialist nurses said that Avril was ready to be discharged and asked me whether I had been to look at homes for her. I admitted that I hadn't as I don't know what I'm looking for. They told me that this meeting was part of the process to determine needs and funding. The conclusions would then go to a Panel, who would decide the final outcome.

What is important to me is the assessment they make of her needs and therefore what level of care and type of home she needs. We discussed each of the eleven categories: from behaviour, communication and cognition, through to medication, continence and ASC (Altered States of Consciousness).

Each interest group presented slightly different perspectives. The result was that she scored one 'severe need', two 'high need', two 'moderate need', four 'low need' and two 'no need'. The nurse had written:

"Mrs Haynes' challenging behaviour has now settled in to a manageable, predictable pattern and no longer requires a hospital. There is a high level of cognitive impairment and all activities of daily living require meeting. Sometimes there are minimal bursts of agitation on nursing intervention. Mrs Haynes' needs could now be adequately met in a community setting with appropriate registration. Requires a 117 aftercare."

"117 aftercare" is the kind of care she will need having come off a 'Section Three'.

She admitted that Mum's behaviour would be much worse if not carefully managed by isolating her away from any noise. She also stressed that Mum cannot make any needs known, nor can she do anything at all for herself. I was surprised to learn that Mum even has to take 'Senna' on a daily basis, as she no longer knows how to push.

So, they are requesting full NHS care funding, but what kind of home do I look for?

The social worker said that he was struggling to think of anywhere in Nottinghamshire where that level of care could be replicated. The nurses were all equally scratching their heads to think of a place with sufficient registration, but where the environment would not be too harsh.

Eventually the social worker said he thought it was wrong of them to have expected me, as just a family member, to be able to find a suitable home for Mum, when they, with all their knowledge and experience, could not think of *one* suitable place between them. Good point.

Still, I do have to look. They gave me a directory of Nottinghamshire homes and discussed the benefits of different registrations, but still they were struggling to name a plausible place. They came up with two suggestions: Kirk Way in Cotgrave and Sunset Copse in Lowdham. They also suggested that I look at the 'CQC link' on the internet to see what the inspectors think of these homes. I will have a browse over the weekend and speak to the social worker on Monday. I don't feel I can do this on my own.

* * *

I went to a friend's funeral today and next week I will take Monica to say goodbye to Alf, her long-standing friend of over fifty-two years. I'm glad I managed to take them both to Newark Market earlier this year. He loved that place.

The social worker is now encouraging me to go ahead and look at a few of these homes. He reiterated how he had found the whole process very difficult.

* * *

This week I went to Sunset Copse in a sleepy little village next to Lowdham. I was very impressed from my first meeting with a member of staff in the car park. The place was welcoming, homely and very enthusiastically and professionally run. I am slightly concerned that Mum would bang in to everything there, but that is my only reservation. I would love her to be in such a homely environment, with what looks like a very stable, generous and committed staff. I put Mum's name down on their waiting list, feeling much more positive again about her future.

A few days later I got a call from the social worker to say, "I'm not putting pressure on you, but..." Apparently, he has been admonished for supporting my case in the MDM.

I was glad to be able to report my positive experience at Sunset Copse and reassured him that I'll see the one in Cotgrave next week.

I was disappointed to also have a letter from Gold Acre, saying:

"A meeting was set up some weeks ago regarding your mother's future care. I would like to arrange another meeting for the 6th November, 2009 at 10:00, with regards to your progress in finding a suitable placement for your mother, as several weeks have now passed..."

It has only been two weeks since the meeting and I do feel they are putting me under too much pressure.

* * *

Mum is clearly now in the late stages of whatever dementia she has.

She was in one of the lounges at Gold Acre with a few other residents, listening to some soothing pan-pipe music. Suddenly a man came in, announcing a "light and sound show", and it occurred to me that I have never visited Mum during an activity morning.

Mum loved the music – a Vera Lyn experience - which you might not expect a sixties girl to enjoy. The nurse was trying to encourage the residents to play percussion instruments, and one resident danced about with a flag. The result was kind of chaotic, but stimulating and encouraging.

* * *

Yesterday I took Monica to Alf's funeral at Wilford Hill. She was pleased to have said goodbye and I was glad to have been able to help. Then I took Monica home and went to my next appointment.

It was an 'Involvement Strategy Group' for the Nottinghamshire Healthcare NHS Trust. Most of the people around the table (about twenty) were 'Leads', representing directorates within Notts Healthcare Trust. A few of us (seven) were carers or service users. I learned that the Nottinghamshire Healthcare Trust (dealing largely with mental health issues) is distinct from the Nottinghamshire University Hospitals Trust, although both are under the umbrella of the NHS Trust.

The discussions and issues raised were very encouraging. I have much to learn about this huge institution and I felt both 'out of place' and yet honoured to have been invited in the first place - like I had gate-crashed a private party. I would like to be involved in influencing and shaping policy decisions; to contribute by offering the perspective of the carer and on behalf of the service user.

* * *

This morning I found Mum slumped over in her chair, looking quite pitiful. I greeted her cheerfully and tried to engage, but she was distressed. She had her eyes shut, but kept shouting, "No, stop it!" and then she would cry soulfully. I was unable to help her today.

They brought her dinner, but she refused to eat more than a couple of mouthfuls. Between sleeping, shouting and crying she was blowing big bubbles through her nose and had a swollen tomato face by the time I left. I think I looked much the same.

I am sure we were a sorry sight when the nurse came in with Mum's medication, saying that the Trazodone should help her. After another hour I went home, having failed again with Mum.

I still haven't been to see the home in Cotgrave either. If I don't go tomorrow I will feel under a lot more pressure, because we are busy for half-term next week. I also feel stressed because I have done nothing for Conor's birthday yet.

* * *

Today I got another call from the social worker to say that Mum has been awarded 'Continuing NHS Funding'.

I need to make sure that they haven't stipulated a different sort of home for her now.

* * *

Today I received a letter to say that Mum's case for NHS funding has been deferred due to insufficient evidence.

I never quite know how I'll find Mum, but I think it depends on who I'm looking for. Many days I am so relaxed and happy to be with her that the whole experience is positive and rewarding for us both. Other days I try hard, get no-where and feel frustrated. I think most of it is my problem of attitude, rather than hers.

I saw the place in Cotgrave this week. The deputy explained how they were full (with a waiting list of five since June) and so "there is little chance of a place" for Mum this side of Christmas. I explained that I had been instructed to look around the places recommended, so they showed me around. I was impressed with the space, the set-up and the quantity of active helpers. There were definite quiet places, and it was incredibly calm at that moment in time and space. I put Mum's name on their list.

* * *

They were very good at Mum's check-up at the Maxillofacial Unit – we didn't wait too long, then a quick look and "fine, see you in six months".

Mum seemed very small and soft and I felt very protective of her.

* * *

I expected to find the same team at today's review, but found myself in another room with three completely different people. The ward manager, who sent me the 'hurry up' letter a couple of weeks ago, a senior nurse and a man I recognised from the St Peter's Wing.

The manager said that the purpose of the meeting was to find out what progress I had made finding a home for Mum. I explained where I had been, why, and what conclusions I had drawn. Then I explained my frustration at not knowing quite what to do next. I tried to follow their responses, but was hearing such mixed messages. They seemed to be saying that the funding will depend on the type of home recommended by the PCT (Primary Care Trust), but nobody knows what that is yet.

They emphasised again how theirs is a "challenging behaviour unit" and Mum "does not have challenging behaviour", worse still, they argued, "as a vulnerable old lady" she was possibly at risk by some of their more challenging residents. They said that they can't just *keep* Mum until a place becomes available in somewhere of my choice, but that I had to find her somewhere – anywhere – and could move her again later if I so desired.

To recap and try to clear my confusion, I said it sounds like they want me to find somewhere before I have been told which category of home I am looking for.

I began to cry (which is really annoying when I have a point to make) and asked if they could find out from the PCT what type of home I *should* be looking for. Whilst handing out tissues, they assigned that job to the man who knew Mum from St Peter's Unit.

I got cross about it all later. One of those days when you feel like everything is left to you.

Feeling sorry for myself I managed to recall some wise person saying "If you want to change the world, you have to start by changing yourself". (Ghandi?)

* * *

The chap from Gold Acre said that he had spoken to someone in the PCT, but that there was no information yet about funding. Apparently they had already decided at the MDM that Mum would need to reside in a home with registered mental-health nurses. He said that Kirk Way doesn't have a mental health registration. I could feel myself becoming frustrated again and asked him to tell me precisely which homes I should look at. He then heartily recommended another home in Cotgrave, which has a newly developed 'Mental Health and Challenging Behaviour Unit' as well as a registered dementia unit.

He thinks I will like this one, and they have rooms available. I told him I would go next week.

I am still getting mixed messages from them: to get her out of Gold Acre they say she doesn't need a challenging behaviour unit, yet the PCT are saying that IS the type of home I am looking for. Does she need a challenging behaviour unit or not?

* * *

Yesterday I took Wendy and Monica to see Mum.

I was a bit spaced out though as I had some shocking news the day before. My beloved friend 'Little John', whom I've known for twenty-three years, died suddenly in Heidelberg on this remembrance day. I had spoken to him just last week and now he's dead. I am still in shock and can't stop crying.

We found Mum slumped in a chair in her room and all greeted her as she started to whimper. After kisses, cuddles and Monica's lively banter, everyone relaxed and we remembered people and times past together. Mum continued to cry out spasmodically, but did seem to vaguely engage.

Nobody else came to Mum's room for two hours, until a cleaner walked straight in and was startled by our presence. She fetched us some chairs and shortly afterwards there was a knock on the door and a nurse entered with Mum's dinner. Well, it was meant to be dinner, but consisted of four dollops of different coloured puree on a plate.

I questioned the nurse, as Mum has all her own teeth and good ones at that. She said that they had "run out of proper food". My silent question was WHY? It's not like they can't predict who'll be there for lunch, is it? I put some green puree with a bit of brown puree on a spoon and tried to feed it to Mum. The spoon was too big and the food was all 'gloopy'. The sponge and custard, on the other hand, went down like a dream.

During the feeding a nurse came in with Mum's midday dose of tablets. Monica asked and we learned that one was the Trazodone and the other an anti-sickness tablet to counteract some of the other medication.

I was struck by the fact that Mum made no attempt at all, during those three hours, to get out of her chair.

Wendy and Monica were glad to have visited Mum and taken another trip down memory lane together. I learned that Mum and Wendy had been to see Gene Vincent, when they were teenagers, and had gone back stage and got an autograph and a kiss from the heart-throb.

I went to put the chairs back in the lounge, which was empty but for two ladies sitting in heavy duty recliner chairs. I spoke to a shouting lady and stroked her shoulder, offering soothing words and immediately she calmed down. What bothered me was that there were no staff around. This lady was so easily placated, but for nearly two hours she had been left alone to cry out.

As I left those rooms I spotted four nurses sitting together in the dining room. Another resident approached them and was told to "go away" as they were having a break.

When I passed the office, I saw at least six nurses sitting in there.

I appreciate that they may have been doing a 'hand-over', a review, or any other legitimate and worthy business; I also appreciate that the staff need to have breaks during their shifts at work, but surely not all at the same time? To be in a 'Challenging Behaviour Unit' with about a dozen members of staff, but nobody available for the residents was to me quite appalling.

Monica and Wendy were also shocked that nobody had come in to see Mum, except to bring food and medication.

* * *

Yesterday Isabelle took me to see the new challenging behaviour unit in Cotgrave. It's not far from Kirk Way, but the Sunny Meadows setting is more tranquil, surrounded by pines and countryside. I was very impressed by the ideology of the new senior nurse. He is all for the challenge and for not doping everyone up. They sound very enthusiastic and, as said, they have beds. The manager took us for a tour of the units and I filled out some paperwork. She said that she would do an assessment of Mum within the week.

Later I had a strange call from a nurse at Gold Acre. She said they had removed Mum's wedding ring and put it in the safe for me to collect, because Mum's hands had gone all puffy "with all the walking around she does".

She also said that Mum had taken a little fall. The doctor had seen her and she was fine, but they had had to sit her down for a while, "for her own safety", even though they prefer her to walk about freely...

She left me wondering if someone had passed on my concerns about the bucket chair again.

* * *

Mum was warm and smiley today. I talked about family and she seemed to respond with understanding and emotion.

A nurse came through to tell me that the manager of Sunny Meadows was in the office doing Mum's assessment.

She came to speak with us and we told Mum she was moving to a nice place in the country. I don't think she understood, because she doesn't know where she is now. The manager said they were considering moving her next Wednesday. It seems very sudden. We don't even know about funding yet.

* * *

November 2009. I spoke to the social worker this morning to see what he knows about Mum's move and if there's any news on the funding issues. He knew nothing about her discharge and was shocked that such a decision could have been made before anyone knows which departments will be paying for Mum's care. He was equally surprised that Sunny Meadows have accepted Mum without clarification of funding too.

At 11:00 I got another call from Mum's nurse at Gold Acre to say that the taxi for Mum has been booked for Wednesday at 10:00, and could I be there to meet them at Sunny Meadows and help her to settle in. I suppose they will sort the funding details later.

Now another phone call from Gold Acre to say that Mum's discharge will have to be delayed until the funding decisions have been made.

Am I surprised? I am disappointed though.

* * *

On the whole Mum is much the same, mostly seeming content, but using less of her capacity and saying very little. She always enjoys hugs and kisses and the occasional massage, but seems half asleep most of the time.

* * *

Happily, I was able to go to Little John's funeral in Heidelberg, to say goodbye and to share some memories with his other dear friends.

Today I got a surprise call from Kirk Way, the home with a waiting list of five when I visited in October. They have a spare room now.

My initial response was to assume that five people had died since I visited, but that was not the case, and I felt rather foolish as they explained that everyone on the waiting list had already secured 'alternative accommodation'. I have also found alternative accommodation, but whether it will still be available when she is finally discharged is anybody's guess.

* * *

At 11:00 I went to a Christmas party for staff and 'friends' of Gold Acre. Mum is still there.

The ward manager sat making small talk, but also said that the psychiatric nurse, who was present at the original MDM, was supposed to have written to me a fortnight ago to explain the final decision and get Mum moved.

But she hasn't and they haven't and therefore, we can't.

I went in with Christmas cards, sherry, mince pies and chocolates. I took a CD of children singing Christmas Carols and Mum cried with joy. She tried to sing along, but no words came out.

Monica came too and we all shared laughter and stories.

* * *

CHAPTER 21

It's the twelfth day of Christmas and time to take the decorations down.

The results of my recent enquiries are as follows:

The discharge coordinator states that Mum should be having her care funded by social services, but they are denying receipt of the necessary information regarding the Panel's decision. I asked him to find out himself from the PCT if possible.

The social worker complained of aggravation and claims that the NHS have made a mess of this. Apparently there is a common procedure – every case that goes to Panel concludes with a decision that is recorded on a standard proforma. Social services can then commission the discharge. However, there is no written evidence of a Panel meeting.

Apparently Sunny Meadows also charge above the standard care-home rate, so someone will have to pay the difference. He says there is nothing I can do, but he anticipates a speedy resolution.

It seems to me that both parties are pointing the finger at the other and we are "piggy in the middle".

* * *

Mum was fast asleep in her chair and I couldn't wake her for ages. The nurse told me they had given her a half dose of Lorazepam "because of her shakes". Despite the 'Cepra', she seems to be jerking more than ever. She managed to wake enough to open her mouth and eat her dinner.

* * *

On the last couple of visits I have found Mum lying in bed in the middle of the day. I know that on previous visits she had been gradually sliding down the chair until her bottom fell off and she landed on the floor. The staff apparently tried all sorts of tricks to keep her upright and said they would ask the Physio for advice.

Mum seemed quite happy in the bed and was very sweet tempered. After talking to her for some time she suddenly said, "I love you!"

It was strangely moving and completely unexpected.

Mammy has incredibly good skin – clear, soft and completely un-blemished, except for the scars from the fire. Her legs have no hairs, no scars and no visible veins. Mine look like a London A-Z map in comparison.

Today she was chuntering away in her semi-comatosed state saying, "Yes I know. That's right..," in a very conciliatory way.

She responded to my funny quips and giggled. I even thought she might get up and dance to 'Heartbreak Hotel'. That would have been great.

I haven't seen her standing for some weeks now, which makes me sad.

* * *

Two weeks ago I phoned to prompt the two guys from NHS and social services.

The man from NHS said that they were accepting responsibility for not informing social services properly. He also said that the manager of Sunny Meadows had been off sick and therefore he hadn't been able to speak to her.

The following day social services had some good news: their manager has commissioned the move on the basis that, although the NHS had lost the original documents, everything was in order. He had also received a copy of the fees from Sunny Meadows, which presumably means that they still have a place to offer Mum.

Three hours later I got another call from the same guy in a very different frame of mind. Having looked at the cost of Sunny Meadows, his manager is now asking, "Why does she need a 'Behavioural Management Unit' when she no longer has behavioural problems"?

Apparently Sunny Meadows charge about £600 per week for that special unit. I don't know what they charge in the nursing unit.

What was the point of the whole assessment process then, if the final decision is determined by cost?

I am content that Mum is at least settled at Gold Acre and is being reasonably well cared for – certainly better than I could do. But I also know that they cannot keep her there.

I had set my heart on Sunny Meadows as a place that could meet Mum's needs positively, but I wonder what type of home they will say she needs now? Probably the cheapest. I feel quite frustrated and disheartened by it all.

* * *

On Monday, Sunny Meadows were asked to reassess Mum's needs to sort out the discrepancies.

The social worker agrees with me that Mum has had severe behavioural needs and has the potential to present them again, especially in a new setting, with more noise and a probable change of medication.

Sunny Meadows also previously said that Mum would need the 'Challenging Behaviour Unit', rather than the general nursing unit there. So now we await Sunny Meadows' reassessment.

My social worker said today: "You could write a book on all this!"

"I am doing!"

* * *

Today I read that carers "save the UK an estimated £87 billion a year through caring at home". I can't say I am surprised, if homes charge £600 per week.

The manager at Sunny Meadows intends to visit Mum today and report back to Panel tomorrow.

* * *

I phoned the ward manager at Gold Acre for an update today:

Sunny Meadows have reassessed Mum and feel that Mum no longer needs a challenging behaviour unit, but that her needs could be met on their nursing dementia unit. He said that he was therefore now looking to discharge her by the end of the week.

I thought it best to phone Sunny Meadows to check. The manager confirmed that, due to Mum's deterioration, their nursing dementia unit would be sufficient to meet Mum's needs, as she is no longer mobile nor challenging. She said she would be happy to offer her a place there.

I reminded her that I had found the nursing dementia unit to be extremely noisy. I also said I was concerned that the reason Mum was no longer mobile was that she has been confined to her room, her chair, her bed and sedatives for so long now, in order to "keep her safe" and manage her behaviour. I shared my concern that Mum would have to stay in her room at Sunny Meadows for the same reasons.

The manager does not think Mum will relearn to walk, because of the loss of muscle tone and the level of her dementia now. She was very sympathetic and said she has noted in her report that I am concerned about the noise level in the bigger unit – it has sixty beds – and that I might want to consider a smaller home. However she feels confident in their ability to meet Mum's needs and intends to bring Mum out of her room into the quieter areas during the day.

She sympathised and said that the ward manager at Gold Acre had been angry about being made to wait so long for this decision. She said I must make up my own mind.

I don't feel I have an option to look for anywhere else, as Gold Acre are ready to discharge her this week.

I feel angry that Mum and I are being pushed about like this. Mum is still so young; she should have been encouraged to walk about and dance. Maybe I should have gone daily to ensure this. I am cross with myself for allowing her to become immobile and not challenging her care plan more, for not giving her more exercise.

I didn't feel I had the right to question her care though – you don't argue with Consultants, doctors and nurses, do you?

I spoke through tears to Debbie and her questions echoed mine: let her go there, where at least she seems to be wanted? Or find somewhere else before the end of the week? She was sympathetic, but the decision and action will remain mine.

I spoke again to the social worker. The Panel are meeting on Wednesday to discuss the new recommendations and I should hear from him on Thursday. He said he was happy with Sunny Meadows' assessments and that it was a good safety net, because if Mum's behaviour does change, she won't have to go far to be cared for in the challenging behaviour unit. He said he trusts the Manager's judgment, but there is no way of gauging how Mum will respond to the complete change of place, smells, carers and noises.

So I await the decision on Thursday morning. I told him I would be at a funeral on Thursday and would want some notice before she was discharged, so that I could be there with her.

* * *

It came as a shock today to find a phone message from the ward manager of Gold Acre saying that Mum would be discharged tomorrow (Thursday) morning at 10:30.

But the funeral begins at 10:30, so I cannot be at Sunny Meadows to greet Mum then. I feel very tearful.

I courageously phoned Gold Acre again, to question the short notice and request some lee-way, but he was adamant. The funding is now in place so they have to discharge her tomorrow.

"She will be well looked after... go whenever you can; that will be fine".

I want to see Mum today. Now, before she leaves there.

* * *

As I arrived, the ward manager was just leaving. I suspect neither of us wanted to see the other. I was not feeling very charitable towards him at that moment, despite choosing to forgive.

He tried to be reassuring and I kept my responses brief: basically, had I known she would end up in a nursing home, rather than a specialist home, then I would have chosen a smaller home nearer to me. He said I can move her again any time I wish.

It was important for me to see her one last time at Gold Acre. I also wanted to log some of Mum's favourite CDs, so that if they don't make the journey to Sunny Meadows, I won't lose them forever, as I did the ones at the St Peter's Wing.

Music is the one thing that clearly links Mum with her soul and her past; it is significant to her well-being, not just any music, but specific: Gene Vincent, Elvis Presley, Buddy Holly, Carl Perkins, Billy Fury, The Everly Brothers and others that I wouldn't know just off the top of my head.

Three of her favourite CD cases were empty and I couldn't locate them.

Some things I had already brought home in anticipation of the imminent move that never happened in the Autumn.

When I found Mum she was sitting up in her chair, which was encouraging, but her face looked so sour. She looked as if she had had a stroke - her eyes were half closed, but her left side, especially the eye and mouth, were drooping down and she had a very grey look.

I tried to be chirpy, but was getting no response at all and, as she couldn't see me, I let the tears fall and prayers rise.

I felt exhausted. If only I knew how to help.

Suddenly she sat bolt-upright in the chair, eyes staring wide ahead.

"You made me jump!" I laughed.

She laughed too, relaxed and then shuffled her bottom back into the chair a little. I was so thrilled. It just got better. She carried on sitting up and shuffling back, and I joked about the 'six-pack' she'd be getting from all the sit-ups.

I was even delighted that she was hallucinating again and talking to Tacker and Cacker about the babbies. I even joined in the conversation as if I understood.

Every time she sat up I hugged her and she smiled or giggled and again she said, "I love you."

I can honestly say that I love you too, Mammy and today you cheered me up so much.

* * *

Whilst I was out, the social worker rang Simon to report that no decision has been made by the Panel as yet – they have not even met – so Gold Acre are clearly acting independently again.

Still, I'll go to the funeral in the morning, then drive straight over to Sunny Meadows. I may even arrive before Mum.

* * *

Now I feel really cross. I was getting ready for the funeral and answered the phone to the ward manager of Gold Acre, who told me that Mum cannot be discharged today, because the funding has not been confirmed.

I was feeling so frustrated, but calmly asked why he thought the funding had gone ahead when the social worker had clearly told me that the Panel would not meet until Wednesday.

"He told you that", he asked, "and you withheld that information from me?"

I reminded him that *he* was the manager and the one with authority, and that I had questioned the short notice yesterday.

"You should have told me about the Panel meeting," he continued accusingly.

"I can't believe you are turning this around now, when you have clearly made the mistakes." I stuttered.

"It means you can go and find somewhere else though, since you said you don't want her to go to Sunny Meadows; you can find her a smaller place."

"I am going to put the phone down and think about this now," I said, shaking, and we both hung up.

* * *

After the funeral service I came home to see what else I could find out. My social worker and his team manager were not available, so I went back to join the funeral crowd at the wake. She was a very loved and well known lady. I was glad to be there.

So many people I know have died since I moved to Nottingham. I don't want anyone else that I know to die for a while.

PART 4

Sunny Meadows Nursing Home

CHAPTER 22

Finally the decision to go ahead was made and Mum arrived at Sunny Meadows on Tuesday 23rd February.

A few minutes later I arrived. Gold Acre staff had left and the new carers were unpacking her belongings. I had brought her "This is your Life" book, a CD player and some more of her music (It looks like her CDs didn't come with her).

I was disappointed to learn that the bedrooms are on the first floor, which means a wheelchair in the lift for Mum.

I stayed for several hours as she was clearly distressed by the journey, the change and the noisier environment.

Mum was sitting in a chair near the door, which was a relatively calm area, but the main entrance was busy with human traffic, phones, buzzers, a TV, a lady banging and there was Kate.

I learned a lot from Kate. She thinks out loud in very clear sentences. I learned that Sunny Meadows is quite understaffed and that one of the cleaners now has to help out with the caring; that second sitting is best for lunch, as it is in the smaller dining room and is much more civilised, and I learned about the contents of the string bag attached to her 'zimmer frame', which she takes everywhere. She is like a sports commentator revealing each thought and observation and made it clear she was unimpressed that they had admitted yet another resident into what she saw as over-stretched resources.

When Mum started to cry Kate shook her head saying, "That's all we need now! No use crying in here, you'd better learn to laugh or something instead."

She also helped as Mum kept sliding out of the wheelchair at lunch. Kate went to find help and came back with the manageress and another lady, who helped Mum get back into her chair. I appreciated Kate and her frankness and thanked her later.

A man, who was feeding his wife, told the carer in the diner that his wife needed the toilet.

The carer said, "She'll have to wait. I'm on my own just now."

On her own? With sixty residents.

After lunch, when Mum was in a recliner, I spoke to the nurse in charge, who appreciated the "This is Your Life" booklet, and away I went.

* * *

It's exactly ten miles each way to Sunny Meadows from home. These last two afternoon visits I found Mum sleeping in her bed. She seemed very comfortable and peaceful. I am told that she joins the other residents through the morning and lunch, then sleeps for a couple of hours and goes back down at about 16:00. They say she is very settled and they haven't had to give her any Lorazepam.

I'll have to come during a morning session to see if I can get Mum standing or walking.

I'm concerned about Monica at the moment. She has been suffering for some time, but has recently been told that she has diabetes and cancer. She had a scan yesterday and goes for surgery on Friday.

* * *

Today I went early and found Mum sitting in the quiet lounge. She was tearful, but doing her 'sit-ups' again.

After cheering her up I took the opportunity to invite her to walk. She responded positively so on her next sit-up I took hold of her hands and asked her to come with me. To my delight she assented and ascended. She stood rather wobbly for some time whilst I hugged her properly and when she seemed steady, I asked her to come walking.

She made the right movements with her legs, but it felt like there was Velcro on the soles of her slippers, which didn't leave the ground. I supported her back with my left arm, guided her hand with the other, whist talking lots of encouragement and a bit of brute force... But she walked. We walked the length of the big lounge and back again.

She was happy to sit back down, but she was aware of having done something good.

I was so happy and the staff and some of the residents were cheering her on too. It was the first time they had seen her walking since she had arrived.

I really hope they find the time to walk with her on a daily basis. It must help them if she gets a little exercise and remains mobile. It may help with the sliding out of the chair habit too.

I will try to visit in the mornings, so I can take her for walks myself and feel a little more useful.

* * *

Sunday evening I got a message to say that Mum had fallen out of bed and landed on her head.

The call came about 20:00, so I have been wondering, if she gets up at 16:00, after her post-lunch nap, has her supper and then joins the others in the lounge, how could she be found on the floor of her bedroom before 20:00? Had they not brought her down for supper? Or had she had the accident earlier in the day, but only just reported it? I'm also not sure *how* she could have fallen out of bed. I usually find her cocooned by pillows, with the 'cot-sides' up as well. I have not seen Mum make that amount of effort or movement for many months.

Apparently she has been checked over and she is okay.

* * *

I felt deflated today. Mum was in the lounge again, but her eyes were closed and I got no response from her at all. No talking, no walking, only tears.

I was able to stay and feed her her lunch . It seems she only gets pureed food now. I must find out whether that is for ease of the staff feeding her. If it is, I could request proper food on the days that I feed her myself.

I asked about the accident: it seems that they do get her up for supper at 16:00, but then they take her straight back to her room afterwards. That means she spends about eighteen hours a day in bed.

I don't think that can be good for her, but I do appreciate that it is difficult for them to manage her if she's constantly sliding onto the floor. I'm sure there must be some chairs that can support her better.

I hope someone puts her music on, if she's in her room for so long. Apparently there is now "no way" that she can fall out of the bed again.

* * *

Saturdays seem to be the best days for visiting Mum. Today we had success with a walk-about and a certain amount of joy.

I found her nearly on the floor when I arrived, but she hardly slipped at all whilst I was there. She does cry a lot. Sometimes with joy, pain, fear, sadness, nostalgia - even some seeming recognition of something provokes a tearful response.

It makes me sad when my words and endearments cause her to sob, but in some inexplicable way she seemed to be glad of my company today.

I spoke again with 'commentary Kate', who said how Mum "can't seem to bend in the middle" and could really do with a different sort of chair.

It's satisfying to be able to say hello to the other residents and offer them a smile and company too.

* * *

Kate is right, Mum doesn't bend in the middle.

She was crying a lot and nearly on the floor when I arrived today. Also there were what seemed like cries of pain, but she cannot tell me where the pain is, so I feel quite helpless.

Last week I asked if it was her head that hurt and she said it was, but it is so difficult to diagnose anything because she cannot communicate reliably.

I mentioned it to the ward nurse, who said she'd ask the doctor to check her over. I asked them to check in case of a urinary infection, which she is prone to, and that she wasn't sore from the incontinence pads.

I did get Mum to walk a bit today, but she stopped a couple of times and made as if to sit down. Fortunately I was able to pull a chair underneath her just in time.

I fed her the pureed meal and blancmange again, whilst looking enviously at Steven's braised steak and vegetables, followed by apple pie and custard. I really must remember to ask about the food.

Steven and his wife are both over ninety and have been married for sixty-nine years. She comes every day to see him and is so lively and encouraging. It seems to be much more heart-breaking when the sufferer is aware of the suffering.

I am not sure whether Mum is now suffering or not. Whether she suffers in silence, trapped inside her head and body, or just exists in each moment oblivious of the last. But I know she sobs a lot.

* * *

Mum looked particularly pretty, freshly bathed and fluffy, but very grumpy today. I couldn't get her to walk - I asked and she said no, and seemed to mean it.

The doctor had said that Mum has nothing obviously wrong, but she still seems to be in discomfort.

I also asked about the pureed dinners. The nurse said that Mum came to Sunny Meadows with instructions from the hospital to have 'soft' meals. We talked it through and, thankfully, I was then able to feed Mum braised steak, carrots, brussels, mash and gravy, followed by rhubarb crumble and custard. Yummy. I could tell she was enjoying each morsel as I named it and put it in her mouth.

On my way out I saw the manager, who said they had tried a beanbag for Mum to sit in, but that it didn't work. I asked about the harnesses that I remember seeing at Gold Acre. She has never seen them but will look into it. It is a problem that needs solving as it causes Mum and the staff an unnecessary amount of stress.

I also managed to manicure Mum's sharp claws, which do get sort of locked into one's flesh.

I went to see Monica today, after seeing Mum. She has her son staying to look after her, which is a blessing. She was in discomfort after her surgery, but was much more positive about it all.

She told me lots of stories about my Haynes' family too. I've heard much of this from her before, but I don't seem to remember the details properly. I love Aunty Monica very much. She wants to come with me to Mum's next time.

* * *

The aim of the NHS Involvement Strategy Group is, as the name suggests, to ensure greater involvement between all the stakeholders in the NHS. That means making sure that the views and opinions of the service users, carers and staff, at all levels, are heard and taken note of in the policies and practice that then ensue.

I am still thinking about what a carer shared with me at the last NHS Involvement meeting: he has been seeking advice on what happens when the Alzheimer's sufferer loses the ability to swallow. Apparently, life is not prolonged by feeding through a drip or peg, so the person is left to starve to death. He said it takes about nine days.

He was asking if, when the time came, he could give his wife something to end her life painlessly and not to have to starve her to death. He reasoned that if you allowed a dog to starve, you would be imprisoned.

He didn't get a favourable reply from the medics, and the thought of watching her suffer is clearly bothering the poor man.

It is such a complex question.

Can you ever condone putting a human out of their misery/ ending their suffering/ playing God?

And why do 'they' not administer food and water intravenously?

Does a dying person get the grace they need to cope? Do they drift into euphoria with the hunger, as they approach the gates of heaven? I don't know.

I suspect that dying is not as bad as we fear.

I *am* afraid of unbearable pain, but not afraid of death. I look forward to the resurrection, to being with God and understanding some of the immense mysteries that life on earth has kept veiled. I'm not in any hurry to leave this life either; it's such a beautiful world and I love so many precious souls here.

I don't think I've fulfilled my purpose yet either. None of us is indispensable, but there is a task just for me and I need to find it and get on with it.

* * *

When we got to Mum's, I introduced Monica to Kate, who I'm becoming very fond of. Mum was sleeping soundly in a super new lounge chair, which was on loan. One of the carers said Mum had managed to fall out of it, but maybe I misunderstood.

We were tickling Mum, talking to her, kissing her, shaking her, but nothing would rouse her.

She woke to be fed, but not enough to really acknowledge anyone around her. I was sad not to be able to get her walking again, but glad that the chair seems to be saving everyone the distress caused by Mum sliding onto the floor.

* * *

Today Mum was much the same – very sleepy and away from the world.

I feel like she has given up, but it may just be the result of the lights gradually going out in her brain.

Apparently having a harness is seen as restraint and loss of freedom, so the super-chair has, I believe, been ordered instead. They seem to be doing their best to solve this problem.

* * *

Change is life.

There was a sadness about the dining room today. Mum and Steven were at the table and Steven was cross. No Jude. Mum was fast asleep and slipping out of the wheel chair again. Steven was frustrated and didn't want to eat his dinner.

Jude came looking frazzled and worried, because she was late. They are so lovely; they kiss and declare their love for one another and she keeps him in line in a very kind way. She instructs him with a gentle reminder that "a gentleman is always polite" and needs to say thank you for the kindness of others.

Jude said that Steven was the first man to ever fly over the North Pole.

They are an inspiration, fighting valiantly this trial. She is worried that they might move Steven into the challenging behaviour unit soon.

There was dignity and treasure in the sadness, but it all felt so heavy.

* * *

On Saturday Mum was already in the dining room, alone, sleeping.

Her face looked terrible – a huge black swelling bulged over her right eye. There was some redness under the eye too, but it looked as if she had taken one neat bash.

I looked around with a question mark on my face to the carers around, but they were all busy. The manager was there, doing the 'meds' and eventually I got her attention. She came over looking shocked at the sight of Mum, as if I had just whacked her myself. She didn't know what had happened . Nobody knew. Surely the person bringing Mum to the dining room must have noticed.

I asked for an ice-pack and some paracetamol, but the best they could do was a wet flannel. A member of staff then brought two paracetamol capsules for Mum and knowing that Mum would chew the foul tasting things, I asked if she could have liquid paracetamol instead? Apparently not without a prescription.

I watched her screw up her upper lip as she slowly chewed the capsules one by one. Fortunately she still had her dinner to wash away the nasty taste.

I wondered whether she could still feel pain, given that she can't have made much of a fuss about whatever had hit her eye, so, as I held the wet flannel gently on her eye, I tried to pluck one of the bristles from her chin. She yelped.

Successful experiment, but unsuccessful in removing the whisker.

Apart from the slow chewing, she was as if asleep and all felt quiet and lonely.

"No Steven today?" I asked a passing carer.

"No, he's gone upstairs."

Their leaving us is a loss. As the carer said, once the funding bodies have made their decisions, you have to comply otherwise you lose the funding. It seems strange that one of the most 'with it' of the residents gets moved to the CBU. I don't know the full story, but again it seems to have been a decision made without the consent of the carer or the 'service user'.

* * *

Monica sounds much better. The stitches have been removed and she goes for radio-therapy in a few weeks.

Simon came with me to see Mum today, for the first time in nearly two years. She had birthday cards all around and seemed to respond a little as I read them all to her.

She appeared uncomfortable again, though more awake and was able to give some possibly appropriate yes/no answers to indicate that she was in pain. Her eye was very purple and still a little swollen, so I requested more paracetamol.

Shortly afterwards a doctor introduced himself and kindly said he would prescribe something soluble. Good.

Simon and I tried to get Mum up and walking, but she wouldn't open her eyes or stand today.

I hate seeing Mum so distressed and tearful and be unable to help in any way. I kept wiping her tears and telling her that she is safe and loved and that all is well now, but I don't know whether all *is* well. Maybe she still has a head full of monsters? Or questions and feelings that she wants to talk about and can't? Maybe she is in terrible physical pain or discomfort inside? I just do not know.

I fed Mum whilst Simon rubbed her back and imitated a goldfish. Mum still enjoys her food and it does seem to be always hot, tasty and nutritious.

I asked about popping up to visit Jude and Steven, but they told me I shouldn't go up there as the residents can be unpredictable and violent. They didn't say that when I went to look around initially.

Simon was glad to have seen Mum again. Obviously he noticed a huge change in her.

* * *

Today I had the review at Sunny Meadows with the social worker and one of the senior nurses. The purpose of the meeting was to review Mum's care and make sure we are all happy with the situation and, if all is well, for him to close the case as far as he is concerned.

Sunny Meadows were satisfied that they could provide for Mum's needs and I expressed how happy I was that they seemed to be addressing the challenges well. I mentioned the chair, which I understood to be on order and asked if it would be possible for Mum to have a bedroom on the ground floor, if one were to become available.

They promised to look into it, as it would make Mum's naps less isolated.

I am thankful that Sunny Meadows are willing and able to meet Mum's needs.

The social worker also reassured me that I can call on him "if normal channels of communication fail" and I need help.

I am grateful for the social worker's help over these two years. He has always had Mum's best interest at heart.

We then went to see Mum and her now rich-purple-and-yellow eye. Again her eyes were closed, but I did see some sweet smiles.

I sometimes think about how I will feel when she does die. Part of me will be happy for her to be free of the limitations and frustrations of her physical disability. I will miss her, but it won't be like missing a mum – I dealt with that a long time ago – it will be like losing a very treasured part of my life. I feel such tenderness towards her nowadays.

Her time, and mine, is in God's hands. I believe we will receive the grace to deal with her loss.

* * *

On Tuesday Mum gave an odd chuckled response to my ramblings. It was strange really, as everyone seemed to be good humoured and light, reflecting the Spring sunshine gently warming the conservatory. People made a bit more sense than usual and there was an air of generosity and hope.

Today I took Monica to be scanned and 'tattooed' for the impending radiotherapy. It is always pleasant to be with Monica and the procedure was painless enough.

* * *

I have had a busy week since I last saw Mum, but I feel guilty not going to see her. I feel I have to go late morning, so that I can do something useful, but maybe I should not be so rigid, if that means waiting a whole week for a free morning.

Anyway, this morning the atmosphere was very different again.

The residents were already occupying some of the places in the main dining hall, as the conservatory was closed off for a meeting.

I looked around for Mum and a carer told me that Mum wasn't up yet. I couldn't quite understand what he was saying as, like many of the carers, he uses English as a second language.

I wondered why she was still in her room, so I went straight up. I found Mum looking disheveled and crying, half dressed with her pants and trousers around her ankles. I assumed that someone had been washing her, but there was nobody else in the room.

I showered Mum with greetings and kisses, and covered her vulnerability with the quilt. I felt very sad for her lying exposed like that. A few minutes later a carer came into the room with a flannel and towel. She was struggling to turn and clean Mum and rang the buzzer for assistance. As nobody came, she accepted my help and we managed to get her clean. Then two more helpers came and Mum was ready.

They said that Mum had been jerking and shaking so badly that morning that they decided it was safer to leave her in bed, but I urged them to bring her downstairs and let me feed her lunch in the dining room.

As they put her into the wheelchair I brushed her lovely, long grey hair and noticed that her teeth were very brown and grubby. On closer inspection I was horrified to see that her tongue was quite black. The carer didn't know why it was so black either.

Mammy was weepy again today and seemed to be suffering from deep, unpleasant memories or sensations. After eating she began to calm a little and I asked her for a Mammy smile. Bless her, she smiled for me. She clearly understands some of what is being done and said around her.

I felt so helpless at not being able to alleviate her distress, frustration and sadness. I kiss and stroke her and tell her familiar stories about people she loves, but it all feels so inadequate sometimes.

The carers decided to leave her in the lounge for a while, but I had errands to do, so I left with a sadness.

I didn't feel there was anyone I could talk to about Mum and I felt we were quite alone.

I'm not blaming the carers, they are warm and friendly and they work hard at a very difficult job. I just wish I could do more for her myself.

Maybe there is nothing else that anyone can do? I don't want to leave her for a whole week again.

* * *

Today I was enjoying a Bank Holiday lie-in when Josh burst into my room demanding that I get up.

"Sunny Meadows said you've got to phone them back!"

I felt a bit panicked, wondering what was so urgent, but was told that Mum had eaten breakfast and then vomited, so they had put her back to bed. She wanted to know whether this had happened before.

I got myself ready to go, but still felt a bit shaky.

I found Mum "as snug as a bug in a rug" in bed, surrounded by padding and pillows and looking very peaceful. She responded sweetly to my kisses and words and even had giggles today. She drank nearly the whole beaker of tea, so they brought her lunch, which she ate most of. I then borrowed some heavy-duty nail clippers and set to work on her toe nails which were in a terrible state. I gave her a foot massage and then warmed her feet in snugly socks. The finger nails were long and dirty, so I attacked them too. Shrapnel flew everywhere from those brittle talons, but I managed to gather most of it.

Finally I fixed the CD player and played some Everly Brothers. Mum was such a sweetheart today and I felt very grateful to be there.

I have been thinking about what to do for Mammy when she loses the ability to swallow.

I spoke to Mary (who is a nurse) about those last days. Her aunt had dementia and she believes they gave her extra morphine to finish her off. She told the doctors that they should be wearing black shirts and swastikas. I asked if it wasn't more cruel to do nothing and she said that you can keep them hydrated, even when they cannot swallow, and that this greatly improves their level of comfort.

I am wondering whether I should bring Mum home for her final days, to do just that and keep her company. I wouldn't like her to die alone, especially because she is responsive to warmth and hugs. I don't think I'd want to be left to die alone, even if I am looking forward to being on the other side.

I will look into what *can* be done; I'm sure I could get some carers in to help with the things that I cannot do. I know that Simon will support whatever decision I do make.

* * *

Again I found a message from the night staff at Sunny Meadows. The nurse said that Mum had been having strong spasms and was unresponsive this morning, so they had called out the paramedics, who then decided to take her to A&E. It sounded a bit over dramatic to me, but it's always better to be safe than sorry. She said that only the paramedics were with her. I know from experience that paramedics look after you on the way, but then leave...

How is anyone going to be able to communicate with her? Who will feed her or change her? I thought I must have misunderstood, so I phoned back to check. They said it was normal procedure not to send staff with a resident into hospital.

I phoned A&E and the doctor said she was struggling to find out what the problem was, because she didn't know her history, how she normally behaves or anything. She had done some routine tests and I suggested that she do a urinary test too.

Simon took me straight to A&E, and I found Mum on a trolley behind a curtain. She had kicked off the blanket and was exposed. She had several blood spots around her wrists and wads of cotton wool, presumably from the blood tests.

A doctor came to tell me that they had done some tests and monitoring, but hadn't been able to get a urine sample - you can't really squeeze out the pad, so it will be difficult. Mum had been very noisy and kept throwing her legs over the sides of the trolley, but she calmed considerably within the first ten minutes of me being there.

She had a strange laughter noise too, which was a bit scary and showed her grubby teeth, but it was good that she was laughing. She was also attempting conversation and responding to things that the doctor and I were saying.

They decided that Mum would be better off in her own comfy bed. I agreed and Mum was happy to hear she was going home again too. Her mouth and lips were quite dehydrated, so I fetched water and they gave me some pink lolly sponges to moisten her lips. Mum kept trying to eat them, which had us both laughing.

I was glad to have been with her for that experience, which she handled remarkably well. A couple of friendly paramedics came to transfer her to the next trolley and off she went home again.

* * *

Conor is now confirmed in his faith and all our wonderful visitors have been and gone.

After seeing Mum today I shall go and rattle a tin for Christian Aid and then take Conor swimming.

When people ask me what I do for a living I say that I am between jobs, but I am really quite busy doing a variety of delightful things and cannot imagine finding time to do a 'proper job'.

I think Mum appreciates the precious moments that we share together, and that it all adds to a certain well-being that takes her beyond what she can remember.

She was particularly responsive today and smelled nice too. Her long, shiny hair looks lovely tied in a ponytail and she was dressed in pink and smiling at the kisses and hugs. She also seemed to be focusing better too, like she was actually trying to look at me.

* * *

I have had more thoughts about Mum's final days. Granny said not to worry, as at that stage one is beyond feeling hunger or thirst. Almost like a different state of consciousness, moving up a level into the more spiritual maybe?

I was also reading something by Bruce Chatwin (See Notes 5). The author tells that animals and humans mauled and eaten by the big cats do not feel pain. The cat apparently nips the back of the neck and paralyses the victim – sort of anaesthetised.

I am sure God did design us in a such a way that we are preserved from unbearable discomfort. But then I remember giving birth to Joshua and again I'm not so sure.

I will talk to the home about it all though and see what they have to say.

* * *

CHAPTER 23

I've been poorly all week with headaches, coughing and just feeling weak. Obviously I stayed away from Mum – definitely not something to pass around old folk.

I was missing Mum, so phoned to explain, and Susan (a keyworker) told me that Mum had had two visitors. It was Mum's sister, and her cousin, Pauline.

They found her unresponsive, thin and sleepy, but I think Julia was glad to have gone. I felt a bit jealous, but I have to wait until I am better.

* * *

When I finally went back to Mum, it was school holidays and Conor came with me.

He was great with his Nana and managed to give her a few hugs and kisses without being too concerned about her lack of response.

Mum has a urinary infection and has been put on antibiotics. She seemed especially hot, but with the antibiotics and the paracetamol she will be fine.

She ate her dinner slowly and steadily. I couldn't keep her head from flopping on the table and my left arm is aching now, having used it to keep Mum's head propped up whilst feeding her.

Conor seemed to enjoy the general interest of the place.

I have arranged a proper meeting with Susan to talk about end of life issues on Friday morning.

* * *

Susan was as reassuring as always as we sat out in the sunshine and she had some forms for me to go through.

She talked me through the resuscitation question that I had been through before with St Peter's Wing.

I still don't have a say in the matter, but fortunately I agree with the policy in principle: if she is dying, do not resuscitate (start invasive surgery or put on life support), but any other accident or sickness should be dealt with as thoroughly as with anyone else. It is a "best interests" policy.

The questions on the form are about what Mum would wish if she should be dying – elements of care that are important and what she would / would not like to happen. I'll try to get Debbie to help me fill this one in, or at least to check that she agrees with what I write.

I asked about what would happen from the home's perspective if Mum were dying. They can't do intravenous fluids, as they are a nursing home; if they were a residential home they would be allowed to. How loopy is that?

I don't want Mum to die in hospital, if at all possible and I don't want her to die alone. They said that I can camp down in her room if it seemed best to me.

So, I have decided that it would not be good to bring Mum home for her final days – it would be too traumatic for her and not as comfortable. I'll just move in there instead. I can hold her hand, read her scriptures, play her music and keep her lips moist.

They cannot tell me how or when it will be, but they think they will know from experience when the time is near. It is all such a mystery.

At the end of the meeting I felt much clearer and more at peace.

We came back indoors and I sat with Mum and Annie (another resident). Mum was not quite so floppy and the strain on my arm was much less when feeding her. Annie is like a child in her simplicity and demanding nature. I managed to distract her from banging everything by simply engaging her in conversation, but it meant that Mum didn't get much out of me. I don't think that it matters, as Mum does listen and it is probably better her hearing a conversation than listening to the banging or to my one sided 'conversation' aimed at her. George and Cecil sat together on the next table, so I engaged them too and it was altogether quite sociable and pleasant in the conservatory.

* * *

I sat with George and Mum at lunch again today. Mum seemed very sweet and happy.

She was sitting up more and opened her eyes from time to time. She was also squeezing my hand tenderly, which felt good.

Sometimes I feel particularly protective of Mum and very close – this was one of those days. I didn't want to leave her.

* * *

I have spoken to Debbie about the 'end of life' forms and filled them in as well as I can.

I decided to finally go to the doctor and see if they can prescribe me something to get me through this current depression. My back has also been very painful and I just want to lie down, read or sleep.

I am finding Simon very difficult too – he is just not available most of the time, and rarely emotionally available. I have been feeling very alone and needing some company and some emotional support, but not finding any. I did not want to resort to medication, but I feel I have to give it a try.

* * *

It was not a good idea after all. I was in bed for nearly a week, with some visits, chats and cuddles from the boys and an occasional, "Can I get you anything?" from Simon. I felt like I might never get up again.

Isabelle then came to see me and she was very cross. She went to make me another appointment and took away the medication, which she thought had made me worse. My back was in agony, I was feeling sick and my skin was peeling off my upper body. The doctor said I should rest from the medication and then he would try me on something different.

* * *

Mum doesn't slide out of her chair so much any more. She has a new trick instead – now she flops her head into her dinner. Sometimes she is amused, but of course it is also very messy.

She seems more alert too, which can mean that she is more responsive, but sometimes she shouts and gets cross with everybody.

* * *

I took Monica to see Mum again today and we had a much better time. The other residents are very entertaining and responsive to visitors, so it livens up the atmosphere with someone as easy going as Monica.

Mum was flopping her head into her food again, but was very alert.

After seeing Mum we stopped at a pub in Cotgrave for a carvery lunch. It was lovely to be out doing something relaxing with Monica and not just being in hospitals and meetings. Monica hardly complains about her own health, but I don't think she is well yet.

Simon has made more of an effort recently, and we are spending more time together again.

My mood is much lighter than it was.

* * *

Mum has been fun of late. Yesterday I got her to stand up twice and managed to walk her into the lift to go back upstairs. She was tired out after that and flopped like a rag-doll into her wheel-chair. She was in great humour though.

Debbie, on the other hand, is very stressed out at the moment and is struggling.

At camp, I decided that I should make the effort to go up to Orkney and spend some real time with her. She is delighted.

Simon won't be coming, but he is letting us take the car. I am excited about the trip.

I am also very excited about a new business prospect, as we desperately need an income.

When we returned from camp, I took my films down to the photo shop for processing. The photo shop business is for sale. I talked with the owner and have been thinking and praying.

I can just about manage to scrape the money together to buy the business and get it started. I love photography and feel I could be of service in the community. And I would still be home enough to share family time, make dinners and clean up, and I would still be able to see Mum regularly, as I would continue to employ Hannah, who works there part-time.

I am very excited. As soon as I get back from Orkney, I will start my training at the shop, so I can learn as much as possible in the three weeks before the current owner leaves.

* * *

The trip to Orkney was fantastic in so many ways.

Debbie is living in a beautiful bungalow just ten minutes from the heart of Kirkwall. She is continuing her trade as a tiler and is rapidly making a good name for herself there. We spent lots of quality time together.

We also went over to Graemsay. Clett looks great since its face-lift, and now houses one very happy tenant. We visited Dad's grave and all the inhabitants of Graemsay, who were eager to hear news of Mammy. They really love her and we shed a few tears there.

I did lots of sight-seeing with the boys too. We went round all the amazing ancient monuments and had great fun driving over sand-dunes and playing on remote beaches. The boys kept shouting, "Fun Mum" as we drove happily about.

It was such a well-needed break and a great family time.

I came back armed with so much to share with Mammy, but she was not able to understand a word of it. Mammy no longer knows anything about Orkney and her life up there. Nevertheless, I passed on the greetings and love as requested by the inhabitants of what was once her island.

There have been significant changes for Mum since I've been away. She is now a permanent resident of the upstairs 'nursing' part of the home. The lounge there is much quieter than the one downstairs and she no longer has to use the lift. Her super-chair is there too, so she is usually to be found reclining in that, in the corner of the lounge. There are some very sweet souls in there.

Monica and Wendy have both been to visit whilst I was away, and they also think that she looks very comfortable.

Mammy doesn't say much at all now. She smiles, cries, frowns, grumbles and giggles, but not much else. She still seems to love chocolate and music, but to dislike other noise.

* * *

I have begun training in what is to be my very own business. It is called 'PhotoPlus'. I am learning how to prepare films for processing and how to use and look after the processing and printing machines. These all need careful maintenance – they have to be fed, watered and emptied at least once a day and need to be kept clean and warm – not unlike a living being. I will also have to sort all the business side of things and paperwork, bills and legal requirements. I am glad I did some business training, when helping Simon.

The business is not as busy as I had hoped, but I am beginning to advertise. I am loving the work and the customers. It is such a privilege to be a part of people's worlds like this. Marriages, births, deaths, holidays, anniversaries – all the special moments when people take photographs – I get to see them all and hear the stories behind them. At the moment there are lots of holiday photos and I do feel like

I get to travel vicariously to all parts of the world as I scrutinise each photograph to make sure it is perfectly framed and colour-balanced, before printing it.

I am buzzing with things I want to talk about when I get home, but there's often nobody available to listen. Nevertheless, I am happy, and keeping on top of housework, boy time and visiting Mammy.

Mum is much the same nowadays – hardly responsive, often seemingly asleep. But she does not seem to be in pain and rarely seems disturbed by the monsters in her head. That at least is good.

* * *

CHAPTER 24

This morning I found a message from Sunny Meadows, telling me that Mum is "out of sorts" with a suspected urinary infection.

I was battling away with the wet-lab printer, thinking about Mammy. I was also thinking about Monica . I got such a shock last week to discover that Monica is very poorly now. She is filling up with tumours spreading from the cancer in her groin. She sounded fairly philosophical as she told me how she's a good age, she has her mind and has her family around her.

I got another call from Sunny Meadows this afternoon, to tell me that Mum does have a urinary infection, and that she is dehydrated, as she hasn't been eating or drinking today. So they have called the paramedics to take her to hospital for some IV antibiotics and to re-hydrate her again.

I felt distracted trying to continue with the usual tasks. I didn't know what to do. I wanted to go to the hospital to see her, but didn't want to change my plans to share some food and time together with Isabelle this evening.

Isabelle came up with a generous solution: she would come a little earlier, drive me to the hospital and we could eat later. Fantastic! I realised then how uptight I was, and I was very grateful not to have to drive and do this alone.

* * *

"You will need to think about what you want to happen next!" she said cautiously, as we drove to the hospital. "You will need to communicate it clearly to the doctors too. Have you given this much thought?"

My head started to spin. I didn't want to think about more than the here-and-now. She was dehydrated and had an infection – the next steps were obvious to me.

"The doctors will have to make their own decisions about the best course of action, unless you tell them differently." She ventured.

I was wondering what Mum was feeling and what she would want. Mammy cannot communicate her thoughts or feelings now.

We walked in silence through the blank corridors to find her. Mum had not been accompanied by anyone from Sunny Meadows. She seemed so vulnerable, just lying there in a booth, unknown and unknowing. Nobody to speak for her, to explain, to champion her cause. After hugging and kissing her, and telling her where she was and why, and what we needed to do, we then waited.

I spoke for Mum to a couple of nurses coming to ask questions. I explained that she was never much more responsive than now, that she cannot eat or drink independently, that she cannot stand, walk or use the toilet. She did look a sorry sight, but I have got used to her like that and I know how precious she is.

As the doctor approached, I felt overcome with the sense of responsibility that I had for Mum at that moment.

I explained again what Mum is like normally, what the doctor at Sunny Meadows had said – a urinary infection and possibly a chest infection – and that I would like Mum to have a chest x-ray, be re-hydrated and put on antibiotics.

"Can I ask a blunt question?" Isabelle threw in, with a direct look in her eye.

I panicked inside. This was not in the script. Was I going to be able to respond adequately?

"Do you want the hospital to resuscitate your mother, or to let nature take its course?" she asked.

"I want them to give her fluids and antibiotics, and to take care of her as they would any patient coming in dehydrated and with a urinary tract infection." I reiterated, relieved that I knew the answer to that one.

"Thank you for letting me know," the doctor said thoughtfully, "we have to make difficult decisions at times, but we will do what you have asked and will give her forty-eight hours to respond before considering any other course of action."

Our two hours' car-park allowance was nearly up, so with the mission accomplished, I said my goodbyes to Mum, feeling bad as I walked away. She seemed so alone there, but I trusted she would be well cared for and would hopefully respond quickly to some fluid and antibiotics. I promised to come back the following day and stay as long as possible.

As we walked back along the corridors, I reluctantly mulled over what the doctors might have done if there was nobody there to speak for Mammy?

Both deep in thought, Isabelle broke the spell as we went outside towards the car park.

"Why do you want to keep her here?" she quizzed.

"Well, because they can't do the intravenous stuff at the home. I wont let her stay longer than necessary. As soon as she responds and can eat and drink again, she can go back home."

But that isn't what she meant.

"I mean, why do you want her to stay in this life? She has no quality of life at all. Naturally she would die now if you didn't intervene, and she could go peacefully. If she recovers from this, she will go home and have to come in again for the next thing. She will continue to suffer. You had the power to make that choice. We are all different!" she added, as if to excuse my poor choices.

I was shocked at Isabelle's perspective. I thought she had been urging me to make it clear to the hospital that I did *not* want them to just leave her to die. How could I play God and tell them when to let her die? Don't doctors have to do all they can to save life? Is the alternative not euthanasia?

I didn't know how to handle these thoughts. I wanted to change the subject and make my unpleasant thoughts and confusion go away.

We ate our supper with an awkwardness. I felt a heavy burden of responsibility and felt accused of doing wrong to my mother, of making a bad decision, of having my head in the sand.

It was true that I wanted to bury my head. I wanted reality to be different.

Isabelle may well have been right, but it felt wrong to me. I did not feel I could make such a decision on her behalf.

I felt exhausted and drained with the responsibility, and as I went to answer the phone to Simon, who was away again, Isabelle went home.

* * *

My sleep last night was disturbed and I was glad that Sunday had come. I went to church needing to find my strength and refuge.

I feel anxious, jittery and rather spaced out.

I need to go back to the hospital. Conor and Josh both want lifts and I want to serve them. They too are precious and I need them to know that they are. I wish Simon were home to help me.

* * *

I found Mum with a needle in her arm, allowing fluids to infuse her in a slow steady drip. The oxygen tube was still at her nose, making it feel so cold to the touch as I kissed her lovely face. She looked so much better today and my anxiety and confusion were dispelled.

I texted Debbie with the good news and felt positive again. Another twenty-four hours of this and she would be well again.

I gave myself up to five hours at the car park and I enjoyed my time with Mammy.

* * *

I should tell Julia, Monica and Wendy that Mum is in hospital. I never thought to tell anyone apart from Debbie until now.

It is Monday and I am back at work. I'm glad the shop is quiet today. I'm waiting to phone the doctor after he's seen Mum on his morning round.

Finally the hospital phoned. It was the consultant, doing his 'morning round' at 15:00.

He said that Mum was not responding to the antibiotics and that we need to talk. He leaves at 17:00, so I closed the shop and went straight up there.

I phoned Julia, who was planning to see Mum after work, so I hoped she'd be there when I was.

I felt nervous.

Please God, let me hear and speak what is true and right.

I put a twenty-four hour ticket on the car and headed up to where they'd put Mum, on the top floor.

Julia was there waiting. She last saw Mum a year ago.

I let the ward staff know that I wanted to see the consultant before he left.

Mum had no oxygen apparatus, no saline drip and nothing going in the needle in her hand. She was looking fairly peaceful though. I was not looking forward to hearing what they had to say.

They had certainly not given her forty-eight hours on antibiotics and saline, even if they had started it the moment I left on Saturday. I suspected that in reality she hadn't had more than thirty hours.

The consultant who had phoned came in, and when he said, "Hello, Avril" she shot him the cheekiest smile. She never could resist a man's voice. Julia and I laughed.

The consultant knelt down on the floor between Julia and I, and told us that Mum had not responded as they had hoped and that it was her time to go.

He said that they could delay death by keeping her hooked up to tubes, but that ultimately she was not going to live without them now. He explained that the kindest course of action was to let her die with dignity and free of pain, now that her time had come.

"But you didn't give her time to let the antibiotics work," I argued meekly, to which he replied that it was not going to make any difference - that her brain and body were closing down, and to prolong her dying would be unkind to her.

He seemed to make sense and Julia seemed content with his prognosis and verdict. He explained that she would be put on a morphine pump which would keep her pain-free, without the need for frequent injections.

He said we need to look after ourselves now and be assured that the ward staff would look after Mum.

Julia left and I phoned Debbie. She was due to come down in a fortnight anyway, but that was obviously going to be too late to see Mum.

I wondered how long she would last without food and water.

Debbie could leave Orkney straight-away, but still not arrive until the following night, by which time Mammy might be gone. She has to do what she can and I have to do what I said I would do – which is to stay with Mum until she dies, so that she does not die alone.

I phoned home to let them know my plans and invited the boys to consider coming to say goodbye to Nana.

I talked to Mum and began to pray for us all, settling into this new space.

I spoke as much hope and encouragement as came to me, then found a Gideon Bible in the side cupboard and began reading scripture out loud.

I was beginning to feel a strong sense of peace.

I knew that Mum was a Christian, and that her future is in God's eternal Kingdom.

She was finally going home.

* * *

Simon, Josh and Conor came over on the bus and the boys looked very solemn and awkward as they said their goodbyes.

Josh seemed most upset by it all and still couldn't bring himself to give her a kiss. They were all supportive of me staying with Nana and as I was so upbeat about it all, they seemed reassured. I was set for my evening vigil and knew that Simon would look after the boys during my absence.

The shop would have to wait, although I had asked Hannah to work whatever hours she could.

Debbie had decided to catch the 06:00 ferry, to be with us the following evening, so I relaxed to enjoy my time with Mammy.

The hospital staff were agreeable to me staying.

* * *

The nurses said they hadn't been trained to use the morphine pump prescribed by the consultant, but said they would inject morphine every hour or so.

Mammy seemed very distressed and uncomfortable, writhing about the bed and moaning, until the morphine calmed her again.

I thought about the long list of medication that she had been taking each day in the home: Haloperidol, Levetiracetam, Lorazepam, Procyclidine, Trazodone and Senna. Three of these cause drowsiness.

Mammy had had none of those drugs since at least Friday night and it was now Monday night. No wonder her body was in distress.

The chair in the room was uncomfortable for me and there was no heating on, which wouldn't normally bother me under a quilt, but it did make it difficult to sleep - next to the huge top-floor window, tired and keeping half an eye on Mammy.

Mum seemed warm enough, although she didn't have a temperature, which surprised me, as I thought the first sign of an infection was always a high temperature.

Mammy's temperature, blood pressure and everything was normal, even on the day she was brought into hospital. I found myself wondering: why the staff at Sunny Meadows had suspected a UTI? When had she last had anything to eat or drink? Why had they not managed to get her to drink even some water?

Silly questions no doubt, and academic at that point, but doubts do begin to creep in, especially in the early watch of the night, when one is tired.

I was glad to see day breaking on Tuesday – the rare event of Dawn seeing the dawn.

I replenished my large mocha, guiltily ate a sandwich in front of my starving mother and looked towards the day ahead with hope and peace. I remembered the consultant's advice to look after myself and decided that rest, exercise and food were going to have to become a part of my vigil too.

When the day-nurse came on duty, she managed to hook Mum up to the morphine pump.

The nurses must have washed and changed Mum a dozen times since I had been there and I had done none of those things for myself. So I went down to the hospital shop and bought myself a clean shirt and came back to wash and change.

* * *

Wendy has been to say her goodbyes and to share her memories and a few tears. Pauline came too.

Mammy seemed very peaceful again.

I was looking forward to Debbie arriving.

Julia came again and brought a favourite Everly Brothers' CD, which she played and sang along to. Apparently she and Mum used to sing duets to The Everly Brothers when they were growing up. Julia shared many beautiful memories with Mammy, and I found myself grateful to hear of those happy times that were before my life began.

I shed some happy tears for the life, music and dancing that Avril had once enjoyed so much.

I read aloud again from the Psalms, sang, prayed and drank countless cups of mocha, but forgot to eat again.

Debbie arrived about 19:00 with her daughter, Rachel, and Rachel's new baby, Skye. Skye was not allowed in the ward.

Debbie and I shared a few hours together with Mum, before I reluctantly left and went to take Rachel and Skye home, to eat and sleep.

I was sure that Debbie needed a good sleep as much as I did, after her long trip down from Orkney, but she insisted that she hadn't come all that way for a good night's sleep anyhow, so I didn't argue.

After accommodating Rachel and baby, enjoying some time with my family, and making sure that my mobile phone was on charge, I gratefully snuggled into my own bed.

Debbie had promised to call me if there was any sign of Mum deteriorating.

* * *

I slept uninterrupted, but was ready to leave for the hospital as soon as the boys were off to school. I left Rachel sleeping.

Debbie had found the chair so uncomfortable that she had attempted to sleep on the window-sill, but she was in good form and had enjoyed her night with Mammy.

Mammy was looking peaceful and more beautiful than ever.

Debbie and I were taking it in turns: the day-times we spent together at Mum's bedside and the evenings we split – one at my house and the other at the hospital.

By Wednesday I felt desperate not to endure another sleepless night, so I asked and they found me a mattress which I sank into and slept like a baby.

Mammy seemed to be getting progressively better and didn't look like she was going anywhere.

I kept playing her music and holding her hand.

"Don't be afraid, Mammy!"

* * *

Spring seemed to arrive whilst I was in there; I was still in boots and a leather coat, whilst the people outside were walking about in summer vests and sandals.

Debbie and I were discussing the next steps, which at first felt a bit strange, with Mum still alive and possibly hearing all we were saying, but on the other hand we hoped she was approving and reassured about the arrangements.

Debbie felt sure that Mammy wanted to be cremated and we both knew that she wanted her remains to be next to Daddy's little plot, in the kirk on Graemsay.

Later, Debbie showed me a photograph of Mammy lying on the grass next to Dad's memorial stone and we smiled.

We decided it would be good to have Mum's funeral here in Nottingham. Her family and friends here would be able to say their farewells and Debbie would arrange a memorial for her Graemsay friends later in the year, when Mum's ashes could then be interred next to Dad's.

It all felt very surreal.

* * *

Last night, I went to ask the nurse what the procedure will be when she actually dies. She seemed a bit surprised, but gave us a booklet explaining everything, saying that she had never given one out *before* death. We needed to discuss it together though and at the rate Mum was going, Debbie would be back in Orkney before Mum finally let go.

I also remembered that Mum and I had talked about her donating her brain to Alzheimer's research. We never did anything more about it, so I went to ask the nurse about that too. She didn't seem to know, but promised to look into it.

* * *

The hospital chaplain visited us again today and has found out about brain donations. It is very straight-forward apparently: I just need to sign a form when I go to get the death certificate at the hospital's bereavement centre.

That's good. I wonder what else I might have forgotten.

* * *

Debbie is heading home again tomorrow morning. So tonight – Friday – she is going to my house to get a good sleep before her journey. I can't believe Mammy is still here. I wonder how her body keeps going with no water or food for nearly a week?

This morning Mum's nose was frosted with white crystals (I had to take a photograph).

Most of the time Mammy is peaceful, sometimes with eyes closed, sometimes open. Always her mouth is open and I use the pink lolly-sponges to moisten around her gums and tongue so they don't crack up.

Yesterday they gave me some saliva gel to use instead of water and it seems more comfortable.

It is strange just watching and waiting, knowing that we can do nothing but be here with her. Mammy doesn't respond to voices now, not even deep, manly voices, but I hope she knows we are here and is comforted by that.

What if she's just waiting to be left alone so that she can die in peace? I'll warn her from now on when I leave the room, in case she wants to slip quietly away in private. Maybe I sound very cold about it all, but I feel very much at peace here and privileged to spend this momentous vigil with her as she passes into her heavenly inheritance. I hope she is not afraid to die, so I keep reassuring her from scripture.

* * *

Occasionally I am overcome with emotion and weep beside her, but that is when I think she is afraid or in discomfort. I have had to request some supplementary shots of morphine today as she seems to be moaning and contorting her body. I don't want her to have any more pain now.

Debbie said her tearful farewells last night, reluctant to go but very glad to have shared this time with Mum. I am grateful to have had Debbie here for these few days too. It has been so good to share this together and have the necessary space to discuss what we want to happen next. It has also allowed me two nights with my family, and in my own bed.

I am becoming a little weary of these walls, noises, bleeps and long corridors, but I don't resent them.

Julia has come to the hospital after work every day to see Mum. I have appreciated that too. It feels good to have some family support.

Simon has done sterling work keeping everything together at home and I am doing what I want to do for Mum, for as long as it takes.

I couldn't even consider not being here with Mum now. I want to see her when she sees Jesus coming to take her home.

I am spending a lot of time reading the scriptures aloud to Mammy and have written down a list of possible verses to read at the funeral.

I hope that someone will read from the Bible to me when I can no longer do it for myself.

Monica has been too poorly to come to see Mum. I know she would have done had she been able.

* * *

The ward sister from Sunny Meadows phoned me at the hospital today to ask when Mammy is coming home. It was hard telling her that she is not coming home and is "on the end of life pathway".

I don't like that expression too much, but can't think of a better one for them to use.

The ward sister seemed genuinely shocked and it set me to doubting and questioning everything again. I did ask about their decision to send Mum into hospital, but I don't recall how she responded.

I am left with many questions. Mammy was admitted with a urinary tract infection and dehydration and now she is on the "end of life pathway". The ward sister's shock has reawakened my own.

* * *

Sunday morning is here again. This is church for me at this moment.

Mammy seems to be weaker today and I get the feeling that turning her and changing her is causing her unnecessary stress. She is no longer passing any waste products and she doesn't seem to be getting any bed sores, so I'm sure they can leave her be. They know better though and I don't want to be critical of the nurses as they do such an amazing job. She does have an enormous blister on her heel though, so we have put a pillow under her calf, to prevent the blister rubbing or bursting.

The last couple of days I keep thinking that perhaps Mammy is just not ready to die. I keep wanting to give her some water to drink, and feel like she would then just get up and walk home with me.

I also wish I had thought to bring Mum home, to die there instead of spending her last days in hospital.

I'm not beating myself up about it, as I don't think Mum knows where she is, and she does have familiar music and voices around her all the time. Maybe it is best as it is.

It is as if her body, mind and soul have gone, but all that remains is her spirit. So my spirit is staying to commune until hers is ready to depart. I really did not expect her to last this long though – she is such a tough cookie and physically there is not much wrong with her.

I can't help thinking that the decision to put her on the end of life pathway was maybe premature. I suppose it is natural to doubt one's decisions and choices?

I think I will write down my questions again and see if I can speak to the consultant, if he's around tomorrow, because now I cannot remember what he said to me and Julia last Monday.

*   *   *

That Monday was a week ago now and even the nurses seem to be amazed that Mammy is still in the land of the living.

I hope I can see the consultant today and am brave enough to ask my questions. I don't want him to think that I am blaming him/them for anything.

I don't know how I feel today.

I don't know how Mum feels either. The nurses say that she will not be aware of anything now, but they also say that the sense of hearing is the last to go, so I must stay positive and reassure her at all times.

I have read most of the New Testament to Mum since being in here – it truly is the most amazing book.

Debbie got home safely last night.

*   *   *

Question 1 – Why did you think she was ready to die?
Question 2 – What do you think she is dying of?
Question 3 – What were the crystals on her nose?

The consultant seemed surprised to see us still here too.

His answer was that ultimately he knew from years of experience that Mum was ready to die, and that to let her go naturally was the best and kindest thing to do. (I think Isabelle knew that too.) He also said that she is dying of "brain failure" – that the Alzheimer's disease has killed her brain.

I mentioned how I wished I had been able to take her home and he apologised for not suggesting it to me. He was very understanding and said that he welcomes these questions, as they keep him in the real here-and-now and keep him checking himself to make sure he doesn't lose touch with the most important aspect of his job, which is people's lives.

I showed the consultant the photo I took of the crystals on Mum's nose and he said it is likely to be urethra, as it does excrete in crystalline form. Urethra is what the liver gives off when it has failed – it is also supposed to make you feel high and happy.

So I am feeling a bit better again now, but very tired.

Julia was also feeling out of sorts today. She hasn't missed one day coming to see Mum in hospital yet.

Each day you think it is going to be her last one.

* * *

Well, today *is* Mammy's last day on earth and the beginning of her life in heaven. Today, 28th March 2011 at 19:30 she slipped away.

And I nearly missed it!

Joshua arrived unexpectedly and flopped down on my mattress, saying that he was missing me and didn't feel right. I was still holding Mum's hand, but talking to Josh, and Mammy gasped and stopped breathing. We both stared at her to see if there was any movement, any pulse, any sign. After what seemed like a couple of minutes, Josh suggested he should go and get a nurse.

While he went I hugged Mum and held her tight, feeling sort of dazed. Suddenly, she took such a loud gasp of breath, right in my ear, that I jumped.

Two nurses came in and looked at Mum, their faces looking suitably composed and sorry, as their glance confirmed that she had gone. They checked her and then left us alone.

"I feel good again now!" Josh said, almost apologetically, "I knew something was going to happen."

"And you can have a lift home too!" I smiled.

I could go home, but was slow getting my things together. I kept looking at Mammy to check that she really had gone. I tried closing her eyes and mouth but couldn't.

To let go myself and leave her empty body there, was harder than I imagined, after such a long vigil.

I felt light-headed and lost. I am glad Joshua was with me to keep me down to earth and to ease me back into the other reality of day-to-day life.

I am looking forward to a long night's sleep and a home rest for a day at least. The thought of facing funeral preparations and my business are a bit too much just yet.

I thought I was well prepared for the final day, but I feel flat and numb now.

I have let family know.

Tonight I will have a glass of wine to celebrate Mum's life and her journey home.

Epilogue

CHAPTER 25

The appointment at the Cooperative Funeral Care was straightforward as we already knew what we wanted to do.

The funeral is booked for Friday 8th April at 15:00. I can hardly believe that Mum is going to have her funeral on the anniversary of Daddy's death. She will like that. I'm sure they are laughing about it in heaven already.

The Bereavement Centre gave me a bit of a shock. I met with a lady to discuss and sign for the brain donation and she asked me if I wanted to see the death certificate. I did. It read: 'Cause of death: Septicemia caused by a UTI'.

"She didn't die of a UTI, she died of brain failure, according to the consultant", I protested.

"I would have understood if it said that she'd died of dehydration or starvation, but not septicemia!!"

Did it matter, I reasoned to myself, but somehow it did. I fought back the tears.

"If she was dying of an infection, why was she not treated for it in the normal way? Why did the consultant tell me she was dying of brain failure?"

It all seems academic, but I felt very confused and like I'd been cheated - like we had cheated Mammy and not given her the correct treatment. Had we let her die unnecessarily? I was crying in my inability to comprehend this.

The consultant was sent for and he did his best to explain why it was written as it was, but I am still not convinced.

There seems little point in asking them to alter it, as we cannot alter anything else.

I arranged to donate Mum's brain to research, as I know Mum wanted to be useful and she certainly doesn't need it any more. If it can help to discover more about this horrid disease and how to prevent or cure it, then this last act will be invaluable.

Nevertheless, I left feeling disgruntled and in just enough time to get to Shakespeare Street for our midday appointment to register her death.

With the paperwork done, I caught up with some work and I bought the Nottingham Evening Post to read the Notice of Death I had sent in.

HAYNES -- Avril. Passed peacefully on 28th March aged 64. Beloved Mammy to Debbie and Dawn, sister to Julia, Nana and friend. We celebrate your life thanking God for all the precious moments. Enjoy the welcome into Glory. Funeral service 15:00 on Friday 8th April at St John's church Oakdale Road.

* * *

Wendy has sent me an article that Mammy herself wrote for her school reunion magazine in 1996, a year after Daddy's death. I think I would like to read that at the funeral – to let Mum give her version of her story. It is amazingly concise to say it spans over thirty years and it expresses beautifully her rose-tinted outlook. It was her story just before the Alzheimer's began to take a hold, just after her "world fell apart... when Dick died aged 49".

I want to write a tribute and I have asked Debbie, Julia, Wendy and Monica to write something too.

I will include any written tributes in the last appendix.

Isabelle has agreed to read the Scriptures. I think I'd like to go with the Psalm I was given in hospital: Psalm 116 .

I have had an overwhelming number of sympathy cards and am amazed at how quickly news travels. I hope that these people will come to the funeral and stay to share their memories.

I have also been to see Monica finally. She is in pain and has an enormous log/leg which inhibits her movement because she cannot bend either the knee or the hip. It was good to see her and share more memories and stories. I hope that she does write some of them down to share at the funeral.

Monica seems to think that she will be following shortly behind Mammy and commented on how they began a life together on Graemsay all those years ago and now will be ending their lives together too.

* * *

I have ordered the flowers to go on the coffin, but I want to pick some flowers from my garden too, as I want Mum to have wall-flowers, daffodils and forget-me-nots, scented garden flowers that Mum would have admired and said, "They don't look real, do they?"

There is a lot of paperwork, arrangements and decisions to be made and lots of expense. I am glad that Debbie and I had enough time to discuss much of this together.

The day before the funeral, Mum's body will be available for viewing in the chapel of rest. I have decided that she should wear the cerise suit that she wore to my wedding. I am not sure that I want to go there, but I will if somebody else would like me to go with them. The boys don't want to go.

The majority of Mum's ashes will be buried alongside Daddy's, but we are going to reserve some to be buried up at St John's and her name remembered alongside her Mum and Dad's on the memorial vase.

* * *

Debbie is going to the Chapel of Rest with Rachel, James and baby Skye, and Conor has now decided to go with them.

My cousin also wanted to go with me, so I met her at the Funeral Parlour. We had a bit of a wait and a good laugh as the people in the Parlour couldn't *find* Mum. My cousin commented that she can't have gone anywhere. It was farcical and we couldn't stop giggling about it.

The formality of the occasion made me a bit nervous, but I remembered how it was seeing Daddy's dead body and how obvious it was that he was no longer in it. So I thought I was prepared, especially as I had also seen Mum as she died.

She did not look like Mammy at all. Perhaps it was because they had removed her brain and had to re-stuff it with something?

Neither of us really wanted to stay long, so we said another farewell and went to the pub for refreshments in the glorious sunshine. I could easily have stayed there, enjoying the company and another pint, but I still had much to do for the morrow.

* * *

Yesterday was Mum's funeral, Daddy's anniversary and Pa's birthday.

There was a good turnout – only Monica, Tony and the Orkney friends were missing. Monica's sons came on her behalf though and we read one of Tony's poems as his tribute for Mum.

Conor gave out the order of service leaflets and Alzheimer's envelopes to the guests at the church. Everybody sang and spoke beautifully. I read two tributes and Julia read hers.

Josh played "Amazing Grace" on the guitar, accompanied by the church pianist. We had Elvis' version of "Amazing Grace" for the entrance and Everly Brothers "All I have to do is Dream" for the exit. The other song that we sang was "Morning has Broken", as that was Mum's favourite song when I was little and Mum had taught me to sing it, word for word.

It was great to finally relax a little and enjoy the company of family and friends, as we all shared happy memories of Mammy's life.

After the pub, we went back home and continued our celebration, with more food, drinks, music and the complete slide show of photographs of Mum. We talked and laughed long into the night.

I think we gave her a good send-off. I could feel her finally smiling and at rest, but sure she was having a good jive too.

I really missed Monica though and want to see her very soon.

* * *

Chapter 26

Monica has gone. Friday 13th May 2011. And she had the last laugh there too. Daddy would have stayed in bed on that day, as he was terribly superstitious about Friday 13th (unfortunately for Mum, her birthday, being 13th April, often fell on a Friday).

Monica was tired and ready to go. At least she was at home and had her family with her. On my last visit, she told me that she loves me and said "Goodbye Dawn". I held her, saying my prayers and goodbyes and then left the room to sob.

It feels very lonely – like the last of that generation is now gone and we have to step up and be the grown ups now.

It is difficult to see my last link with the Haynes' family go. But for Monica, I would never have known much about the Haynes' lot. I really wish I had written down some of her stories.

* * *

Monica's funeral was on 26th May in Arnold. It was a beautiful sunny day. There were other family members, whose names I knew, but that was all.

I read the Gospel at the funeral, but I couldn't stop the tears. After the service many of us went for refreshments and a family get-together.

* * *

August 2011. We all went up to Orkney for the burial of Mum's ashes.

I have now made the journey by plane, train, coach and car, over the years. This time we went on the train.

I was carrying the big, green plastic jar containing Mum's ashes, a couple of books for Debbie, but very little else in my back-pack.

On one of the trains, I was chatting with a lady, telling her all about Orkney and how remote and beautiful it was, and she asked me "Where is your Mum now?"

I bluntly pointed to my back-pack and said "She's in there! We are taking her up to be buried."

The poor lady didn't seem to know how to respond, so I laughed and apologised for being so direct, but explained that Mammy had been so poorly, was now at peace in Heaven, and we were fulfilling her desire to be buried next to her beloved. The lady relaxed then, but she wasn't quite as chatty after that.

* * *

The service was all set and the islanders on Graemsay were going to be at the Kirk, having prepared a spread for us all for afterwards.

Mine, Debbie's and the Pastors' family nearly filled the little boat to Graemsay.

We walked through sunny tranquility to the Kirk and, from the top of the hill, we could see the little patch dug out in preparation, with the hills of Hoy creating a serene but stunning backdrop.

It felt strange for our family to all be there together – the first time ever.

After the simple service, I was driven up to the community hut by a 12 year old. The folk on the island had many memories of Mammy, Roger and Monica to share.

It was all such a fitting tribute and Mammy's ashes are now lying next to Daddy's, just as she wanted it to be.

* * *

Debbie was baptised two days later. She was terrified of going into the sea and was nervous about giving her testimony, but it was glorious and Debbie was so brave. She was glowing (and shivering) when she came back out of the water.

I felt so privileged and blessed to be there.

Later we went out for dinner to celebrate a momentous week of journeys, endings and new beginnings.

Rest in Peace, Mammy.

* * *

Finally... March 2014. Three years after Mum's death, I put Mum and Dad's remaining ashes all into a sealed box and wrapped it in hearts, then we went up to St John's for a short service.

Debbie, Rachel, Olivia, Skye, Conor and cousin Pauline were present. I did a reading from Revelations 21 (about there being no more pain or tears in heaven and all things being made new) and placed the box in the pre-dug hole. The service finished with a blessing and hugs all round.

I was surprised to find myself choked with emotion when I put the box in the ground. I had not felt anything until that moment.

It began to rain as we departed and the most beautiful rainbow then appeared and stretched over the expanse of sky in front of us as we made our way home. It was a sign of hope and promise to me.

* * *

Five days after the burial of Mum and Dad's ashes was my forty-ninth birthday. I realised then that Dad died five days before Mum's forty-ninth birthday. Just another one of those 'coincidences' that has run throughout all these deaths and anniversaries.

I am so grateful to have been able to get to know my mother and have the privilege of caring for her when she most needed it.

I still struggle with doubts and questions about choices along the way, but I have to remind myself that I *did* do my best for her with what was available to me.

This is all we can do: to trust God, do our best in love and accept responsibility for the choices we make.

* * *

A NOTE FROM THE AUTHOR.

Between writing these memoirs and their publication, more than time has past.

A lot of painful things happened in our lives (as in so many people's lives) and I had mountains of insecurity and fear, which, until I exposed it honestly and brought it to God for healing, caused me to seek reassurance and comfort by having others feel sorry for me. I complained about my burdens instead of allowing God to heal me and set me free. I was a mess.

I knew I had forgiven my parents, but I wasn't healed of the pain or of out-dated coping strategies.

Many said "Why? She doesn't deserve it, it's not your duty."

Others sympathised and assured me that I was doing a great job.

But, through it all, God began to expose my motives and heal the deep, underlying issues.

As the Holy Spirit gently reveals my issues, I am able to own them and bring them to God for healing.

I did my best for Mum and my family, but my pain and attitude robbed me of much of the joy that we could have all enjoyed. I was always trying to prove to myself and the world my self-worth. Often I did the right thing, but for the wrong reasons.

This year I turned fifty and I am finally moving into my destiny and enjoying life without striving, fear, and worrying about what people think. I have the assurance that God planned for, wants, and loves me just as I am.

I thank God for His persistent love and patience and for giving me the courage and strength to take one step at a time.

I thank Jo Naughton for her powerful "Healed For Life" ministry; my therapist for her honesty and holding; my church for being human; and all my loving family and friends, who reflect that love and patience and have never given up on me, despite my sin and mess.

I am still a work in progress, but I am now living my life to the full, as Jesus promised.

My heart can now echo St Paul's, as he writes, "This causes me to be confident that, because the Lord has begun such a good work in you, He will enable you to complete the purpose He has for you." Philippians 1:6 (The Truth Bible)

I pray that you will be richly blessed by His grace and truth.

IMAGES

Front Cover painting: - 'Fork In The Road' by Michael Tolleson, Autistic Savant Artist, Kent, Washington, USA. <u>www. MichaelTollesonArtist.com</u>

Author photograph: - by Alexander O'Riordan

Photograph of Mum:- by Debbie Haynes

* * *

Bibliography

[1] Reproduced with kind permission from Carers.org/key-facts-about-carers <accessed April 2015>.

[2] "Alzheimer's at your fingertips" by Harry Cayton, Dr Nori Graham, Dr James Warner. [Class Publishing, 1997]

[3] BBC2 Terry Pratchett: "Living with Alzheimer's" 03/02/09 9pm.

[4] "RCN neutral on assisted suicide" from the BBC News channel 25/07/09.

[5] "Songlines" by Bruce Chatwin

APPENDIX 1

Early, Middle and late stages of Alzheimer's (page 10 of Alzheimer's At your Fingertips) (Note 2)

Early Symptoms: "Because the onset of the disease is gradual, it is difficult to identify exactly when it begins. The person may:

* show difficulties with language;
* experience significant memory loss – having particular problems with short-term memory;
* be disorientated in time;
* become lost in familiar places;
* display difficulty in making decisions;
* lack initiative and motivation;
* show signs of depression and aggression;
* show a loss of interest in hobbies and activities.

* * *

Middle Symptoms: "As the disease progresses, problems become more evident and restricting. The person with Alzheimer's disease has difficulty with day-to-day living, and:

* may become very forgetful – especially of recent events and people's names;
* can no longer manage to live alone without problems;
* is unable to cook, clean or shop;
* may become extremely dependent;needs assistance with personal hygiene, including visiting the toilet, bathing and washing;
* needs help with dressing;

* has increased difficulty with speech;
* wanders and sometimes gets lost;
* shows various behavioural abnormalities, such as unprovoked aggression or constantly following the carer around the house;
* may experience hallucinations.

* * *

Late Symptoms: This stage is one of total dependence and inactivity. Memory disturbances are very serious and the physical side of the disease becomes more obvious. The person may:

* have difficulty eating;
* not recognise relatives, friends and familiar objects;
* have difficulty understanding and interpreting events;
* be unable to find his or her way around in the home;
* have difficulty walking;
* suffer bladder and bowel incontinence;
* display inappropriate behaviour in public;
* be confined to a wheelchair or bed.

* * *

Choosing a Nursing Home

For many caregivers, there comes a point when they are no longer able to take care of their loved one at home. Choosing a residential care facility—a nursing home or an assisted living facility—is a big decision, and it can be hard to know where to start.

- It's helpful to gather information about services and options before the need actually arises. This gives you time to explore fully all the possibilities before making a decision.
- Determine what facilities are in your area. Doctors, friends and relatives, hospital social workers, and religious organizations may be able to help you identify specific facilities.
- Make a list of questions you would like to ask the staff. Think about what is important to you, such as activity programs, transportation, or special units for people with AD.
- Contact the places that interest you and make an appointment to visit. Talk to the administration, nursing staff, and residents.
- Observe the way the facility runs and how residents are treated. You may want to drop by again unannounced to see if your impressions are the same.
- Find out what kinds of programs and services are offered for people with AD and their families. Ask about staff training in dementia care, and check to see what the policy is about family participation in planning patient care.
- Check on room availability, cost and method of payment. You may want to place your name on a waiting list even if you are not ready to make an immediate decision about long-term care.
- Moving is a big change for both the person with AD and the caregiver. A social worker may be able to help you plan for and adjust to the move. It is important to have support during this difficult transition.
- A Social Worker will also arrange for a nursing assessment to determine the needs of the person and suitable homes that can meet those needs.

Appendix 2:
Where to go for help

Things to find out about:

1. GP – for a referral to psycho-geriatric Consultant
2. Lasting Power of Attorney – someone close and trustworthy should have it! (See next section)
3. Social Worker – for a needs assessment and help coordinating all levels of support.
4. Attendance Allowance or Disability Living Allowance/ Pension Credit (See next section)
5. Carers Allowance – not much, but it is for you, the carer.
6. Respite care – so that you can go away and have a break from caring, with peace of mind.
7. Day centres – where trained carers offer activities and company for your cared-for.
8. Volunteers – Alzheimer's Society (Befrienders); Age Concern (Volunteers)
9. Trent Crossroads – 'sitting service': Your Social Worker can refer you for this.
10. Home help for the cared-for.
11. Carers' groups: Social Services run these locally, according to need.
12. Local Support Groups: eg.: 'Take-a-Break' in Nottingham.

Useful Websites for information:

http://en.wikipedia.org/wiki/Dementia a definition of dementia

http://www.alzheimers.org.uk

http://www.alzinfo.org

http://www.alzheimers-research.org.uk/ for info about current research.

http://www.nhs.uk/conditions/dementia/Pages/Introduction. aspx?url=Pages/What-is-it.aspx

http://www.nice.org.uk/Guidance/CG42

http://www.rcpsych.ac.uk/mentalhealthinfo/olderpeople/ memoryanddementia.aspx memory tips

http://www.fordementia.org.uk/ carers issues

http://www.bbc.co.uk/health/conditions/dementia1.shtml

http://www.neurologychannel.com/dementia/treatment.shtml

http://www.dementialink.org support services

http://www.mednwh.unimelb.edu.au/tips on ageing/ dementia_tips.htm managing symptoms

http://www.guardianship.gov.uk information on Lasting Power of Attorney.

Helpful organisations

Age Concern: 1268 London Road, London SW16 4ER. Helpline: 0800 009966 (7 days a week, 7am-7pm) Tel: 020 8765 7200 Fax: 020 8765 7211

Provide information and advice to older people and their carers. Promotes a positive attitude to older people.

http://www.ageconcern.org.uk/

Alzheimer's Society: Gordon House, 10 Greencoat Place, London SW1P 1PH.

Helpline: 0845 300 0336 Tel: 020 7306 0606. Fax: 020 7306 0808

Email: info@alzheimers.org.uk

Care and Research organisation for people with Alzheimer's disease and other forms of Dementia.

http://www.alzheimers.org.uk/

Alzheimer's Society of Ireland: 43 Northumberland Avenue, Dun Laoghaire, Co. Dublin, Ireland. Tel: 00 353 1 284 6616

Gives support to families and provides information on Alzheimer's Disease and dementia.

http://www.alzheimer.ie/

Alzheimer Scotland: 22 Drumsheugh Gardens, Edinburgh EH3 7RN. Tel: 0131 243 1453; Fax: 0131 243 1450; 24 hour Freephone helpline 0808 808 3000; E-mail: alzheimer@alzscot.org.

The leading Scottish charity working with, and providing support to, people affected by Alzheimer's and other forms of dementia.

www.alzscot.org

Help the Aged: 207-221 Pentonville Road, London N1 9UZ

Tel: 020 7278 1114 (Monday-Friday 8am-6pm then answer phone)

Helpline: 0808 800 6565 (Monday-Friday 9am-4pm)

Fax: 020 7250 4474 Email: info@helptheaged.org.uk

Provides practical support and help for older people to live independent lives, particularly those who are frail, isolated or poor.

http://www.helptheaged.org.uk/en-gb

Carers UK: 20-25 Glasshouse Yard, London, EC1A 4JT. Tel: 020 7490 8818;

Fax: 020 7490 8824; info@carersuk.org; **Carers Line:** Tel: 0808 808 7777

Wednesday and Thursday 10am-12pm and 2pm-4pm.

To help anyone who is caring for a sick, disabled or elderly frail friend or relative at home.

http://www.carersuk.org/Home

'for dementia'

6 Camden High Street
London

NW1 0JH **Tel:** 020 7874 7210 **Fax:** 020 7874 7219 **E-mail:** info@fordementia.org.uk

The mission of 'for dementia' is to improve the quality of life for people affected by dementia.

http://www.fordementia.org.uk/

Admiral Nursing DIRECT –

Telephone or email advice and support for family carers, people with dementia and professionals.

Email:direct@fordementia.org.uk

Telephone:0845 257 9406

Mind (The National Association for Mental Health) –

Website:www.mind.org.uk

Telephone:0845 766 0163

Trent crossroads

Unit 2.1, Clarendon Business Park, Clumber avenue, Sherwood Rise, Nottingham, NG5 1AH

Tel: 0115 9628920

Financial help/benefits

Carers in the UK are entitled to Carers Allowance and could also be entitled to other benefits from the government.

The benefits system is complicated. Claiming can be difficult and time-consuming. If you are not sure whether you can claim, get advice from your local Citizens' Advice Bureau, a disability organisation, a carers' project or an Age Concern branch.

- Carer's Allowance
  The main benefit for people looking after a family member or friend who is ill or disabled.
- Help with council tax
  Carers may be able to reduce their council tax bill and / or claim Council Tax Benefit
- Incapacity Benefit
  For people who are unable to work because of illness or disability.
- Income Support / Pension Credit
  For people on a low income who do not have to look for work e.g. carers or people aged 60
- Employment and Support Allowance (ESA)
  ESA has replaced Incapacity Benefit and Income Support for those who are not well enough to work and making a claim on or after 27th October 2008.
- Disability Living Allowance
  For disabled people under 65 who have difficulties with their personal care and / or mobility
- Attendance Allowance
  For disabled people aged 65 or over who have difficulties looking after themselves
- Working Tax Credit
  To claim you should usually be over 25 and work for at least 30 hours a week.
- Child Tax Credit
  For people who look after a child under 16 (or under 19 in education).
- Help with health costs

People on a low income or who have certain medical conditions may be able to get help with health costs

- Help with fuel costs
  How to get help with heating costs and what to do if you receive a large bill.

- Social Fund
  Helps people to pay for one-off costs e.g. funeral, winter fuel payments or cold weather expenses

- Housing Benefit
  Helps people on a low income to pay their rent

- Jobseeker's Allowance
  For people who are unemployed or work part-time and are expected to find full-time work."

(from Carers UK financial help website.)

Appendix 3: Tributes

Dawn: This is really a tribute of thanks

Thanks to my Mammy for giving me life and, despite many hardships, for doing her best, as such a young mum, to give us what we needed in life. I am grateful for all the skills she passed on to me – for teaching me to read, write, draw and speak French – even before I ever started school! For teaching me to mend and sew and knit. For giving me a love of plants and gardens and for teaching me how to make something good out of what many would have thrown away.

But here today I want to thank all of you who have come to celebrate Avril's life with us. I know you all have your own special memories of Avril. It is a comfort to me to see you all here. Many of us were mourning the loss of Avril long before she died.

I also want to thank all those caring people who looked after Mammy when her early onset dementia began, especially the good people of Graemsay, whose care and oversight kept Mammy in the home that she loved so long after she could have survived there alone. I am especially grateful to the late Roger, to Tony, Cathy, Mick, Ethel and the other islanders.

When I moved back to Nottingham and Mammy came to live with us, we received so much help for which we were all very grateful. Social Services, doctors and occupational therapists were patient and understanding and opened the way for me to provide the best care. Mum had some wonderful befrienders too – Liz, Val and some excellent 'sitters' from Trent Crossroads who made it possible for me to have some independent time to myself, but they also were able to bring out some of the playfulness and humour in Mum in a way I could not. We were also provided with occasional breaks of 'respite care', allowing me and the boys to go camping and do some of the things that Mammy could not have safely enjoyed.

I would like to say a very special thank you to Simon and to Joshua and Conor, for making it possible for me to welcome Nana into our home for all that time and for helping me to entertain her...

Eventually we had to admit defeat and Mammy had lots of other carers – at Broad Glade, St Peter's Wing, Gold Acre and then latterly at Sunny Meadows in Cotgrave. I want to thank all of those carers, on Mum's behalf, for all those acts of kindness and love. I could go on with the list of people I wish to thank and even then I would miss somebody out.

So thank you all; for caring, for visiting, for praying, and for remembering Avril today.

The article that Mum wrote in May
1996 Avril Haynes

I last saw the majority of my classmates in July 1962. I began work at Raleigh in August and 3 months later I left to have Debbie! She was born in May and in the July I married Dick – far too young and loads of problems, but absolutely no regrets. Dawn came in 1965 and completed our family.

After a house fire in 1969, we moved to Calverton, to a caravan in a lovely quiet and isolated spot – our first taste of 'country living'. Four years later, the girls were growing and we moved to a house in Mapperley, where we spent the next 14 years. Dick was working as a motor mechanic and me running a little clothes shop called 'Nine till Five', on Woodborough Road. I learned a lot there and developed my knitting and designing skills.

The girls grew up and moved on and we once again thought about the 'good life' somewhere – an island to ourselves appealed to us! We didn't find one, but got a close second with Graemsay, a small offshore island with 10 households – 27 people including ourselves – with a tiny Post Office and a one-roomed school which had 4 pupils at that time, but only one now. Clett is an old stone croft house with 8.5 acres stretching down to the shore. We look out to the Hoy Hills and across to Scapa Flow; the landscape changing constantly with the changing light and seasons. It's generally mild, but quite wet and certainly windy! The summer sky doesn't darken and the winter sky sometimes shows us the Aurora Borealis – a magnificent sight! There is no crime, no pollution, no hassle. I created gardens and sold my knitwear to local shops and Dick kept the island's cars running.

On the 8th April 1995 my world fell apart when Dick died very suddenly, aged 49.

Debbie whisked me off to Spain where she lives with her husband and the grand-kids – Rachel 9, James 4 and Olivia, who was born just hours after Debbie heard of her Dad's death. Spain is quite nice, but

I couldn't live there, nor in London where Dawn is with Eddie and their son Joshua, nearly 2, and another to come in October. Dawn is a teacher there.

I am getting my life back together again now with the help of Dick's sister Monica, who has come to live here too. We have 10 sheep, 4 goats (2 adults and 2 mischievous kids) and a cat. My job as Postmistress keeps me busy for all of 4.5 hours a week and now we are planning a caravan park!?...

Julia's Tribute

I have a very vivid memory of being in the coal house with Av. I must have been about a year old and I was trying to do what Av was doing and that was eating coal. Mum said that Av had tried to get me to eat some, but as I didn't have many teeth it was proving to be pretty difficult.

Av was five and a half years older than me so when we were younger she always thought I was a nuisance and according to some, that was possibly true. As I got older I would torment the life out of her in one way or another. When Av was expecting Debbie, Malcolm would come round to our house and because she was not allowed to see him because of the situation she was in, Malcolm would ask me to pass Av a letter. This I did, but not before I had managed to persuade him to give me some money for doing this important job. I have to confess that sometimes if he did not give me money I would take the letter and then taunt him that I was not going to give it to her. Malcolm would chase me down Dickenson Street and up St Anns Well Road, but I was like a whippet in those days and he never caught me.

Av eventually married Malcolm and went to live with him at his mum's house. I then realised how much I missed her and would often go round to see her and Debbie. Av then had another baby that unfortunately died at birth but was named Avril – the same as her. Dawn arrived shortly after that and I loved to go out with them; Av pushing this massive Silver Cross pram and both girls in the pram.

Av had many hurdles to get over in her life. She was badly burnt in an accident when the girls were very young and she always struggled for money, but she never complained and she just got on with it.

I remember Av was happiest when she was dancing and singing. She loved to watch her cousin Micheal jive with Val and so she would practise with me. She would lead and be the man and I would spin round and round and I thought it was great. We would dance to Elvis's 'Jail house Rock' and she would be so happy and I would get dizzier and dizzier. We would also harmonise to the Everley Brothers song

'Dream'. We got it off to a T. That was one of the songs I sang to Av when she was in hospital.

As I got older I began to realise what an amazing woman she was. When she moved to Graemsay in the Orkneys I think Av was the happiest she had ever been. She loved living there. We would talk together on a Friday for hours on end about this and that and what our families were doing. When Av was diagnosed with this awful disease that eventually killed her, she was very philosophical about it and seemed to take it day by day. As it turned out, her torment was to last for 12 years.

Av gave birth to two beautiful daughters of whom she was very proud. She had five lovely grandchildren and one great grand daughter. This remarkable sister of mine made a difference to everyone she came into contact with and she was an inspiration to me. She was kind, she was silly and liked to do silly things. She did not have one ounce of bitterness for what had happened in her life.

Av is my big sister. She is my hero.

About the Author

Dawn Fanshawe lives in Nottingham, England, where she grew up and lived until she was nineteen. She then worked for two years in Germany as an au pair, before doing a degree in education and art in London. For fifteen years Dawn was as an early years teacher and Foundation-Stage manager in London. Dawn remains passionate about education and was a school governor for over twenty years and a county governor for the NHS in Nottinghamshire.

As a student, she worked as a care assistant in many elderly & mentally infirm homes across London, and in 2006 she brought her mother – who was at the time living on a remote island in the Orkney Isles and had early onset Alzheimer's Disease – to live with her in her new family home in Nottingham. At this point Dawn became her mother's full-time carer, which was to turn her life around in so many ways.

Contact with mental illness has been integral to Dawn's life and relationships; as a child she suffered abuse at the hands of her parents and this had long-reaching implications for herself. Dealing with the challenge of caring for her mother as she became more and more incapacitated by dementia has been a big part of Dawn's own journey of healing, forgiveness, and self-discovery.

More recently Dawn ran her own photography business in Nottingham and is a trustee for a Nottinghamshire charity looking to help disadvantaged families and children in her neighbourhood; she was also actively involved in the NHS Involvement Strategy.

A key part of Dawn's life is her Christian faith and her active involvement within her local church community. Dawn's other passions include learning and speaking languages, travelling, reading, writing, photography, and gardening. Dawn's mission is to become fully the person she was created to be and feels she is on a life-time adventure of healing, loving, and seeking to become the change she wants to see in the world. She feels blessed with her family, friends, and the community around her.

FIC : FAN

Printed in Great Britain
by Amazon.co.uk, Ltd.,
Marston Gate.